Biblical Economics...

...BEGINNING AT SQUARE ONE

E. Jay O'Keefe

Westcliff Press
P.O. Box 1521
Amarillo TX 79105

Biblical Economics

First Edition 2006

Copyright 2006 by E. Jay O'Keefe

Westcliff Press
P.O. Box 1521
Amarillo TX 79105
1-806-359-6362
www.webtheology.com

ISBN: 0977405109
Library of Congress Catalog Card Number 2006934800

Printed in the United States of America

Unless otherwise indicated, all Scripture quotations are taken from the *Holy Bible*, New International Version, Copyright 1978, the New York International Bible Society, [www.ibs.org].

Scripture quotations marked KJV are taken from the *Holy Bible*, King James Version.

Scripture quotations marked NASB are taken from the New American Standard Bible.

Table of Contents

Table of Contents, Continued

FOREWORD

The first seeds of truth which led to the writing of this book were planted in my heart by a sermon which I heard on a Sunday morning in 1978. Our pastor was out of town that day so we had a guest speaker. His text was Luke 16:1-13, sometimes referred to as the Parable of the Unjust Steward. The only thing I remember today from that message are his comments on verse 9.

> I tell you, use worldly wealth to gain friends for yourselves, so that when it is gone, you will be welcomed into eternal dwellings [Luke 16:9].

I don't remember what he said word for word about this verse, but the general idea of it was that people you minister to by means of your money will be a welcoming committee for you when you enter heaven, to greet you and help you celebrate your reward for giving. He mentioned several examples of who these people could be: ministers in churches, poor people you helped feed, people won to Christ because you supported some missionary or ministry ...... anyone to whom you minister by giving your money. Many of these people you will never see in this life, but they will welcome you when you arrive in heaven. The first part of the verse urges that we use our money to make these friends.

I don't remember anything else the preacher said that day, but what I remember as clearly as if it were yesterday, is the profound impact that message had on my heart. I could not get it out of my mind, and a few weeks after hearing it, I committed myself to finding all the Bible says about handling money. Over the next two years, I read through the Bible twice and made a list of every passage which touched on the subject of economics. That list contains 534 passages and aggregates more than 2000 verses of Scripture. I'll be referring to many of the more important of these passages throughout this book.

After studying the passages in that list, I put together a twelve session seminar under the title, "Biblical Economics, what the Bible teaches about handling money." I taught that series in my home church in 1980, and in several other churches during the 1980s, the last time being 1989. That seminar, along with what I have learned since then, has resulted in this book.

Suggested Cataloging-In Data

O'Keefe, E. Jay
Biblical Economics, E. Jay O'Keefe
238 p. 24cm
Includes biblical references
ISBN 0977405109
1. Money - Religious Aspects 2. Finance -
Religious Aspects 3. Finance, Personal -
Religious Aspects 4. Tithes 5. Stewardship -
Religious Aspects
Suggested Library of Congress Number:
BU772
Suggested Dewey Number: 248.6

ACKNOWLEDGEMENTS

As I studied this subject, I read the writings of a number of authors. The ones who made the most significant contributions to my understanding were Larry Burkett, Howard Dayton, Jr., Ron Blue, George Foshee, Randy Alcorn and John Alexander. I am indebted to all of them, and recommend their books to you. There are a few quotes from some of them in this book.

Until now, I never considered writing a book. Tape recordings of the Biblical Economics Seminar sessions done in the 80s have been in our church tape library all these years. I felt that God could use them, if He wanted to, to help anyone seeking help with his finances. But I now realize that was very short-sighted thinking. God used one man to bring me to that conclusion, my friend and fellow church member, Dan Bentley. In the late 80s, Dan and his wife, Susan, listened to the Biblical Economics series at our church. For the past five years, Dan has been urging me to put the series in writing. More than any other person, God has used him to bring that about. He is a dentist, a busy man, yet he was always there to read, correct and suggest revisions and additions to the text. He read every word of every chapter many times, and he actually wrote a significant portion of the text, including all of the Epilogue. Usually when you see the word "we," the other half of the "we" is Dan. Thanks, Dan, from the bottom of my heart.

I must thank Barry Bedwell, who has been such a vital part of my life. Ten years ago he and I entered into a mentoring relationship, which is still ongoing as this is written. We meet weekly for lunch to discuss Scripture, pray, and deal with life's challenges in all areas, including the subjects discussed in this book. I am supposed to be the mentor, but I suspect I have learned more than he. What a blessing he has been to me.

Early in our relationship, Barry introduced me to Walt Henrichsen, who has been mentoring businessmen for 45 years. For nine years, Barry and I sat in a monthly class, along with several other businessmen located in three cities, brought together by telephone conference call. Over the years, we studied verse by verse through several New Testament books, as well as the Sermon on the Mount. Each man in the class agreed to study twenty hours during the month, and memorize the text for the next class.

In spite of all that study and memorizing, I still missed most of the vital truths and applications (you will probably understand why when you read Chapter 2). Not until we got on the phone with Walt, and he took us through the text (using primarily Socrates' teaching method) did they finally begin to take root in my soul. Those nine years transformed my life. Most of the truth in the first three chapters of this book came from what I learned during those nine years ... while I was in my 70s. I readily admit that I am the slowest learner on the planet. I thank and praise God for you, Walt. You will never know how God used you in my life.

My nephew, Britt Jones, also listened to the economic series by tape as a twenty year old, before he married Debi and started a family. They began their marriage with a commitment to live debt free, and with the exception of a mortgage on their modest home, they have fulfilled that commitment, even though Britt's income has been modest, and Debi has not worked in an income producing job. They are a rare exception to the typical baby-boom family in our culture today.

Not only has Britt consistently shared the principles contained in this book with others, but it was his vision to get this book into audio format, which he says is the way to reach his peer group. I had absolutely no inclination to attempt that, but he persisted, and I finally relented. We faced a logistical problem. Britt lives in Colorado Springs, and I live in Amarillo. We didn't find an easy way to get together to do the recording.

God led us to Glenn Storlie, who has a recording business (and ministry) here in Amarillo. He produces music, preaching, seminars, etc., for churches and other ministries. For three months, Glenn and I met for two or three hours a day, three days a week, and recorded the book. Glenn really sacrificed, making literally hundreds of edits in order to get it into a usable product. As I said, I had no inclination to do an audio. I'm the last one I would choose to do so. I just kept praying, "Lord, here are my five loaves and two fishes. Only you can multiply them. Please do so if it is Your will."

My son-in-law, Karl Wheeler, has been a youth speaker for Dare to Share Ministries, Int'l., and currently pastors a church in the Denver area. He read through the manuscript, and spent many hours discussing it, and the Scriptures, with me. This was special to me, as well as spiritually profitable. Thanks, Karl.

Thanks also to Ted Spaeth, one of Walt's students, who took the time to read several of the chapters and offer some excellent suggestions, some of which found their way into the final version.

All of my former pastors played a role in molding my understanding of the Bible, but none as much as my current pastor, Dr. Steven Waterhouse at Westcliff Bible Church in Amarillo. I have worshipped and studied under him for the past twenty years. Without even being aware of it, I will undoubtedly say things I've heard him say from the pulpit, or in discussions. He read a portion of the manuscript and helped me with some of the more difficult theological issues. Thanks, Pastor Steve, for your counsel and your faithful teaching of the Scriptures over these twenty years.

I am indebted to and grateful to Alan Good, business manager of our church, and editor of the books published by Westcliff Press. He worked tirelessly to get the manuscript into suitable form for publishing, correct the grammar, suggest better ways to express some of the text, and talk through some of the theological issues, all with exemplary patience and persistence. Thanks, Al.

Finally, I thank and praise God for my life mate (of 48 years), and best friend, Mary Ann. Though she made no suggestions regarding the content of the book, her support, encouragement and prayers will surely earn her a greater reward than mine. Those who know me (and her) will understand why I say that.

Biblical Economics

PREFACE

I think it is appropriate to include a brief overview of the contents of the book. I consider the first three chapters to be by far the most important part of the book, even though they do not even deal specifically with financial stewardship. They contain no "new" truth in them, for there is no such thing. It's just that the truth they contain so dramatically impacted my life, when I was in my 70s, that I am anxious to integrate them into the biblical financial principles which I taught years ago. I consider them to be the foundation of the study, and in fact the foundation of all aspects of the Christian life. I pray that God will use them to bless your life as He has mine.

▶ Chapter 1 is titled *Let's Go Back to Square One.* It deals with the theology of our relationship with God and other people, and explores the simple proposition that God is in control and He has our best interest at heart.

▶ Chapter 2 is titled *The Problem – Our Lust for Autonomy.* It's really about pride and humility, both good Bible words, but they have become so familiar that I wonder if we really understand their biblical meanings. This chapter attempts to define the problem we face as we try to be good stewards of the gifts and assets God entrusts to us to manage for Him. It also proposes the solution to the problem, which leads naturally to the next chapter.

▶ Chapter 3 is titled *All I Have Commanded (What Jesus Expects of His Followers).* It contains a complete list of all the commandments of Jesus and the apostles which relate specifically to financial stewardship. I have read many good books on finances (presented from a biblical perspective), but I have never seen one which presents this focus on the commandments. I'm not saying it hasn't been done. I'm just saying I've never seen it, and I think it's important, especially in our day.

I am convinced that unless we are serious about the material presented in the first three chapters, it really won't make a lot of difference how well we know all the biblical principles of handling money. Their theme runs through all the other chapters.

▶ Chapter 4 is titled *God's Management Agreement with Man.* It is a study of the parable of the talents, and, in my opinion, gives one of the clearest pictures of the owner – manager relationship, both from our perspective and God's.

► Chapter 5 is titled *The Sin of Materialism*. This is the "respectable sin" in the church today, a sin almost impossible for our conscience to identify. It is very important to understand how the Bible defines this sin and what its consequences are.

► Chapter 6 is titled *Presuming on the Future*. In the list of Jesus' commands dealing with economics, this is the very first one. He calls presuming on the future evil, and so does the apostle James in his commentary on this command. I believe it is so important that I devoted a chapter to it.

► Chapter 7 is titled *Standard of Living*. I suspect the average Christian thinks he is responsible for determining his standard of living on earth, while God determines his standard of living in heaven. In fact, the Bible teaches exactly the opposite. It's really important to get this one straight.

The first seven chapters are mostly theological in nature. All the rest of the chapters deal with the practical principles of handling money, including giving, paying taxes, borrowing and lending, getting out of debt, houses, saving for the future, investing, retirement and estate planning, in that order. Throughout the book I will share with you some of the mistakes I made in handling our finances. I do that because it is possible to learn from other people's mistakes. That's my prayer for you as you read the chapters.

Financial decisions you have made in the past, and those you will make in the future, speak volumes about the seriousness of your relationship with Jesus Christ. This work is an attempt to give you the necessary biblical truth required to be a good manager of God's assets. Your willingness to obey the Lord's commandments will, in part, prepare you to give an affirmative response to the question Jesus asked Peter, "Do you love me?" Remember that Jesus said to His disciples, and thus to us all, "If you love me, you will keep my commandments."

May the Spirit of God move in your heart as you begin at Square One.

E. Jay O'Keefe
October 15, 2006

Biblical Economics...

...BEGINNING AT SQUARE ONE

E. Jay O'Keefe

CHAPTER 1

LET'S GO BACK TO SQUARE ONE

God is in control and He has my best interest at heart. The first time I heard that statement, I was sitting in a businessmen's Bible study ten years ago. That day my life changed and it has never been the same since. The teacher who made the statement called it "The Twin Pillars of Faith." You can tell how important it is to him by that title. I have given it a different name because of the way it has impacted my life. I call it "My Square One Theology," or simply "Square One" for short, hence the title of this chapter, "Let's Go Back to Square One." I consider the information in this chapter so important, and so foundational to the Christian life, that I urge you to read and carefully consider it as you begin your study of Biblical Economics. God is in control and He has my best interest at heart. I'll be making frequent references to Square One throughout this book.

Square One is not a new truth. It is not a new doctrine. It is the application of an old truth to life, an application I had largely missed during the years I had been a Christian up to that time. It has to do with two of God's attributes, His sovereignty and His goodness. If you enrolled in a seminary as a student, you would sit in a class entitled Theology Proper, which is a study of God Himself, His attributes, His nature, His activities as revealed in the Bible. Let's say that you do this, and you show up for theology class the first day. The professor begins to list God's attributes and explain them to you, sovereignty, goodness, justice, love, eternal life, omnipotence, etc., down through the list. And you leave class that first day with a little better understanding of what God is like.

Two or three days later you encounter an unexpected crisis in your life, a major problem of some kind. And it's the kind of problem you have to share with somebody, someone you trust, someone who might act as a counselor for you. So you get with this person and tell him or her the story, all about this crisis. You come to a pause, and your counselor looks up at you and looks you in the eye and says, "Don't you realize that God is in control and has your best interest at heart?" And like a bolt of lightning you think, "Wow, is that what I learned in theology

1

class earlier this week?" Actually it was, but it was presented quite differently. In theology class you learned it as a statement of theology, or a statement of faith. But in the visit with the counselor, you heard it as the application of theology to real life. If God is sovereign, then He is in control of everything, not just some things. He's in control because He created all things. To think of God as having created this world, and not be in control of it, doesn't make sense. That wouldn't be the God of the Bible. If God is good, if He's absolutely righteous, then He's incapable of doing anything with your life, or letting anything happen in your life that's not in your best interest. Hence the phrase, "God is in control and He has my best interest at heart."

I am learning that every issue in life, every relationship in life, every experience in life should be approached from the foundation of Square One. As each day begins, I try to go to Square One and start there. I try to affirm my belief in it and reinvest my faith in it. If I fail to do that on a given day, it's a different kind of day. The problem is not in my statement of faith, or what I say I believe. The problem is my failure to live consistently with what I say I believe.

PRACTICAL ATHEISM

The great British theologian, Charles Spurgeon, who ministered in the middle and late 1800s in England, taught a concept that he called "Practical Atheism". He said even though a believer is not an atheist, he can sometimes act like one. He can act as if one or more of God's attributes were not true. Consider an illustration of this that has been helpful to me. Let's suppose you learn the attributes of God in Bible class. Some teachers have His attributes divided into ten. Let's say you go down to the store and buy ten attractive plaques. And you have one of the attributes of God engraved on each of these plaques. Then you hang the plaques up in your house in a conspicuous place where you pass by them every day. Each day as you pass by them on your way to work they remind you of the nature of God.

But suppose that one day you start to go past those plaques, and you just reach up and take one of them down ...... you take down the plaque that has "sovereignty" engraved on it, and you take it to a back room of your house and put it on a shelf in the closet. Then you walk back by those plaques and go to work, but you live that day as if God were not sovereign. That's practical atheism. And you might encounter a problem in that day, and you reason in your mind that it is of human origin ...... somebody did this, or somebody caused that. Or you might reason that it's happening by chance, that it is an accident. That's practical atheism. That's living as if God were not sovereign.

Let me ask you a question. Search your soul. Are you living today as if God were not in control? ...... as if He does not have your best interest at heart? Are you living today as if God were not omniscient? ...... as if He did not know every thought in your mind and every decision you will ever make? That's practical atheism. I find in my own life that I have to be constantly reminded that God is sovereign, that He is in control, that He is good, that His goodness is absolute. He does or permits nothing in my life but that which is in my best interest.

Let's look at a few passages which teach us about God's sovereignty and His goodness, and I suggest that you be especially on the lookout for the word "all."

One of the most remarkable verses in the entire Bible is Psalm 139:16. Here's what it says (David speaking to God), "Your eyes saw my unformed body. All the days ordained for me were in your book before one of them came to be." I admit that I do not understand how the sovereignty of God interacts with the responsible choice of man, but the Scripture teaches both. God created us in His image. Part of that image is the ability to reason and choose. I would certainly admit that our choice is not the same as God's. He's the Creator and we are the creatures. Our choice is limited. It has boundaries on it. But within those boundaries, we're free. And what is important for us to understand in connection with this study is that we are free to sin, or free to obey.

God in His foreknowledge knew every decision that we would ever make in our lives. And God knew every decision of every person that would touch our lives. He wove all of it together into a detailed plan, spoken of in this verse. And then He ordained that plan for us before we were ever born. And how much of our life was ordained before we were born? Well, the verse says "all." "All the days ordained for me were in your book before one of them came to be." Do I understand that? No, I don't. But I believe it. And if I am interpreting correctly, it has profound application for our daily lives.

A FAVORITE TEXT

One of my favorite passages as a text for this truth is Romans 8:28, "And we know that God causes all things to work together for good to those who love God, to those who are called according to His purpose" (NASB). Notice how sovereignty and goodness are coupled together in this verse.

There are three things that Romans 8:28 does not say that we should understand if we're going to interpret the verse correctly. First, Romans 8:28 does not say that all things **are** good. It says that God **causes** all things to work together for good, which is quite different. There are bad things that come into our lives. But God works them along with all other things for our ultimate good.

Second, Romans 8:28 does not say or imply that God causes sin. Scripture is clear. God is not the cause of sin. We are the cause of sin by our own choices. But God is the cause of the **effects** of sin in any life and in any situation. In other words the sins, though they are bad, are part of the "all things" that He causes to work together for good for those who love Him and are called according to His purpose. On a number of occasions, I have heard my pastor say from the pulpit, "God manipulates evil". In my opinion, this is a good way to put it.

And third, Romans 8:28 does not say God causes all things to work together to bring about His (God's) best. When we sin, we get something less than God's best. But even when we sin, the promise that God causes all things to work together for good stands. By our sins we can damage our lives and reduce our reward in eternity, but for the elect God will cause things to work out the best they can given the level of sins and disobedience of which we are guilty. Only God could be the cause of such an outcome! What a bold statement is Romans 8:28.

Notice in Romans 8:28 the word "all." We must decide what "all" means in this verse. Of course we know the definition of the word "all." But we don't always act as if "all" means "all" in Romans 8:28, do we? And if "all" means "all" in Romans 8:28, then there is no such thing as

4

chance, or an accident. To the world, things sometimes look like an accident or chance. And I would admit that the idea of an accident might be a useful concept for the world. It's useful in insurance, in determining liability, and in other ways. But for a believer in Christ it's not a valid concept. When I was young, I can remember seeing the phrase "acts of God" in secular documents such as insurance policies. Even the world, at least to some degree, accepted the biblical view. I don't remember seeing this phrase much in recent years.

One of the great application verses for what we're discussing here is 1 Thessalonians 5:16-18, "Be joyful always. Pray continually. Give thanks in **all** circumstances, for this is God's will for you in Christ Jesus." This study has given new meaning to that passage to me. If Square One is not true, then this passage makes no sense whatever. It's a cruel joke for God to command us to give thanks in all circumstances, if the premise is not true. But if God is in control and has our best interest at heart, then not only does this passage make sense, but it's a sin not to obey it. I believe that "all" means "all" in this verse. Give thanks in ALL circumstances. And let us remind ourselves that thankfulness is not only spoken, it is a disposition that others sense as they touch our lives, with or without a word being spoken.

SQUARE ONE AND INTERPERSONAL RELATIONSHIPS

Up to this point in this discussion we have looked at verses that emphasize our relationship to God. But the Christian life involves interpersonal relationships as well. And the question is, how do God's sovereignty and goodness apply to interpersonal relationships? I'm going to make a statement that may shock some of you. It did me the first time I heard it. Some of you will accept it as truth. Some of you will dismiss it out of hand. You will reject it immediately. And some of you will take it in and put it on probation and meditate on it for the next few hours or days, and come to your own conclusion. That's what I hope you will do if you have trouble accepting it now.

Don't accept it. Don't reject it. Take it in. Meditate on it.

All right, are you ready for the statement? Here it is as it came to me ten years ago, "If you truly believe that God is in control and has your best interest at heart, then biblically **there is no such thing as a**

problem with another person."

Think about that for a moment. I admit that it's a shocking statement, and I want to tell you how I reacted to it. There was an initial shock and rejection from my heart, but within 30 seconds after I heard it, I knew it was true. And the Holy Spirit bore witness with my spirit that I had heard the truth, an application of the truth that I had largely missed during most of my Christian life. And my life changed at that instant, and has never been the same since. And I have spent many hours over this past 10 years meditating on this truth, and searching the Scripture, and my conviction grows stronger by the day that it is in fact the truth.

WHAT CAN MAN DO TO ME?

Here is a verse that I think teaches the truth contained in the statement, "There is no such thing as a problem with another person." Hebrews 13:6, "So we say with confidence, the Lord is my helper, I will not be afraid. What can man do to me?" The last phrase of that verse is a rhetorical question that solicits a negative answer by implication, something like, "What can man do to me?" Implied answer, "Nothing without God's permission." I think that's the essence of it. Every believer in Christ must face this question, "To what extent can another person influence my life without God's permission?" You must answer that for yourself. And I believe that Scripture teaches that the answer is, "To no extent can another person influence my life without God's permission."

That being true, then our problem is never with another person, our problem is with God, and the other person is God's agent placed in our life for God's purposes, to participate in His plan for our life. Now to be sure, other people can and will sin against us, but when they do, they are simply participating negatively in God's plan for our life, **but they do not alter our destiny.** People who sin against us will face the consequences of those sins, but God will use them in our life for our good, and they will not alter our destiny. We must realize that every financial difficulty is ultimately from God, and He causes it for our good. When somebody else's irresponsibility affects my wallet, I have to remember that God is in control, and I should not let my anger affect my relationship with the irresponsible person.

I close this chapter with nine conclusions that I believe are supported by Scripture relating to the application of Square One to our relationship to God and man. Some will be difficult to accept, and even more difficult to apply to daily life. Please understand that I am not trying to convince you that they are true. I ask only that you face the issues involved, meditate on them, pray and search the Scriptures for yourself.

• If you feel that you have a problem with another person, it is a sign that you do not understand God, because other people who impact your life are God's agents in your life for God's purposes to mold you into the life plan that God ordained for you in eternity past.

• Other people can and will sin against you, but when they do they merely participate negatively in God's plan for your life. They will face the consequences of their sins, but they will not alter your destiny. God will not delegate your destiny to another person.

• If God can act only in our best interest, and if He will not let anyone else act contrary to our best interest, then we are forced to the conclusion that we alone can hurt or destroy our life, and we do that by sin and disobedience.

• Since our problem is not with other people, we should always take our complaint to God, not to people. If we complain to God without rebelling against or threatening Him, He will hear us with an understanding, loving ear.

• For a believer in Christ, there is no such thing as being a victim. If I am harboring a victim mentality, then I am engaging in practical atheism. There is nothing happening to me that God has not ordained.

• Understanding Square One, and applying it to daily life, is the path to peace with all people.

• When we enter eternity, and faith becomes sight, we will look back over our lives on earth and not regret a single circumstance

God ordained. Our only regret will be our own lack of faith, and disobedience.

• Discontentment with my circumstances is practical atheism, living as if God were not in control with my best interest in His heart.

• Unless we understand and believe in Square One, we will have great difficulty navigating the storms of life, and great difficulty obeying all the commandments.

ADDITIONAL PASSAGES FOR STUDY AND MEDITATION

I know, O Lord, that a man's life is not his own; it is not for man to direct his steps [Jeremiah 10:23].

Trust in the Lord with all your heart, and lean not on your own understanding. In all your ways acknowledge Him, and He will make your paths straight [Proverbs 3:5-6].

Commit to the Lord whatever you do, and your plans will succeed [Proverbs 16:3].

In his heart a man plans his course, but the Lord determines his steps [Proverbs 16:9].

A man's steps are directed by the Lord. How then can anyone understand his own way? [Proverbs. 20:24].

Consider what God has done. Who can straighten what He has made crooked? When times are good, be happy. But when times are bad, consider: God has made the one as well as the other. Therefore, a man cannot discover anything about his future [Ecclesiastes 7:13-14].

... I am God, and there is no other; I am God, and there is none like Me. I make known the end from the beginning, from ancient times, what is still to come. I say: My purpose will stand, and I will do all that I please [Isaiah 46:9-10].

CHAPTER 2

THE PROBLEM – OUR LUST FOR AUTONOMY

The thesis of Chapter 1 is, God is in control and He has my best interest at heart. If this thesis is true, then it must follow that I am not in control. But the problem is, I want to be in control. I thirst for autonomy, independence, self-rule, self-realization. Why is that? What is the origin of this lust? What are the consequences of it in our lives? Is there a solution to this problem? What part does God play in the solution, and what part do we play?

These are the questions we will seek answers to in this chapter. The answers are more important to the management of your finances than you might imagine.

WHAT IS THE ORIGIN OF OUR LUST FOR AUTONOMY?

The answer is, in a word, God created us with the desire for autonomy. A teacher I studied under in a businessmen's Bible class had the best way of expressing it I have heard. I begin with a quote from him so that you may hear it in his words.

> "When God created Adam and Eve, He placed them in a perfect environment; no sin, pollution, opposition, and no prohibitions—with the exception of eating of the tree of the knowledge of good and evil. Genesis records no other command given to our first parents. The issue of the tree was who gets to determine what is good and evil: what is in my best interest and what is not? This issue focused man's struggle with God. Satan said that if they were able to decide what was good and evil for themselves they would be "like God." You can see why taking of the fruit was such a temptation. Note that Adam and Eve's thirst for autonomy came before the fall: it brought about the fall. God created them with a desire to be autonomous, and then asked that they limit this appetite by allowing God alone to determine what

was and was not in their interest. This same struggle remains with us today"[1]

Satan is still suggesting to us that God does not need to be taken seriously. His excuse for such a suggestion among those in our circles today is that grace eliminates accountability in eternity for temporal behavior, a dangerous assumption, which we will deal with in Chapter 3.

We are told that man was created in God's image. I assume that the desire for self-rule is a part of that image. Another part of that image is volition, the ability to make choices. And when Adam and Eve violated the one command God gave them, they exercised their choice, causing the fall, which created the problem we have lived with ever since.

So the origin of our desire for independence is creation. The problem is our unwillingness to surrender that desire and submit to God ...... to let God decide what is in our best interest and what is not.

SOME CONSEQUENCES OF OUR QUEST FOR AUTONOMY

I will mention just three. The first is anger. One day in Bible class, the teacher used some very strong language to describe the seriousness and danger of our refusal to surrender our autonomy-lust. I think his words are worth considering.

> "Know that man's fundamental problem with God has always been that man is angry with God because God is God, and man is not. Put another way, men rebel against God in anger because God got there first. Man ought to have been God. I should have been God, but God beat me to it, and it ticks me off."

And on another occasion, this quote.

---

[1] Walter A. Henrichsen, *Thoughts from the Diary of a Desperate Man* (Ft. Washington: Christian Literature Crusade, 1977), p. 207.

"I want to be in control. I want to be in charge. It seems to me that God is arbitrary and capricious in the way that He handles Himself. Not only are His standards arbitrary and capricious, the whole doctrine of election is. I want to be able to elect. I want to be able to make those decisions. It makes me angry that God does that. And not only that, but how dare God make me sick, or give my wife cancer, or take my child prematurely, or cause my business to go bankrupt. How dare He do that? And so men say, 'I will not worship a God who does that. My God could never kill a little baby.' That's utter nonsense. Of course God kills babies. That is the arrogance that is hard to suppress. It lies just below the surface in every man's life."

These are hard words. Some will not be able to accept all of them. Not many years ago, I would not have accepted all of them. But I believe we need to hear them because of the seriousness and danger of our refusal to surrender our autonomy-lust. The theologians of old called this "pride." The Scriptures say, "God resists the proud but gives grace to the humble." Often I meditate on that statement. I asked myself, what does it really mean for God to resist me? Can you imagine the Creator God of the universe resisting us puny created beings? What does that mean? I think we'll get some insight on that as we continue to list the consequences, and then consider God's part in the solution to our problem, which is essentially **pain**, but I'm getting ahead of myself.

A second consequence of our failure to surrender our lust for autonomy is discontentment. The lure which Satan used to entice Adam and Eve was the prospect of becoming like God. They may even have thought it possible to become God Himself. We would never admit to anything like that today, and yet the craving for autonomy that is in us, as depraved human beings, unless dealt with in God's way will approach wanting to be God, whether we're conscious of it or not. Let me ask you as you hear this to examine your own heart. Perhaps you've never thought of it in this way. Can you think of yourself, in some sense at least, as wanting to be God? I can.

A third consequence of our failure to surrender our lust for self-rule is pessimism and despair.

It seems to me that Christianity today cannot accept these statements. Without the answers and truth we are attempting to present in these first two chapters, our thinking is likely to run something like this: The circumstances in my life indicate that God is not acting in my best interest. If I were in control, I would do things differently. I am not in control, therefore life is a cruel joke, and it's God's fault for letting it happen. This is the conclusion Job reached before God explained what we are referring to as Square One. In the end Job repented and admitted that God knew what He was doing and had Job's best interest at heart, even though he never understood the reason for all his suffering and tribulation. In eternity, we will all admit the same thing.

STOP! TIME OUT. THINK ......

Go back to Square One. Do you really believe that God is in control and has your best interest at heart? Can you accept that you are locked into a system over which you have no control? Did you have any control over where you were born, or the family you were born into? The color of your hair or eyes? Your IQ?

Do you believe that God has you exactly where He wants you right now?......

Perhaps you're thinking, I've made some really bad mistakes, that's why things are in such a mess? Or more likely, you have shifted the blame to the actions of one or more other people who have sinned against you. Do you understand that God knew every decision you would make in your life, and every person who would touch your life, before you were ever born? And that He ordered all the circumstances which would arise in your life on the basis of that foreknowledge? ...... "All the days of my life were written in your book before one of them came to be" (Psalm 139:16) ...... and that He has brought you to where you are today?

Go back and re-read and meditate on the Scriptures given in Chapter 1: Psalm 139:16, Romans 8:28, 1 Thessalonians 5:16-18, Hebrews 13:6, Jeremiah 10:23, Proverbs 16:9, Proverbs 20:24, Ecclesiastes 7:13-14, Isaiah 46:9-10.

You can take your first step toward the surrender of your autonomy-lust by understanding and believing Square One ...... God is in control and He has my best interest at heart. Until you can take that step, you will have to endure the consequences of your quest for autonomy.

THE SOLUTION TO THE PROBLEM – GOD'S PART

Now let's talk about the solution to the problem. Obviously, the solution is for us to surrender our lust for autonomy and submit to the absolute authority of Jesus Christ. Unfortunately, without intervention from God, our sin nature predisposes us toward refusal to surrender. So what is the nature of God's part of the solution to the problem? In short, it is the administration of pain and opposition. God engineers circumstances in our lives which motivate us to surrender our autonomy-lust. Let's begin with Adam and Eve.

> To the woman he said, "I will greatly multiply your pain in childbirth. In pain you shall bring forth children. Yet your desire shall be for your husband, and he shall rule over you." Then to Adam He said, "Because you have listened to the voice of your wife, and have eaten from the tree about which I commanded you saying, 'You shall not eat from it'; cursed is the ground because of you. In toil you shall eat of it all the days of your life" [Genesis 3:16-17 (NASB)].

Though it did not appear to our first parents to be the case, these new conditions God instituted following the fall were in their best interest. No discipline for the moment will appear to be in our best interest, declares Hebrews 12:11. Will you trust God that He is acting **always** in your best interest? Remember the many times the word "all" appeared in the Scriptures we studied in Chapter 1?

God cooperates in this lifelong process of bringing us to surrender and to submit to His commandments. I personally believe this is the best description of the sanctification process. And as I read through Scripture, it seems to me that His primary role is the administration of pain - pain of all kinds, physical, emotional, financial, war, natural disasters, chaos and many others. Quite simply, we learn obedience by suffering pain. Although Jesus never committed a sin, even He learned obedience by suffering pain. "Although He was a Son, He learned obedience from what He suffered" [Hebrews 5:8].

Israel suffered immeasurably as they repeatedly went through the following cycle: (1) disobedience, (2) pain, (3) repentance, (4) obedience, (5) repeated disobedience, etc. Stop and think about this for a moment. A key to understanding Jewish behavior, as well as our own behavior today, is what happens following step 4 (obedience) that causes step 5 (repeated disobedience)? This is something for every believer to ponder for himself.

WHAT IS THE GOAL OF GOD'S PART?

More than any other author whom I have studied, Paul E. Billheimer has articulated the great value and benefit of suffering and sorrow in the life of the Christian in his book, *Don't Waste Your Sorrows.*

> "Because tribulation is necessary for the decentralization of self and the development of deep dimensions of agape love, this love can be developed only in the school of suffering. It grows only by exercise and testing. This may explain the relationship between sainthood and suffering by showing WHY there is no sainthood without suffering. It may also show why the greatest saints are often the greatest sufferers. It is an attempt to answer the age-old question, 'Why do the righteous suffer?' " [2]

> "Thus, the supreme purpose of life on earth is not pleasure, fame, wealth, or any other form of worldly success, but learning agape love. In the ultimate social order of the universe (the kingdom of God) rank will be determined, not by talent, magnetic personality, intellectual acumen, earthly success and affluence, but by one thing and one alone – agape love." [3]

Here, in my opinion, Billheimer has beautifully stated the process by which God does His part in bringing us to the point of surrendering our lust for autonomy. We must be brought to a state of total brokenness

---

[2] Paul E. Billheimer, *Don't Waste Your Sorrows*, (Ft. Washington: Christian Literature Crusade, 1977), p. 10.

[3] Ibid., p. 35.

before we will finally turn loose of our craving for self-determination. This is a life-long process for most of us. It is different for each of us. For some of us, this lust is so entrenched, so embedded in our souls that it has to be blasted or bulldozed out of us before we will finally surrender. What is meant by "brokenness?" Here is Billheimer's definition.

> "One is not broken until all resentment and rebellion against God and man is removed. One who resents, takes offense, or retaliates against criticism and opposition or lack of appreciation, is unbroken. All self-justification and self-defense betrays an unbroken spirit. All discontent and irritation with providential circumstances reveals unbrokenness. Genuine brokenness usually requires years of crushing, heartache, and sorrow. Thus self-will is surrendered, and deep degrees of yieldedness and submission developed, without which there is little agape love."[4]

It seems I have read that paragraph at least a hundred times. I return to it often and meditate on each sentence. What a great tool for self-examination. I commend it to you.

All of my Christian life I have struggled to understand and resolve what seems to me to be a paradox ...... the sovereignty of God and the responsible choice of man. As I get older I am becoming more resigned to the fact that I will never understand it. Certainly there are people with far greater intellect and theological knowledge than I who may understand it better than I, but I detect in their writings their own struggle. I suspect God does not intend for any human being to understand it, and several Scriptures hint in that direction. In those times when I am most confused and unsure of my own understanding, I find peace and rest in reading and meditating on some of the Scriptures that I have cited in this book.

> I know, O Lord, that a man's way is not in himself; nor is it in a man who walks to direct his steps [Jeremiah 10:23 (NASB)].

> The mind of man plans his way, but the Lord directs his steps [Proverbs 16:9 (NASB)].

---

[4] Ibid., p. 75.

...... I am God, and there is no other; I am God, and there is none like Me. I make known the end from the beginning, from ancient times, what is still to come. I say: My purpose will stand, and I will do all that I please [Isaiah 46:9-10].

How can God know the future unless He causes it? ...... We must believe in the sovereign control of God, but also in the responsible choice of man, though we may never be able to resolve the coexistence of both.

Some will question whether certain forms of pain and suffering are caused by God, or come as a result of other causes that God has nothing to do with. This seems especially so for things like natural disasters and wars. Some would even include diseases, accidents, financial reversals, and other things, as events God is not responsible for. The church has long debated these questions. I do not have the wisdom or knowledge to make any meaningful contribution to the debate. I can only search and meditate in the Scriptures, hoping for better understanding.

WAR AND CHAOS

Could war and chaos be a form of pain and opposition God would initiate? Consider the following quotes:

"Genesis 11:6, And the Lord said, 'Behold they are one people, and they have all one language; and this is only the beginning of what they will do; and nothing they propose to do will be impossible for them.'

"The whole earth spoke one language, and united the people built the Tower of Babel. I have never been sure what this tower looked like, or how the people thought it would accomplish their objective, but God responded to them with this startling comment, 'If We don't stop them, there is nothing that they won't be able to do.' So God scattered the people by confounding them with a multiplicity of languages.

"This scattering produced at least the following: a diversity of cultures and religions – the inability to understand one another, not only because of language, but also culture-war. Diversity breeds divisiveness. There is no indication of war prior to the Tower of Babel. You find instances of violence, such as Cain killing his brother, but no organized group warfare. God instigated much of the chaos you find in the world.

"People have always worked toward solving the problems of the world through unity and union. We formed the League of Nations, the United Nations, and some look to the union of European nations as another step towards one world government. We sign nuclear proliferation treaties, seek to eliminate poverty and injustice, etc. If God were to allow success, it would seal the eternal damnation of the world, for the path from God is independence; the path to God is dependence. God uses chaos to teach people their need of Him. Never cease thanking God for chaos." [5]

You may sense that I believe God is the cause of war. Even if I do, I also believe that man has choice, which, within the boundaries God has established, are free. It may be accurate to say that men choose to fight each other. What more natural expression of their refusal to surrender their autonomy could there be? Nevertheless, according to the Genesis passage, God clearly created the circumstances under which men would want to fight each other.

Again, the Genesis passage clearly implies that God's confusion of the languages was a good thing, not a bad thing. It led to a restraint on evil. It put men in a position of being dependent on God, making it more likely they would turn toward God rather than away from Him. Pain has a tendency to turn us toward God. When the pain lets up, or we go through times when things are going well, usually we drift right back toward our lust for independence and self-rule. As my mentor once said, "You are never in greater danger than when all is well in your life. The satisfied life has no need for Jesus."

---

[5] Walter A. Henrichsen, *Thoughts from the Diary of a Desperate Man* (Ft. Washington: Christian Literature Crusade, 1977), p. 350.

When I read the quotes on the Tower of Babel, it reminded me of some of the statements Paul made to the Colossians.

> For by Him all things were created: things in heaven and on earth, visible and invisible, whether thrones or powers or rulers or authorities; all things were created by Him and for Him. He is before all things, and in Him all things hold together [Colossians 1:16-17].

This passage clearly teaches that Jesus Christ has authority over everything, and that one of the results of that fact is that "in Him all things hold together." And that is a very good thing. Were it not for the fact that Jesus "holds things together," they would fly apart, or blow up, so to speak. Were it not for Jesus' restraint of evil, likely mankind would long ago have completely self-destructed. To me, the amazing thing about this fallen world is not how bad it is, but how much better it is than it would be without Jesus and His authority over all things.

NATURAL DISASTERS

I also see natural disasters in much the same way as war and chaos. Since He created the heavens and the earth, God has the same absolute control over nature and the physical universe that He has over nations and individuals.

> It was you who opened up springs and streams; you dried up the ever flowing rivers. The day is yours, and yours also the night; you established the sun and moon. It was you who set all the boundaries of the earth; you made both summer and winter [Psalm 74:15-17].

Notice that first phrase, "It was you who opened up springs and streams." As this is being written, the giant tsunami wave disaster in Asia, which killed more than 200,000 people, is still fresh in our memories. Many people, even Christians, will find it impossible to believe that God deliberately caused that disaster, intending for each one of those victims to die. Of course, no one can answer the question, "Why?" But we can believe, based on what Scripture asserts, that God had complete control of it and that it worked in the best interest of every life affected by it. Already there are reports of many turning to

Jesus as a result of the disaster. Perhaps many Christians who survived the tragedy have been motivated to surrender their lust for autonomy and submit to Jesus' authority over their lives. What I do believe is that when we enter eternity and look back on our earthly lives, we will not regret any circumstance that God ordained in our lives. Our only regret will be our disobedience and lack of faith.

> That at the name of Jesus every knee should bow, of those who are in heaven, and on earth, and under the earth, and that every tongue should confess that Jesus Christ is Lord, to the glory of God the Father [Philippians 2:10-11 (NASB)].

THE SOLUTION – OUR PART

What is our part in the solution to all the misery, heartache, dissatisfaction and sinful behavior that flows from our lust for autonomy?

> Then He said to them all: "If anyone would come after Me, he must deny himself and take up his cross daily and follow Me. For whoever wants to save his life will lose it, but whoever loses his life for Me will save it" [Luke 9:23-24].

How could Jesus have possibly made it any clearer? He is asking me to deny myself ...... to surrender my lust for self-rule. When I do this, I "lose" my life (my right to myself) for His sake. When I refuse to surrender my autonomy-lust, I am attempting to save my life (retain my right to myself), and I lose my life instead.

What does He mean by taking up our cross and following Him? First and foremost it must mean unconditional obedience to all the commandments of Jesus and the apostles. This is so important, we will explore it further in Chapter 3. But I must share my favorite passage indicating our part in the solution to the problem.

> Come to Me all who are weary and heavy-laden, and I will give you rest. Take My yoke upon you, and learn from Me, for I am gentle and humble in heart, and you shall find rest for your souls. For my yoke is easy and My load is light [Matthew 11:28-30 (NASB)].

There is certainly nothing wrong with quoting these verses to an unbeliever who is seeking to enter a relationship with God, but I'm going to suggest an interpretation that you may not have heard. I believe the primary application is for believers who, having been born again, have been made aware of the lifelong process of warfare with their lust for independence. It is this warfare that makes us weary and heavy-laden. It is surrender of this lust that will give us rest.

Jesus' use of the word "rest" reminds me of what the writer to the Hebrews said, "And to whom did He swear that they should not enter His rest, but to those who were disobedient?" [Hebrews 3:18 (NASB)]. I believe the rest Jesus is referring to in Matthew 11:28-30 is the rest of obedience, and His yoke to which He refers are His commandments. We take this yoke by surrendering our autonomy-lust and submitting to His commandments.

Notice what He wants us to learn about Him, that He is "gentle and humble in heart." That is the path to surrender and submission. Finally, notice in verse 30 that He says, "My yoke is easy." On the surface it may seem to us that obeying all the commandments is anything but easy. But when you compare it to the weary and heavy-laden life of self-rule, truly His yoke is easy and His burden is light.

HOW GOD'S PART AND OUR PART WORK TOGETHER

The surrender and submission that comprises our part in the solution will be taken as we respond to God's part, the administration of pain and opposition. We aren't likely to initiate our part until He initiates His part. When things are going well, our tendency is to drift right back into our thirst for control. If things are going well for you, my advice is, thank God for the good times, but realize they won't last. Best that we anticipate the coming pain and sorrow, and prepare for it by understanding it will be lovingly administered upon us by God. It will be discipline and testing, not punishment. It will be remedial, not punitive.

Another of my heroes of faith is the South African theologian, Andrew Murray, pastor, missionary, writer and educator, who ministered in the 19th century. I have read several of his books. I think that he had a wonderful understanding of what we are referring to as "God's part in the solution to our problem," and it permeated his writing and preaching. I don't remember where I read it, but somewhere in his writings I ran upon his counsel to us on how to respond to God's administration of pain and sorrow. I share it with you here.

"In time of trouble say:

First, He brought me here. It is by His will I am in this straight place. In that fact I will rest.

Next, He will keep me here in His love, and give me grace to behave as His child.

Then, He will make the trial a blessing, teaching me the lessons He intends me to learn, and working in me the grace He intends to bestow.

Last, In His good time He can bring me out again ...... how and when He knows.

Let me say I am here,

     (1) By God's appointment.
     (2) In His keeping
     (3) Under His training
     (4) For His time."

A PERSONAL TESTIMONY

I trusted Jesus Christ as my Savior when I was nine years old. I was taught in Sunday School about the sin of pride and selfishness, that serving others rather than self was the essence of the Christian life, that it was more blessed to give than to receive. And I understood these truths, in some sense, at least. But it is with regret and shame that I confess that I was approaching my 70th birthday before the truth we are discussing in this chapter penetrated my soul in a way that transformed my life.

One day in Bible class, my mentor said, "Your problem is that you want to be God, and you're mad that God beat you to it. You want to decide what is in your best interest rather than submit to what God says is in your best interest." When I heard those words, the truth finally registered in my soul, and I've not been the same since. That day I took my first meaningful step toward surrender of my quest for independence, and submission to the absolute authority of Jesus over my life. I confess that I am among the slowest learners on this earth. My only consolation is God's grace in allowing me to live long enough to say, better late than never.

BIBLICAL ECONOMICS AND SQUARE ONE

We will be unable to prevent others from competing with us regardless of how we live our lives. What is our responsibility toward those who will compete with us, and what should be our response to them? Our autonomy-lust will predispose us to take our focus off of excellence (self-competition), and instead focus on those with whom we compete. What does Square One teach us? One who competes with me with all the world's fury is acting as God's agent in my life by God's permission and under His control. Though he may sin against me or cause pain in my life, he will not alter my destiny. God is still in control, superintending all the circumstances in my best interest. God will not delegate my destiny to another human being.

Prayer: Heavenly Father, we understand from your Word that You have created us with the desire for independence and self-rule. But it is also clear to us that you have asked us to surrender that desire, and submit to your authority over us ...... to let you decide what is in our best interest and what is not. When Your Son instructed us to obey "all that He commanded," He removed any doubt about what would be in our best interest. We've also learned from this study that You will administer pain and opposition and sorrow in our lives, not as punishment, but as a motivation to surrender. We understand Your goal for us is a state of perpetual brokenness, in which state we will finally find true rest and joy and peace, and as a by-product usefulness in the ministry of Your kingdom. Please use this study to lead those who read it a step closer to that surrender. In Jesus Name, amen.

CHAPTER 3

ALL I HAVE COMMANDED
(What Jesus expects of His followers)

The conclusion reached in Chapter 2 was that our part in the solution to all the misery, heartache, dissatisfaction and sinful behavior which flows from our thirst for autonomy, is a total surrender of our autonomy-lust and total submission to the absolute authority of Jesus Christ over our lives. That would translate into unconditional obedience to all the commandments of Jesus and the apostles. There can be no doubt that Jesus intends this to be our goal. Right in the middle of His discussion of the commandments in the Sermon on the Mount, He said, "Be perfect, therefore, as your heavenly Father is perfect" [Matthew 5:48].

As we "Come unto Him ...... humble ourselves ...... learn of Him ...... take His yoke upon us ...... He will give us rest." I believe the *rest* Jesus speaks of in that passage is the rest of obedience. As He administers the pain and opposition and testing required to bring us to surrender our craving for independence, we will grow closer to the goal. This is the sanctification process spoken of in Scripture. In my 78 years on this planet, I have seen it miraculously occur in many lives.

This chapter will focus on the commandments, and will include a complete list of those which relate specifically to financial stewardship. As mentioned earlier, I have never seen this focus in any of the books which I have read on the subject of finances.

The day before Jesus was crucified, He gathered his disciples together in a room and delivered to them what has become known as the Upper Room Discourse. It covers John Chapters 13 through 17 in the Bible. During this discourse, he used the word *commandment* nine times, making statements like, "If you love me, you will keep my commandments." And, "If you keep my commands, you will remain in my love." Then a few days later, following his resurrection and just before he ascended into heaven, he commissioned his soon-to-be church with its mission in the world. He instructed us to do two things. Go into all the world and preach the gospel (evangelism), and teach the converts to obey all that He commanded (discipleship). Wouldn't you conclude that keeping all His commandments and teaching others to keep them was a high priority for the church in Jesus' mind?

A friend and I began meditating on this a few months ago. We asked ourselves some questions. How can we be obedient disciples of Jesus if we don't know all His commandments? How many are there? How can we teach others to obey all his commandments if we don't know them all? How well is the church doing today at fulfilling the second half of the great commission? Frankly, we would answer, "miserably," based on our observations. We wonder if a lack of respect for and a lack of obedience to the commandments might not be the number one problem in the church today. We decided to research the New Testament for answers to these questions.

THE APOSTLES' COMMANDS VS. JESUS' COMMANDS

One question had to be answered before we could complete our list of commandments and make it a practical study guide to motivate the believer to obedience. That question is, what about all the commandments the apostles gave us in the remainder of the New Testament? Are they part of, equal to, or subordinate to the commandments of Jesus?

Look carefully at the first two verses of the book of Acts, "The former treatise I made, O Theophilus, of all that Jesus began both to do and teach, until the day in which He was taken up, after He through the Holy Spirit had given **commandments** unto the apostles whom he had chosen" [Acts 1:1-2 (KJV)].

The word "commandments" there in Acts 1:2 is the same word used to quote Jesus in the great commission when he referred to "all I have commanded." Just before he left this earth, he commissioned the Holy Spirit to give commandments to the apostles whom he had chosen, so that as the church age began, these commandments wound up in the remainder of the New Testament. We concluded that all the commandments of the apostles must be added to the commandments Jesus spoke to form a composite "all I have commanded" as referred to in the great commission.

The apostles seem to agree with this interpretation as is clear from passages like the following.

Finally, brothers, we instructed you how to live in order to please God, as in fact you are living. Now we ask you and urge you in the Lord Jesus to do this more and more. You know what instructions we gave you by the authority of the Lord Jesus [1 Thessalonians 4:1-2].

[T]hat you should remember the words spoken beforehand by the holy prophets and the commandment of the Lord and Savior spoken by your apostles [2 Peter 3:2 (NASB)].

One of the more interesting things we discovered in our study was that many of the apostles' commandments are commentaries or applications of Jesus' words. This should be no surprise in light of Acts 1:2. For example, "Now flee from youthful lusts, and pursue righteousness, faith, love and peace, with those who call on the Lord from a pure heart" [2 Timothy 2:22 (NASB)]. This seems to be a commentary on Jesus' words, "whoever looks on a woman to lust for her has committed adultery with her already in his heart." And notice that Paul adds counsel on how to obey the command. ("Pursue righteousness, faith, love and peace, with those .... in fellowship with those .... who call on the Lord from a pure heart.") By the time several apostles have commented on or stated a command of Jesus in their own words, the believer should be better equipped to obey it.

IS DISOBEDIENCE EVER IN MY BEST INTEREST?

Our deepest concern is that many of the commandments are being widely disobeyed in the church today. It seems that the church is not taking the commandments seriously. The phrase that describes the church today, we believe, is "selective obedience," and the church in the main is tolerating it.

Remember our discussion in Chapter 2 about our lust for autonomy? The real issue is, do I decide what is in my best interest, or do I let God decide? More accurately, do I accept what God has already revealed to be in my best interest? What is that? His commandments are the simplest and clearest statement of what is in my best interest.

Obedience is always in my best interest, and God gave us no commandments which are impossible for us to keep.

The message of grace, at least in our circles, is well understood and clearly proclaimed, and that is as it should be. But grace invites abuse. Paul understood this and addressed it as an issue in the entirety of the 6th chapter of Romans, which he began with the words, "What shall we say, then? Are we to continue in sin that grace may increase? May it never be."

Like the Israelites in the Old Testament, most serious Christians today intend to keep the commandments, and often do, until they find themselves in a situation in which they perceive the pain of obedience to be greater than the pain of disobedience. That's when they are likely to make the fatal misjudgment that willful disobedience of a command will be in their best interest. Sometimes they disobey anticipating that they can later repent and receive God's forgiveness. This is dealing recklessly with the commandments. God hates willfulness. At best, such a person is saved, but faces severe discipline by the Lord, as Hebrews 12:5-12 clearly teaches. At worst, he has no basis for assurance of his salvation, and may not in fact be saved. Let us not forget that Jesus made it clear that some who think they are saved are in fact not saved, but they will not know it until they stand before Jesus in eternity and hear Him say, "I never knew you."

But many Christians are convinced that grace eliminates accountability in eternity for our behavior on earth. This is a misunderstanding of what theologians call, "The Law of the Harvest," taught throughout Scripture, and perhaps best stated in Galatians 6:7, "Do not be deceived: God cannot be mocked. A man reaps what he sows." The Law of the Harvest has nothing to do with salvation. And note, this was addressed to Christians.

Paul said, "God will render to every man according to his deeds ..." [Romans 2:6 (NASB)]. Both lost and saved will give an account of their behavior when they reach eternity. Hell will not be the same for all unbelievers, and heaven will not be the same for all believers.

Before you conclude that it might be in your best interest to disobey a command, consider the following:

Jesus said, "But I tell you that men will have to give account on the day of judgment for every careless word they have spoken" [Matthew 12:36].

For we must all appear before the judgment seat of Christ, that each one may receive what is due him for the things done while in the body, **whether good or bad** [2 Corinthians 5:10].

Whatever you do, work at it with all your heart, as working for the Lord, not for men, since you know that you will receive an inheritance from the Lord as a reward. It is the Lord Christ you are serving. **Anyone who does wrong will be repaid for his wrong, and there is no favoritism** [Colossians 3:24-25].

If you think that God's forgiveness eliminates accountability in eternity for temporal behavior, you are reading a different Bible than we are.

COMMANDS RELATING TO FINANCIAL STEWARDSHIP

We conclude this chapter with a list of the commandments of Jesus and the apostles relating to financial stewardship. This is only a small percent of the more than 2000 verses which I found on money in the Bible, but they are by far the most important ones, because they give direct instructions and commands on how to manage our finances. We hope you will read them many times, and refer back to them during the course of your study of this book. Just reading and meditating on them will give you a running start toward an understanding of Biblical Economics.

Important Note: These "one-liners" for each command are provided in order to get a quick grasp of all of the commands relating to the managing of money. They can be read at a single sitting, which we recommend doing. But obviously, most have been shortened. This involves some paraphrasing and some interpretations. We could be wrong in some of our interpretations, therefore we invite all comments, suggestions and criticism from the body of Christ. And these are not intended to be a substitute for the full text, which we suggest you read from the Scriptures in its context.

FROM JESUS

MATTHEW

5:33-37   Fulfill your promises. Do not make any vows which presume on the future. Such vows are evil.

5:42   Give to him who asks of you, and do not turn away from him who wants to borrow from you.

6:2-4   Do your giving in secret and your heavenly Father will reward you.

6:11   Pray this: Give us this day our daily bread.

6:19-24   Do not store up for yourselves treasure on earth, where moth and rust destroy, and thieves break in and steal.

6:19-24   Store up for yourselves treasure in heaven, where moth and rust don't destroy, and thieves do not break in and steal.

6:25-34   Do not worry about what you will eat, drink or wear.

6:33   Seek first the kingdom of God and His righteousness, and all these things will be added as well.

22:17-21   Render to Caesar the things that are Caesar's and to God the things that are God's.

25:21,23   Well done good and faithful servant. Come and share your master's happiness.

LUKE

6:38   Give and it will be given to you, for by your standard of measure, it will be measured to you in return.

12:15   Guard against every form of greed, for a person's life does not consist in the abundance of his possessions.

12:32-33   Don't be afraid. Sell your possessions and give to the poor, which will secure you treasure in heaven.

16:1-13   Make friends for yourselves by means of money, that when it fails, they may receive you in eternal dwellings.

16:1-13   If you have not been faithful with your money, who will entrust the true riches to you?

JOHN

6:27-29   Do not work for the food which perishes, but for the food which endures to eternal life, which Jesus gives you.

OBSERVATIONS ON JESUS' COMMANDS

You probably noticed the emphasis on giving. It is one of the primary ways of storing treasure in heaven. Probably the most important command relating to money is store for yourself treasure in heaven, not on earth. That being the case, Jesus put a lot of emphasis on how our earthly needs are to be met. If we are faithful with His money, He will meet our needs. There is a strong implication that our job or profession is our pulpit, our place of ministry. But our employer is Jesus. He will supply our needs. Be a faithful servant and He will meet your earthly needs. And did you notice the heavy emphasis on accountability and reward in eternity based on how we handle our money on earth?

FROM THE APOSTLES

ACTS

4:34-35   Those with a surplus share with those in need that the work may go forward.

20:35   Work hard, helping the weak, remembering Jesus' words, "It is more blessed to give than to receive."

ROMANS

12:13   Contribute to the needs of the saints.

1 CORINTHIANS

9:1-14   Contribute to the financial support of those who minister the word to you.

9:24-27   Discipline yourself in such a way that you may earn a maximum reward for your ministry.

16:1-2   As God prospers you, set aside each week your gift toward the offering for the saints in Jerusalem.

2 CORINTHIANS

8:7-8   Just as you abound in all other spiritual gifts, see that you also abound in giving.

8:11-15   Follow through and make good on your giving commitments. Those with a surplus share with those in need.

9:6-11   Give what you purpose in your heart to give, not grudgingly or under compulsion, for God loves a cheerful giver.

9:6-11   Understand those who sow sparingly will so reap, and also those who sow abundantly will reap abundantly.

EPHESIANS

4:28   Don't steal any more, rather labor to perform what is good, so you can share with those in need.

6:5-8   Employees, be obedient to your employers, as unto Christ, knowing that you will receive back from the Lord.

6:9   Employers, treat well your employees, knowing their Master and yours is in heaven, and He is impartial.

COLOSSIANS

3:1-4   Set your mind on things above, not on earthly things.

4:1   Employers, give your employees justice and fairness, knowing you too have a Master in heaven.

1 THESSALONIANS

4:11-12   Lead a quiet life and mind your own business, that you may behave well toward outsiders, and not be in need.

2 THESSALONIANS

3:10-12   If anyone will not work, neither let him eat. Some are undisciplined, doing no work, acting like busybodies.

1 TIMOTHY

5:3-7   Honor widows, but if she has children or grandchildren, let them first care for her.

5:8   Whoever fails to provide for his own family has denied the faith

5:9-10   To qualify for help, a widow must be 60, the wife of one man, and have devoted herself to every good work.

5:11-15   Do not provide for the younger widows, who should marry rather than be idle.

5:16 If a believing woman has dependent widows, let her assist them.

5:17-18 Compensate generously the elders who rule well, especially those who work hard at preaching and teaching.

6:1-2 Let employees regard their employers as worthy of honor, that the name of God not be spoken against.

6:1-2 Let those who have believers as employers not be disrespectful because they are brethren, but serve them well.

6:11-14 Flee the love of money and the desire to get rich, rather pursue righteousness, faith, love. Keep the commandment.

6:17-19 Instruct those who are rich not to fix their hope on their riches, but on God who gives all things to enjoy.

6:17-19 Instruct those who are rich to do good, to be rich in good works, to be generous and ready to share.

TITUS

2:9-10 Employees, be subject to your employers in everything. Be well-pleasing, not argumentative, showing good faith.

HEBREWS

13:5-6 Let your character be free from the love of money, being content with what you have.

13:5-6 He has said, "I will never leave you nor forsake you." Therefore, I will not be afraid. What can man do to me?

13:16 Do not neglect doing good and sharing, for with such sacrifices God is pleased.

JAMES

1:9 You who are of humble circumstances, glory in your high position.

1:10-11 You who are rich, glory in your humiliation, because like the flowering grass,you will pass away.

4:13-17 Do not presume on the future saying, "Tomorrow we will do this or that." You do not know what tomorrow holds.

4:13-17 Say, "If the Lord wills, we will do this or that," rather than boast in your arrogance. Such boasting is evil.

5:1-6 You who are rich, weep for the miseries which are coming upon you. Your hoarded riches have rotted.

---

1 PETER

2:18-21   Employees, be submissive to your employers, not only to those who are good, but to those who are unreasonable.

2:18-21   Employees, if you suffer unjustly, you were called for this purpose, your example being Christ.

1 JOHN

3:16-18   Whoever sees his brother in need and closes his heart to him, how does the love of God abide in him?

3 JOHN

1:5-8   You do well to minister to the brethren, especially strangers, and send them out in a manner worthy of God.

OBSERVATIONS ON THE APOSTLES' COMMANDS

As was the case with Jesus' commands, there is a major emphasis on giving, but we notice the apostles' use of the word *need*, which appears a number of times. Giving is to be based on need (spreading the gospel, feeding the poor, supporting the ministries of the church). The apostles' commands also touch on the work ethic and the relationship between employers and employees. And like Jesus, the apostles focus on the eternal rather than the temporal, and warn strongly against the sin of greed and the desire to get rich.

A FOUNDATION OF THREE PILLARS

This concludes the first three chapters, which we consider to be the foundation for our study of Biblical Economics. That foundation rests on three pillars. First, we must understand and believe that God is in control and has our best interest at heart. Second, we must surrender our lust for autonomy, independence and self-rule. Third, we must submit to the absolute authority of Jesus Christ, making our goal unconditional obedience to all He has commanded. Only a financial plan which rests on these three pillars will bring honor and glory to God and reward in eternity.

FOR MEDITATION ON THE THREE PILLARS

First Pillar – Square One

Do I really believe Romans 8:28? "God causes all things to work together for good to them who love God, who are called according to His purpose." Do I believe "all" means "all" in that verse? Review the nine conclusions at the end of Chapter 1. Which ones am I unable to accept? Do I believe that every circumstance of my life, and every person who touches my life, is there by God's permission, for His purposes and under His control? Read and meditate on Hebrews 13:5-6. It says, "Let your character be free from the love of money, being content with what you have, for He Himself has said, 'I will never leave you nor forsake you.' So that we say confidently, 'The Lord is my helper, I will not be afraid. What can man do to me?' "

How do you answer that question?

Second Pillar – Surrender of my Autonomy-Lust

Do I understand that I am in a life-long process of sanctification, which is really a process by which I am progressively being brought to surrender my lust for autonomy, my lust for independence and self-rule? Do I understand that God's role in this process is the administration of pain and opposition, and that my part is surrender, humbling myself under the mighty hand of God? Do I understand the vital role of sorrow and suffering in this process, as expressed in countless passages in the Bible, such as Romans 5:3-5, "We also rejoice in our sufferings, because we know that suffering produces perseverance; perseverance, character; and character, hope." Do I understand that the ultimate goal of this process is brokenness? I recommend that you read *Don't Waste Your Sorrows*, by Paul Billheimer, for the best presentation of this truth I have seen.

Third Pillar – Obedience to the Commandments

Do I understand that once I have begun the process of surrendering my autonomy, then my whole duty becomes submission to Jesus, which means obedience to all He has commanded us? It is so easy for us to think of our duty as evangelism, bearing fruit, ministry, the exercise of our spiritual gifts, or even abiding in Christ. But these are not goals in themselves, but rather results of obedience, as Jesus so carefully explained in His last discourse to His disciples (John Chapters 13 thru 17). Here are some of His statements. "If you keep My commandments, you shall abide in my love, even as I have kept My Father's commandments and abide in His love." "You are my friends if you do what I command you." "If you love Me, you will keep My commandments." Do I understand that selective obedience is not an option in the mind of Jesus? Am I familiar with all the commandments of Jesus and the apostles?[1]

In the remaining chapters of this book, you will find truth which will challenge you as you manage your finances. However, it will make little difference eternally if you forget or brush aside this summary. On the other hand, if you copy and memorize these ideas before you proceed, the burdens that can be lifted from you in this present life, and the weight of blessing that can be transferred to your eternal account, will be inestimable.

May God protect and watch over our hearts as we now move into the study of Biblical Economics.

---

[1] A complete list of commands of Jesus and the apostles is available free upon request by email to muff-jd@cox.net. Put "Command List" in the subject line.

CHAPTER 4

GOD'S MANAGEMENT AGREEMENT WITH MAN

When I taught a seminar on this subject in the 1980s, I made a list of questions which I wanted to find biblical answers to and share with those who would attend the seminar. The first question in the list, which became the subject of the first session, was, "What is the central truth in the Bible regarding the handling of money?" The short, one-statement answer which I came up with was, "God entrusts His wealth to man to manage for Him." A slightly fuller version of this was, "God owns and controls all wealth. He entrusts His wealth to man to manage or steward for His purpose, which is to enlarge His estate (the kingdom). And He holds man accountable for his stewardship, rewarding those who do well and penalizing, or withholding rewards from those who don't."

As I read through the list of commands in Chapter 3, I asked myself this question, "Do they support the statement of the central truth which I came up with 25 years ago?" And my answer is, "Yes, they do." And I remember that at that time, the passage of Scripture which seemed to me to best present this central truth was Jesus' parable of the talents recorded in Matthew 25:14-30, which begins, "Again, it (i.e., the kingdom) will be like a man going on a journey, who called his servants and entrusted his property to them."

The illustration is of an estate owner who went on a journey, and during his absence, left portions of his property in the hands of three managers, obviously hoping they would not only protect his interests but enhance the value of his estate. As I studied the passage, it struck me as being almost in the form of a management agreement or contract. And I could see four basic provisions in the contract.

1. A duration provision

In the illustration, the duration is the time between the estate owner's departure and return from his journey. But this is a parable, and Jesus probably intends for us to see this as representing the time between His first and second advents, what we commonly refer to today as the "church age." But further, I believe He intends for each believer to see the duration as beginning with his new birth and ending with his death, or the return of Christ, whichever first occurs. In other words, I'm under this management agreement from the time I become a Christian until I die.

2. A purpose and responsibility provision

In the illustration the purpose of the arrangement was to preserve and increase the value of the owner's estate. And each servant was responsible to employ the assets entrusted to him in investments or activities designed to best carry out that purpose. Likewise it is the responsibility of each believer to employ the assets God has entrusted to him (time, energy, gifts, abilities, financial resources, etc.) in ways which will enlarge the kingdom. A simple reading through the list of commands suggests to me the primary ways in which we do this are evangelism, sharing with those in need, supporting various ministries, meeting the needs of our families, discipling others, etc. Not all, but a significant portion of our responsibilities will involve the management of money.

3. A reward provision

This is the incentive or payoff provision, and it lets us know that we can expect to be rewarded for good stewardship. The parable mentions two specific rewards for good stewardship, more assets to manage for the estate owner, and more joy and happiness.

4. A penalty provision

What we can expect if we are poor stewards. What happens if we waste God's assets, or consume them on things which produce nothing for the kingdom? What happens if we hoard God's assets (storing them on earth instead of heaven)? In the parable, one of the servants buried the money entrusted to him, giving the excuse that he was afraid to subject it to risk. He was severely rebuked and lost his reward. His mismanagement was simply failing to invest a sum of money in a way that would produce a return for the owner. But he may be representative of a believer with a musical talent who does not use it to glorify God, or a believer who overspends his income, or a believer who hoards wealth in such a way that very little of it ever gets into the kingdom, or a Christian parent who does not prepare his children for good stewardship of God's assets. In the parable four specific penalties are mentioned, or implied, for mismanagement: rebuke, loss of joy and peace, loss of management responsibility, and loss of reward.

CAUTION: THIS IS A NEW TESTAMENT PARABLE

Here we must be very careful. Because this is a parable, we cannot press every detail of the story to teach doctrine. Often many of the details of the story are there merely to make the story internally consistent. For example, we cannot conclude that God will entrust more wealth to us if we are good stewards, on the basis of the fact that one of the stewards in the parable received the talent that was mismanaged by the poor steward. In the Old Testament God promised temporal blessings - such as health and material prosperity - for obedience.

But in the New Testament, although God does promise things like peace, contentment, joy and assurance for obedience, we are promised nothing in the way of material wealth beyond our basic needs. This is clear from many passages, but none clearer than Matthew 6:19-34, where Jesus commands us not to store for ourselves treasure on earth, but rather treasure in heaven.

I will never forget sitting in a Bible study on this passage, and the teacher said, "It is so important to Jesus that we concentrate on storing treasure in heaven that He has taken upon Himself full responsibility for meeting our earthly needs." And this is exactly what verse 33 says. God may or may not give us wealth beyond our basic needs, but He has not obligated Himself to do so.

Likewise, in the Old Testament, God told Israel that not only would He withhold temporal blessings for disobedience, but He would send curses. (See especially Deuteronomy 28 for His promise of both blessings and curses.) There is no such language in the New Testament. We have entered into a father-son relationship with God through the new birth. Although He does discipline us for disobedience (Hebrews 12), its purpose is not punitive, but rather remedial. Therefore, we cannot interpret the penalty imposed by the estate owner in the parable to teach that God will remove wealth from the poor steward in this life. He may or He may not. What we know for certain is that eternal reward, or loss of it, is what is at stake in the stewardship arrangement. This is consistent with the whole of the New Testament.

Look for a single theme or truth to be conveyed by a parable, but don't try to build doctrines on each of the details. The overall truth of this parable is that we are managers, not owners, of all God entrusts to us, and we will be accountable to Him in eternity for our stewardship of His gifts and assets here on earth. We will be rewarded for good stewardship and lose rewards for poor stewardship. Our only promise for this earthly life is that obedience will bring spiritual blessings and the meeting of our basic needs.

THE TEMPTATION TO TAKE POSSESSION OF GOD'S WEALTH

So summarizing, the management agreement has four provisions: duration, purpose, reward and penalty. And as we read the agreement in the pages of the Bible, one of the first things we notice is that God entrusts his assets to us, but He does not give them to us. God does not transfer title to his property to the believer. He does not convey ownership. He only conveys stewardship. Psalm 24:1 says, "The earth is the Lord's and everything in it, the world and all who live in it." Most of us get off the track at this point. We immediately take possession of God's property when any of it falls into our hands. We clutch it, and soon it becomes an idol, and we begin to instinctively think of ourselves as owners of God's wealth rather than managers. And the moment we do, we're in violation of the management agreement.

It has been helpful to me since I learned this to make myself recall this central foundational truth every time God entrusts anything to me ...... to stop right then and say, "Thank you Lord, I understand that this is yours. What do you want me to do with it? How much of it do you want me to surrender today, and how much of it do you want me to hold and manage for your purposes?"

When God entrusts income, ability, knowledge, energy, health to you, do you do this? Do you look at it in this perspective? When you get up in the morning, do you do this? Do you realize that every new day is included in the term "God's property?" It's a sacred trust from God to be used in a certain way to glorify Him. When a child is born into your home, do you do this? Do you think of your children as being included in the term "God's property?" **And think about this**. Our children will be a form of God's property which we will have under management for only a short time. Do you consider yourself an owner of your children? Are you willing for them to be used as God directs? This is a tough question ...... a soul-searching question. Are you teaching your children how to live a life of stewardship of God's property. You have at most 18-20 years to do that. After that they are no longer under your authority. If you will stop and recall this central truth every time God entrusts any of his assets to you, it will begin to transform your life. Don't wait until you have taken possession of it, and it has become an idol.

GOD'S CONTROL AND DISTRIBUTION OF WEALTH

How much do we know about how God distributes and controls His wealth? The short answer to this question is, "Some, but not much." What we know for certain is that He is in complete control, and that everything He does is with our best interest in His heart. What is far more difficult, and usually impossible to know, is how and why He distributes wealth and all other forms of His assets among individuals and nations.

No one from the east or the west or from the desert can exalt a man. But it is God who judges: He brings one down. He exalts another [Psalm 75:6-7].

An age old question we have heard is, "Does God intend for all Christians to be rich materially?" Some would answer this question, "Yes," especially in our day.

Rich and poor have this in common: The Lord is Maker of them all [Proverbs 22:2].

Consider what God has done: Who can straighten what He has made crooked? When times are good, be happy. But when times are bad, consider: God has made the one as well as the other. Therefore a man cannot discover anything about his future [Ecclesiastes 7:13-14].

Ponder this question: Can we marshal all of our mental resources, mobilize the power of positive thinking, and set our minds on becoming rich and have it happen? For a hundred years or longer, books have been written declaring that we can. Sales of these books are still strong today. I don't believe the Bible supports this idea.

Who can speak and have it happen if the Lord has not decreed it? Is it not from the mouth of the Most High that both calamities and good things come? Why should any living man complain when punished for his sins? Let us examine our ways and test them, and let us return to the Lord [Lamentations 3:37-40].

In his heart a man plans his course, but the Lord determines his steps [Proverbs 16:9].

There is nothing wrong with planning in and of itself. It is a wise practice, as long as we are obedient to God's commandments.

There is no wisdom, no insight, no plan that can succeed against the Lord [Proverbs 21:30].

Through the centuries men have tried to leave God out of their plans and succeed, but if these verses are true, no one has ever pulled it off. God makes rich, and He makes poor. He controls the transfer of wealth. He always has the last say.

THE NEW TESTAMENT ALSO HELPS ANSWER THIS QUESTION

Command those who are rich in this present world not to be arrogant nor to put their hope in wealth, which is so uncertain, but to put their hope in God, who richly provides us with everything for our enjoyment [1 Timothy 6:17].

Here Paul expands on Jesus' words that treasure on earth is subject to loss ...... from moth, rust and thieves.

God may take wealth away from the faithful steward to teach him he can have contentment without material wealth. This is one way of testing His steward and teaching him to live in daily dependence on God. Nowhere in Scripture have I found anything to indicate that wealth or poverty are intended to be permanent conditions in life, but either can be a stage in the development of godly character. The apostle Paul learned this lesson.

> I am not saying this because I am in need, for I have learned to be content whatever the circumstances. I know what it is to be in need. And I know what it is to have plenty. I have learned the secret of being content in any and every situation, whether well fed or hungry, whether living in plenty or in want [Philippians 4:11-12].

Notice he used the word "learned" twice here. I don't suppose this was natural for Paul any more than it would be for any of us. It is something that has to be learned over a period of time as God puts us through the tests.

Sometimes God puts people through a complete cycle from wealth to poverty and back to wealth. A good illustration of this was Job. Surely the greatest example of some one who went through this cycle is the Lord Jesus.

> For you know the grace of our Lord Jesus Christ, that though He was rich, yet for your sakes He became poor, so that you through His poverty might become rich [2 Corinthians 8:9].

Jesus went through this wealth-poverty cycle, and He wants us to be able to go through it.

> In the same way, any of you who does not give up everything he has cannot be my disciple [Luke 14:33].

I think you can see that God's distribution and control of wealth on this earth is not as simple as some would have us believe. I believe that the theological system which declares that God intends for every believer to be healthy and wealthy is unscriptural because it is built on half-truths. We cannot understand all of God's ways. We cannot always know why God does what He does. Yes, He has seen fit to reveal some of His truth concerning His distribution of wealth. These few statements and Scripture passages are an attempt to convey some of the more simple concepts. It has been a blessing to me to meditate on them.

SIX RECOMMENDATIONS FOR MANAGING GOD'S PROPERTY

- Recognize God as the owner and controller of all wealth.

- Sign the stewardship agreement, which means in effect that you deed everything back to God.

- Remember that owners have rights and managers have responsibilities, so give up your rights and accept your responsibilities.

- Hold all wealth with an open hand. Consider it on call to God. Be ready to surrender it when He calls (for He *will* call).

- Never forget that God is in control and has your best interest at heart.

- Never forget that unless you surrender your lust for autonomy and submit to the authority of Jesus, you have not signed the stewardship agreement.

A PERSONAL CONFESSION

Every time I make a financial decision in life and forget the one thing that is the subject of this chapter, I cannot possibly please God. I need to realize whose assets I'm about to spend. When I am considering investing in a business, or purchasing an automobile, or whether to rent or purchase a home, the decision will be affected by whether I see an owner or manager in the mirror. This will be an ongoing struggle in my life. The true Owner has been absent physically for many generations, but He retains 100% control of all the holdings of His universe. This arrangement really is in my best interest.

CHAPTER 5

THE SIN OF MATERIALISM

Usually we tend to think of our problems in terms of symptoms. In the case of financial stewardship, some of the symptoms would be overspending, compulsive buying, failing to give generously, hoarding wealth, cheating on our income tax, failing to budget, failing to save for the future ...... These are all symptoms of the problem, but they are not the root problem. The root problem is spiritual, not economic, and there are no economic solutions to spiritual problems. There are no political solutions to spiritual problems. A spiritual problem must be dealt with spiritually.

We established in Chapter 2 that our problem is with God. We want to decide what is in our best interest and what is not, rather than submit to what God says is in our best interest and what is not. We called this our lust for autonomy, and our part of the solution to this problem is to surrender our autonomy-lust and obey His commandments.

The Bible has a lot to say about how this lust manifests itself in relation to the management of money. It describes a specific sin, the sin of materialism. In this chapter we want to try to answer three questions about this sin. How does the Bible define it? What are its consequences in our lives? What is the way of victory over it?

HOW DOES THE BIBLE DEFINE THE SIN OF MATERIALISM?

There are eight words in the King James Version of the Bible, (five, New Testament, three, Old Testament) translated by the English word "covet," or one of its forms, and usually translated by the word "greed" or "greedy" in the later translations. Sometimes the old English word "covet" or "coveteousness" is retained in the later translations. Although "covet" is sometimes used in a good sense, e.g., "covet earnestly the best gifts," this discussion is restricted to its use to describe the sin of greed.

Of these eight words, the most prevalent is the Greek word *pleonexia*. That is the word which appears in Luke 12:15, where Jesus said,

"Watch out! Be on your guard against all kinds of greed; a man's life does not consist in the abundance of his possessions." W. E. Vine, in his Expository Dictionary of New Testament Words, defines this word, "a desire to have more." In the Amplified translation of the New Testament, this word is translated by a phrase, "the greedy longing to have more." After reading several scholars, I get the feeling that this translation is very close to the true meaning of *pleonexia* as it was used in the Koine Greek language.

As I studied all eight of these Bible words and looked up the references, two attitudes of heart emerged in my mind as the essence of the sin of materialism as presented in the Bible. First, a desire to have more arising out of a dissatisfied or discontented heart. Second, the envy of someone else's possessions. If you marry these two attitudes together, I believe you have the essence of this sin.

WHAT ARE ITS CONSEQUENCES – HOW DANGEROUS IS IT?

I think it is almost impossible to overestimate the danger of this sin in our lives. Jesus had a lot to say about money, most of it warning of its danger. He never taught that money is intrinsically evil, but He repeatedly taught that it is intrinsically dangerous. It formed a prominent part of His Sermon on the Mount (especially Matthew 6:19-34). In that passage He made it clear that the love of money is idolatry, the worship of a false god. He said, "Where your treasure (money) is, there your heart will be also ...... you cannot serve both God and money." We will study that key passage in Chapter 15 of this book.

If I had to select Jesus' strongest warning of the danger of covetousness, it would be what He said to his disciples following his conversation with the rich young ruler. You are familiar with the story. The young man asked Jesus what he needed to do to gain eternal life. Jesus told him to keep the commandments. The young man asked which ones. Jesus named six of the commandments. The young man said he had kept them and asked if there was anything else he lacked. Jesus told him to sell all his possessions and give to the poor, then come and follow Him. Then the text says:

> When the young man heard this, he went away sad, because he had great wealth [Matthew 19:22].

He could not give up his wealth for Jesus. He could not surrender his lust for control. Then followed a brief discussion between Jesus and His disciples which holds the key to how man enters into a relationship with God.

> Then Jesus said to His disciples, "I tell you the truth, it is hard for a rich man to enter the kingdom of heaven. Again I tell you, it is easier for a camel to go through the eye of a needle than for a rich man to enter the kingdom of God" [Matthew 19:23-24].

Did Jesus intend this to be taken literally? It has been debated throughout church history. Some have suggested ways of getting around the difficulty of a literal interpretation. I incline toward a literal interpretation based on what immediately follows in the text.

> When the disciples heard this, they were greatly astonished and asked, "Who then can be saved?" Jesus looked at them and said, "With man this is impossible, but with God all things are possible" [Matthew 19:25-26].

A camel could go through the eye of a needle if God performed a miracle, otherwise it would be impossible. A rich person can get to heaven only if Jesus performs a miracle, otherwise it's impossible. How could Jesus have possibly better communicated the intrinsic danger of possessing riches?

But wait, you and I, and all other people are in exactly the same position. Salvation is impossible for everyone, with or without money and regardless of the amount, unless God removes the blindness of Satan (See 2 Corinthians 4:4).

That having been said, Jesus leaves no doubt that the rich face an additional temptation not faced by the poor. The rich young ruler would not have been saved by the good works of charitable giving. However, in his case he had to overcome greed in order to believe. Money was his god and a barrier to faith. The key phrase is "... come, follow me" [Matthew 19:21]. The first step in following Christ is faith, but money blocked any faith from the rich young ruler. Many in our time have the identical problem.

Jesus didn't define rich. Obviously He didn't intend to. Couldn't a person with very little money still let his desire for money keep him from trusting Christ? I would say, of course. So why did Jesus make such a point of it? My opinion is (just opinion), He wanted to strike fear into us of the danger of wealth.

PAUL AND THE DANGER OF MATERIALISM

The apostles also sounded warnings of the danger of the sin of greed, especially the apostle Paul. If I had to pick one passage which best sounds the warning, it would be Paul's well known and lengthy discourse on the love of money found in 1 Timothy 6:3-19. Let's let Paul tell us in his words how dangerous this sin is. Verse 9 says, "People who want to get rich fall into temptation and a trap and into many foolish and harmful desires that plunge men into ruin and destruction."

The word translated "destruction" is translated "perdition" in the King James Version. Webster's New World Dictionary defines "perdition," (1) complete and irreparable loss; ruin, (2) In theology, (a) the loss of the soul or of hope for salvation; damnation, (b) hell. The Greek word is *apoleia*. J. H. Thayer, in his Greek-English Lexicon, defines this word, "the destruction which consists in the loss of eternal life, eternal misery, perdition, the lot of those excluded from the kingdom of God." Does that sound dangerous to you?

We know Paul was familiar with the words of Jesus, for he begins this discourse, "If anyone advocates a different doctrine and does not agree with sound words, those of our Lord Jesus Christ, and with the doctrine conforming to godliness, he is conceited and understands nothing" [1 Timothy 6:3-4a (NASB)]. I suspect Paul was familiar with what Jesus said to the rich young ruler, and to His disciples. What he writes to Timothy seems to be a commentary on Jesus' words. He makes the point that the desire to be rich sets a person on a path that leads to hell, the same destiny as the man who has riches referred to by Jesus, a destiny impossible for men to avoid without the intervention of God.

Have you ever said, or thought in your mind, I don't really want to get rich; I just want to have enough money to be secure? Be very careful with that position, because Paul clearly defines what he means by the desire to get rich. Verse 8 says, "And if we have food and covering, with these we shall be content." Paul's phrase "food and covering" is his way of describing the strict essentials of survival. He wants us to understand that we must be content if we have nothing more than that. Then he begins verse 9 with the word "but," setting up a contrast.

Thus he is defining a person who wants to get rich as anyone who wants more than the strict essentials. I think that one must manipulate the text to get around this definition.

But Paul isn't finished with his warning. He goes on to say in verse 10, "For the love of money is a root of all kinds of evil. Some people, eager for money, have wandered from the faith, and pierced themselves with many griefs." The love of money is a root ...... meaning it can spawn or lead to ...... just about any other sin imaginable. And it leads to grief, heartache, and defeat in life.

Let me summarize what we have said about the danger and seriousness of the sin of materialism. It is idolatry, the worship of a false god. It ruins lives and leads countless men to hell. It is the source of every brand of sin in the catalogue. It brings sorrow, heartache, defeat, loss of contentment, sometimes death, and eternal loss of reward. I submit that that is dangerous.

HOW CAN WE GET VICTORY OVER THE SIN OF COVETEOUSNESS?

Is there a way of victory over this sin in the Christian life? Of course, the answer is "yes." There is a way of victory over any sin in the Christian life. God has a way out of entanglement with any sin. Let us not forget Jesus' words, "With men this is impossible, but with God all things are possible." If we take these words at face value, our only hope for victory over this sin is by the power of God. And let us not forget that God loves to do the impossible. It is His specialty.

Then what will bring about His doing the miracle required to deliver me from the bondage of this sin? I was visiting about this with my friend who is helping me write this book. He looked at me and said, "Tell me how to disengage from an intimate, sinful relationship to money." For several minutes I was at a loss for words. I did not have an answer for him. We discussed the question for quite a few minutes, and we both realized that the Bible gives us clear and explicit instructions on how we should proceed ...... that is, our responsibility in the matter. If He chooses to do so, God will work the miracle that will bring deliverance, but there is a part we must play, actually a series of steps we must take. What follows is the best I have been able to put it into words.

First, we must realize we are guilty of this sin. We must understand that the desire for money has blinded us and deceived us, else why would we seek deliverance from it? Then how are we to come to this realization? The apostle Paul clearly commands us to examine ourselves and to judge sin in our own lives. Meditate on the following.

> Therefore, whoever eats the bread or drinks the cup of the Lord in an unworthy manner will be guilty of sinning against the body and blood of the Lord. A man ought to examine himself before he eats of the bread and drinks the cup. For anyone who eats and drinks without recognizing the body of the Lord eats and drinks judgment on himself. That is why many among you are weak and sick, and a number of you have fallen asleep. But if we judged ourselves, we would not come under judgment. When we are judged by the Lord, we are disciplined so that we will not be condemned with the world [1 Corinthians 11:27-32].

That's pretty clear isn't it? Paul commands us to examine ourselves (obviously he means examine our hearts for any sin that is there), and makes it clear that until we have done so, we are not eligible to participate in communion (the Lord 's Table).

So what does this self-examination look like in relation to the sin of materialism? Personally, I would think it means I should ask myself some questions. Am I content with what God has given me? Or, do I want more? Am I grateful to God for the circumstances I am in? Do I believe He has providentially ordered them with my best interest at heart? Am I envious of someone else's wealth? Do I desire to get rich? Have I fallen for the illusion that money will bring fulfillment of my dream for control?

A few years ago I watched by video recordings, a twenty-session Bible study on finances. In one of the sessions the teacher was discussing the sin of covetousness. He suggested that each student examine his own heart in relation to this sin by answering ten questions. Here are the ten questions, each to be answered "yes" or "no."

• When you need some item (of more than token value), is your first thought to buy it rather than pray for it?

• Are you expecting money to give you peace of mind, influence or happiness?

• Do you find it more exciting to get money than to gain insight from the Bible?

• Do you allow the cares of this world to choke out a daily time in God's word?

• Are you content with your present income?

• Do you look forward to retirement more than the return of Christ?

• Do you spend more time each week reading secular or business material than you do reading the Bible?

• Would those who know you best say that your job is more important to you than your family?

• Do you have a secret desire to be rich?

• Have you ever dedicated all of your money and possessions to the Lord?

As my friend and I discussed these questions, he suggested an 11th question. It struck me as being one of the best, so I want to include it.

• Is your lifestyle inextricably linked with your giving? In other words, when your income rises, how much of it goes to giving and how much goes to increased standard of living?

I suggest meditating on these questions. It can give you an indication of where you stand in relation to this problem.

Having "failed" this self-examination, then what do I do? Answer: confession, repentance and prayer for deliverance. "If we confess our sins, He is faithful and just and will forgive us our sins, and purify us from all unrighteousness" [1 John 1:9]. It is important to understand the meaning of the word "confess" in this verse. The Greek word is *homologeo*, literally, "to say the same," thus meaning that we agree with God about our sins. If we are not honest in our self examination, perhaps having no real intention of forsaking the sin, then we have not met God's condition for forgiveness and cleansing, and we will not get victory over this sin.

Let me make two observations. First, since we are told to repeat observance of the Lord's Table until Jesus returns, it follows that we must also repeat self-examination, confession and repentance.

Second, failing the exam is evidence that we have not surrendered our autonomy-lust. When Jesus spoke of "the deceitfulness of riches," He was putting us on notice that the desire for wealth would be one of the greatest hurdles we would face in this life. Part of the deception to which He referred is the notion that wealth will give us the control we crave ...... the notion that our dream for autonomy can be realized. The further one is drawn into this deception, the greater the pain and opposition God must administer to bring the deceived believer to realize his dream is an illusion.

You don't have to attain affluence to get sucked into this trap. You need only desire it. "Trap" is Paul's word in 1 Timothy 6:9, "People who want to get rich fall into temptation and a trap and into many foolish and harmful desires that plunge men into ruin and destruction." Had it ever occurred to you that the heartache, ruin and tribulation Paul describes in this passage could be the very thing God is using to motivate you to get off the path of seeking autonomy (and riches)? And that until you surrender that desire and submit to Jesus, you are on the path to self-destruction?

A poor person can be as guilty of the sin of materialism as a rich person, but Jesus left no doubt which would face the greater challenge. He left no doubt that the "wealth test" would be far more difficult than the "poverty test." Since learning this, my heart goes out to the wealthy every bit as much as to the poor. Apparently Jesus' heart went out to the rich young ruler. In the account recorded by Mark, it says, "Jesus looked at him and loved him" [Mark 10:21].

I want to be as honest and balanced as I can be here. Certainly there are wealthy people who are not guilty of the sin of covetousness. But I believe this sin is the "respectable" sin and the "near-universal" sin in the church today, and that the message of this chapter is the message the church needs today.

Verses 8-10 of 1 Timothy 6 are among the strongest words in the New Testament addressed to believers. I suggest you spend some time meditating on them. They are nothing less than terrifying to me. I want to share with you some of my observations on them. They are undoubtedly written to believers, but Paul knows that some of his readers who profess Christ are in fact not believers. He may be warning any unbeliever, who thinks he is a believer, that if he wants to get rich, and does not repent of his sin, he will go to hell. He has been deceived ...... blinded ... fallen into the trap, and is on the path that leads to hell as verse 9 says.

Paul may intend for those who are in fact true believers to take these words as a strong warning that if they are guilty of this sin, they have no reason to enjoy assurance of their salvation. And unless they repent, they will inevitably endure the ruin, heartache and griefs spoken of in verses 9 and 10.

But let me come to my primary observation. What difference does it make what the correct interpretation is? Why would any person today who professes faith in Christ, who believes the Bible to be the Word of God, and who is familiar with this passage, do anything other than examine his heart, confess and repent if the Holy Spirit convicts him? Why would he not take up a prayer vigil and beg God to deliver him from materialism lust? And how could such a person come to any conclusion other than that he still clings to his lust for autonomy, his thirst for self-rule?

Why wouldn't such a person ask God to do whatever it takes to free him from the trap? Many in the church today are already experiencing the ruin, harmful lusts, and griefs Paul describes in this passage. I believe they are being purposefully administered by God in the lives of those caught in this trap. God is in control, doing what is in each one's best interest. I believe God intends for this passage to scare us ...... no, to terrify us. It may be the only hope for some.

In my personal opinion, the evangelical church of our day has well proclaimed the gospel of grace, which teaches that salvation comes by faith alone in the redemptive death of Christ, not by works. I believe this with all my heart. If my salvation depended in any degree whatsoever on any work or deed that I could perform, I would be absolutely without hope.

But we have remained far too quiet on the words of Jesus and Paul discussed in this chapter. Genuine conversion is presented in the New Testament as a regeneration, or transformation, as "becoming a new creation; old things have passed away; all things have become new." I get the impression that many believe that once they go through the motions of professing Christ by signing a decision card or walking an aisle ... they can continue as they are and feel safe. Is that the conclusion you reach reading the words of Jesus and Paul?

Turning away from the love of money, by itself, doesn't save anyone. Trusting Christ as sin-bearer saves us. But our attitude toward money is a litmus test of *saving* faith, an evidence of the genuineness of faith. As we write this book, my burden is for that multitude (including, no doubt, many identified with the church) who are on the broad way leading to destruction, unaware that they are, who will hear Jesus say, "I never knew you," after it's too late. I'm not concerned about those who are truly born again, who may be attempting to serve both God and money. God will deal with them. He will chastise them, scourge them, administer pain and opposition to them, and do whatever it takes to bring them to surrender and brokenness, or remove them to heaven (sin unto death). My burden is for those who are "without chastisement, who are illegitimate children, not true sons" (Hebrews 12:8). They can believe they are saved, and still be blind to their lost condition. It seems to me that a major portion of the Sermon on the Mount, other teachings of Jesus, and Paul's teaching in 1 Timothy 6 are addressed to them as a warning of the danger of materialism. We don't know who they are. We cannot judge any heart or condemn any individual. Only God knows those who are His, and which ones will repent (perhaps at some future date). All we can do is make the warnings clear, and when someone openly disobeys a commandment, confront him, administer church discipline, restore fellowship when there is repentance, or withdraw fellowship when there is not. (A practice almost non-existent in much of the body of Christ today, it seems to me.)

None of this gives me any comfort or pleasure, but I believe Jesus will not allow anyone to be comfortable attempting to serve both Him and money. I believe He intends us to fear (in the sense of terror) when we attempt to, and I admit having such fear as I read these portions of Scripture. If you fit the description of the person Paul describes in 1 Timothy 6:8-10, and you feel secure and have assurance of your salvation, these are the words you need to hear, for you could be in grave danger.

HOW WILL I KNOW I AM BEING DELIVERED FROM MATERIALISM?

If I am being delivered from this sin, I should notice that some of the answers to my self-examination questions are changing. Am I content with what God has given me? Or, do I want more? Am I envious of someone else's wealth? Do I desire to get rich? Have I fallen for the illusion that money will bring fulfillment of my dream for control? Is my attitude toward money changing? Am I attempting to serve both Jesus and money, or have I deeded all my wealth back to God, holding it with an open hand for God to call on at any time? When that becomes my experience, then I will know I am being delivered from materialism lust. I will have made a dedication shift from the riches of the Owner to the Owner Himself. Let's ask God for it.

Dear Lord, we acknowledge our sin. We pray for Your forgiveness. We cast ourselves on Your mercy, and beg You to once and for all deliver us from our lust for autonomy and money. By Your almighty power we ask You to intervene in our lives and do whatever it takes to deliver us from our materialism lust. We realize from reading Paul's words what this could mean, and it is scary. But we must have it, so we ask You to perform the miracle to make happen what will otherwise be impossible. Do the miracle that would make it possible to put a camel through the eye of a needle. We pray in Jesus name. Amen.

CHAPTER 6

PRESUMING ON THE FUTURE

The very first command in the list of commands dealing with economics is Jesus' command on vows.

> Again, you have heard that the ancients were told, "You shall not make false vows, but shall fulfill your vows to the Lord." But I say to you, make no oath at all, either by heaven, for it is the throne of God, or by the earth, for it is the footstool of His feet, or by Jerusalem, for it is the city of the great King. Nor shall you make an oath by your head, for you cannot make one hair white or black. But let your statement be, "Yes, yes," or "No, no"; and anything beyond these is of evil [Matthew 5:33-37 (NASB)].

As you know, I have interpreted the essence of this command as stated by the following "one-liner":

"Fulfill your promises. Do not make any vows which presume on the future. Such vows are evil."

Like several of His commands in the Sermon on the Mount, Jesus refers back to a command from the Law of Moses, and then revises it. Here are two Old Testament references to the law concerning vows.

> If you make a vow to the Lord your God, do not be slow to pay it, for the Lord your God will certainly demand it of you and you will be guilty of sin. But if you refrain from making a vow, you will not be guilty. Whatever your lips utter you must be sure to do, because you made your vow freely to the Lord your God with your own mouth [Deuteronomy 23:21-23].

> When you make a vow to God do not delay in fulfilling it. He has no pleasure in fools. Fulfill your vow. It is better not to vow than to make a vow and not fulfill it [Ecclesiastes 5:4-5].

A vow was simply an oath, or promise, or commitment to do something in the future. You will notice right off that God did not command men to make vows to Him. He did not even suggest that they do so. His only command was, if you do make a vow, be sure that you keep it. You will be held accountable for keeping it. It seems obvious that God knows men are going to make vows, and that often such vows will be foolish (Ecclesiastes 5:4).

One of the things that we can be certain about in this life is that the future is uncertain. That's what makes vows foolish and dangerous.

WHAT PREDISPOSES US TO PRESUME ON THE FUTURE?

I asked myself, why is there such a tendency in us to make promises regarding an uncertain future? My guess is, because we are created in the image of God. God is sovereign (completely autonomous, independent and self-determining.) As we discussed in Chapter 2, by dent of Creation, there is within us a lust for autonomy, for independence, for self-rule. God put it in us, but then told us that we must surrender that lust and submit to the absolute authority of Jesus Christ, "to obey all He has commanded."

As one of my teachers said, "We actually want to be God, and we're mad because God got there first." I believe the whole of the Christian life is a process by which God brings us to surrender our lust for autonomy (usually a little at a time over a long period), and submit to the authority of Jesus Christ. This process is also referred to in Scripture as "being conformed to the image of Christ," or "being controlled by or walking in the Holy Spirit," or simply by the word "sanctification." I personally feel it's one of the best definitions of the sanctification process.

The following is a quote the teacher made in a businessmen's Bible class.

> "Let me suggest three things. (1) To promise the future is intrinsically evil. It is cruel and it is unnecessary. When you make a promise in an area over which you have no control, you sin. When you make a promise in an area in which you do have control, Jesus said let it be a simple yes or no. Don't complicate

it with oaths. (2) Oaths have their origin in men's propensity to deceive. Some men make oaths simply because they've got limited vocabulary. So it's not mere style of speech that Jesus is addressing in these verses, I suggest to you He's discouraging exaggerations and any other form of speech that communicates ambiguity. Do not cover equivocation with an oath. (3) The hubris of youth causes foolish oaths. Somehow in my immaturity I think that I am more spiritual if I make promises, such as, I'm going to spend an hour a day in prayer. That's just utter stupidity. It's not necessary. You're not impressing God."

WHEN WOULD A VOW NOT BE PRESUMING ON THE FUTURE?

Jesus probably intends His teaching to apply to **initiating** promises involving an unknown future, which is different from responding when people require an oath. In a court of law we may be required to promise to tell the truth. At the marriage altar we may be asked to promise to remain faithful to our spouse. These are promises within our power to keep without presuming on the future.

APPLICATION OF JESUS' COMMAND TO NEW TESTAMENT GIVING

In Chapter 9 we will examine the New Testament principles of giving, but I would like to briefly discuss here the application of this command to our giving. Without specifically commanding us to not presume on the future, Paul says nothing that I can find which would suggest ever doing it, in fact, just the opposite. His instructions seem to suggest determining your giving day by day or week by week based on God's provision and blessing, and then only what you can give with the approval of your heart, "not reluctantly nor under compulsion." Furthermore, he suggests that those with a surplus share with those in need, and neither condition is guaranteed to continue.

This is an area in which my thinking has changed completely over my Christian life. Early on, when I became interested in being a good steward of God's money, I strongly believed I should vow to tithe for my entire life. Later I came to the conviction that the tithe should be a minimum for my giving, and that I would seek to give above that, but I did not vow to give above the tithe. Today I do not believe it is wrong to desire to give a certain amount or percent of one's income in the future, nor wrong to plan one's finances in such a way that it be possible to do so, but to **promise** to do so, I believe, is a direct violation of Jesus' command and therefore sin. Besides Jesus' clear command, the remainder of this chapter contains many scriptures which fortify this conviction.

JAMES' COMMENTS ON JESUS' COMMAND TO NOT VOW

It seems to me that a significant portion of the epistle of James is a commentary on portions of the Sermon on the Mount. Obviously, James was there and heard Jesus preach the sermon. I feel that James' comments in 4:13-17 are almost certainly a commentary on Jesus' command not to make a promise involving an unknown future.

> Come now, you who say, "Today or tomorrow, we shall go to such and such a city, and spend a year there and engage in business and make a profit." Yet you do not know what your life will be like tomorrow. You are just a vapor that appears for a little while and then vanishes away. Instead, you ought to say, "If the Lord wills, we shall live and also do this or that." But as it is, you boast in your arrogance; all such boasting is evil. Therefore, to one who knows the right thing to do, and does not do it, to him it is sin [James 4:13-17 (NASB)].

Let me point out several things which stand out to me from this passage. James' illustration involves the conduct of business, while Jesus' illustration involves the giving of offerings to God. Both involve the stewardship of God's money, and both are very relevant to the Christian life today.

James uses Jesus' word "evil" (same Greek word) to describe presuming on the future, but also calls it "boasting" and "sin." James' warning that we know nothing of the future and that our earthly life is like a vapor that can vanish at any moment is really a rather strong rebuke, especially when considered along with his words boasting, sin and evil. I wonder if we have assigned a high enough level of seriousness to this sin today.

We go about our day to day businesses and professions as if everything would function like a well-oiled engine for the next 30 or 40 years, making forecasts about how much we're going to sell, or make, next year, without knowing if we'll even wake up tomorrow morning. And most of the time it never occurs to us to follow James' command to say (and believe), "If the Lord wills ..." In recent years I have made a concerted effort to use and mean this phrase when I speak of the future, even when it's something like, "I'll see you at the YMCA tomorrow," or, "I'll meet you for lunch next Friday."

PRESUMING ON THE FUTURE BY GOING INTO DEBT

Going into debt may be the most prevalent form of the sin of presuming on the future in the Christian community today. The subject of Chapter 11 will be "Borrowing and Lending." In that chapter I will try to cover most of what the Bible says on that subject. But it is my conviction that understanding the danger of presuming on the future is so important, that we will be well served by including it briefly in this chapter, having it in mind as we embark on the study of borrowing and lending. Following are additional passages on the danger of presuming on the future, with special emphasis on going into debt. They give us further insight into the mind of God.

It is a trap for a man to dedicate something rashly and only later to consider his vows [Proverbs 20:25].

This verse gives us the wisdom of thinking long and hard before making a promise we may find out later we are unable to keep. An example would be a debt, which because of circumstances beyond our control, we are unable to pay when it comes due.

A prudent man sees danger and takes refuge, but the simple keep going and suffer for it [Proverbs 22:3].

A prudent man has insight on what could happen in the future. He knows that he cannot forecast the future. So before promising to perform in some way in the future (such as payment of a sum of money), he prepares a "what if list" and carefully thinks through it. What if I lose my job? What if I become disabled? What if I die? Will my estate be able to make good on the liability? What if interest rates increase by 3 percentage points before the debt becomes due? Will that affect me? It will if I have a variable rate mortgage. So the prudent man goes down his "what if list." He knows that we are fallen people living in a fallen world, and things don't always go from bad to better, in fact they can go from bad to worse, especially when we have presumed on the future.

> Do not be a man who strikes hands in pledge or puts up security for debts. If you lack the means to pay, your very bed will be snatched from under you [Proverbs 22:26-27].

A word of clarification is needed for this verse. The phrase "puts up security for debts" does not mean putting up collateral. There's nothing wrong with that. What it means is to make yourself personally liable for a debt to be paid in the future. And the reason it is dangerous is because we don't know the future. Notice how clearly this is stated in the following verses.

> Do not boast about tomorrow, for you do not know what a day may bring forth [Proverbs 27:1].

> Consider what God has done: Who can straighten what He has made crooked? When times are good, be happy, but when times are bad, consider: God has made the one as well as the other. Therefore a man cannot discover anything about his future. [Ecclesiastes 7:13-14].

If we take to heart this passage, especially the last statement, we should be very reluctant to presume on the future. As James 4:13-14 and Proverbs 27:1 point out, we cannot even see ahead one day, much less to the end of a thirty-year mortgage. Long term debt can be very dangerous, and the longer the term, the more uncertain repayment becomes. The higher a debt is in relation to your financial net worth, the more dangerous it is.

PRESUMING ON THE FUTURE AND OUR LUST FOR AUTONOMY

We have established that our problem with God is that we want to decide what is in our best interest rather than submit to what God says in our best interest. I believe that probably the best way God communicates to us what is in our best interest is through His commandments. It is always in our best interest to obey every one of

His commandments. We will one day regret every time we were disobedient, but we will never regret obeying His commandments.

One of the commandments is, "Keep your lives free from the love of money and **be content with what you have,** for He has said, 'I will never leave you nor forsake you' " (Hebrews 13:5). Our culture is full of young couples with two, three or more children. By design, God has entrusted them with differing amounts of material wealth and income. Think of the couple with the heavy responsibility of raising three children, but whose income is at the very bottom of the middle class income spectrum. They are under the same command as those at the top, "Be content with what you have." God is telling them it is in their best interest to be content with their income ...... to live within the means He has provided.

They look around. They see the house and car their peers have. They see the entertainment they participate in. They see where they travel, the clubs they belong to, and on and on. And of course everything they see or hear in the media is designed to make them feel dissatisfied with their standard of living. They have no difficulty getting one or more credit cards, and begin buying the things they feel they should have.

They are disobeying the commandment. They are presuming on the future. They do not know the future. They do not know whether the husband will have a job in a year or two, whether he will be disabled, or even whether he will be alive.

If we believe that God is in control and has our best interest at heart, and if we take seriously Jesus' and James' commands, and if we take to heart all the wisdom quoted above from the Proverbs and Ecclesiastes, why would we ever want to presume on the future? Answer, because it is in our nature to do so. The lust for autonomy is born into us. Add to that the sin nature, and the marvelous intellect God has given us, and soon enough we begin to believe we can predict the future ...... well not really, but we think we can analyze our world well enough to know much of what is likely to unfold. Or perhaps we feel we're smart enough or skillful enough to plan and take actions which will cause to happen in the future what we want to happen. Notice how starkly and bluntly God's word refutes all such notions. Notice the consequences and warnings against trying to do so.

Real security, contentment and joy is found only in unconditional obedience to the commandments of Jesus and the apostles, and serious meditation on the wisdom of the Scriptures.

CHAPTER 7

STANDARD OF LIVING

How should I determine my standard of living? I suspect the average Christian thinks he is responsible for determining his standard of living on earth, while God determines his standard of living in heaven. In fact, the Bible teaches exactly the opposite. The answer to the question is, we don't determine our standard of living in this life. God does. We have no control over that. Re-read the parable of the talents (Matthew 25:14-30) and that should become clear. God, by design, entrusts different amounts and different types of His kingdom assets to different stewards to manage. Then he holds each steward accountable for his management of what is entrusted to him. At the Judgment Seat of Christ, where this accountability is reviewed, the steward is not compared with any other steward. He is accountable for his stewardship of only that which was entrusted to him, and he has the same opportunity as every other steward to earn a maximum reward. He has complete control over his standard of living in eternity.

In our capitalistic culture today, people compete for a limited supply of goods and services. God's supply of rewards in heaven is unlimited, therefore there is no reason to compete with our fellow believers in ministries or spiritual endeavors.

Thus the first step to getting on the right track toward the right standard of living is acceptance of the truth contained in Chapters 1 and 2. That is, God is in control and He has my best interest at heart, therefore I will surrender my lust for autonomy, and trust Him to set my standard of living as He sees fit.

THE RIGHT QUESTION

Therefore, the question, "how do I determine my standard of living?" is the wrong question. Then, what is the right question? The right question is, "what should my stewardship be"? Everything should center around my stewardship commitment. Many Christians are constantly fooling with their standard of living. They are obsessed with changing it, with seeking the ideal ...... trying to find the right house, or a second house, or the right car, or more of this or that ...... a third or fourth TV set ...... and it just goes on and on. It's obvious that we are making standard of living a goal or objective in our lives. And when we make standard of living the focus, we don't ever find the ideal standard of living, that is, the one that brings contentment. There's no particular house or car that brings contentment when our goal in life is wrong ...... when our focus is not on God's stewardship. God withholds contentment because we're mismanaging His property.

But once we change the goal and the focus to a maximum increase in God's estate with the material resources He's entrusted to us, then the standard of living takes care of itself. It becomes the result of a changed life, not a goal.

One of the best illustrations I have ever found of this redirected focus is the life of Hudson Taylor. There is a book called *J. Hudson Taylor (God's Man in China)*. I highly recommend it for insight on the Christian life. Hudson Taylor was a missionary who went from England to China in the nineteenth century. The theme of the book is missions, as you would expect. But the life of Hudson Taylor was a masterpiece of the stewardship of money. It is evident all through the book. Here is a quote from that book.

"Before leaving Barnsley, my attention was drawn to the setting apart the firstfruits of all one's increase, and a certain proportion of one's possessions for the service of the Lord. It seemed to me desirable to study the question, so, with Bible in hand, I was led to the determination to set apart not less than one-tenth of whatever money I might earn, or become possessed of, for the Lord. The salary that I received as a medical assistant would have allowed me to do this without difficulty. But in addition to my salary, I received a board and lodging allowance. Now arose in my mind the reflection, ought not this also to be tithed? It was surely a part of my income, and had it been a question of government income tax, would certainly not have been excluded. But to take a tithe from the whole would have left me insufficient for other purposes. And for a time, I was embarrassed to know what to do. After much thought and prayer, I was led to leave the comfortable home and pleasant circle in which I resided, and engage a little lodging in the suburb, a sitting room and bedroom in one, undertaking to board myself. I was thus enabled to tithe the whole of my income. And while one felt the change a good deal, it was attended with no small blessing. More time was given in my solitude in the study of the Word of God, to visiting the poor, and to evangelistic work on Sunday evening, than would otherwise have been the case. Brought into contact in this way with many who were in distress, I soon saw the privilege of further economizing, and found it possible to give away much more than I had first intended." [1]

Hudson Taylor was 19 years old when he made these decisions. What he was doing was letting his standard of living come as a result of his stewardship goal instead of the other way around. Although not required to do so by commandment, he was applying the Old Testament principle of firstfruits, apparently by conviction. Briefly stated, to apply the firstfruits principle, we set aside the first portion of every dollar of income. We earmark it for God. We do not spend it on anything else. We make that as a commitment and let everything else in life adjust to fit it. It is my conviction that if we do not practice the principle of firstfruits, we will never become top managers for God. If we wait until our income reaches that level at which there is "something left over," it won't happen. It's a mythical level that does not exist. God's portion must be looked at as holy. It must be set aside first.

Here is a continuation of the quote from the Hudson Taylor book.

"I soon found that I could live on very much less than I had previously thought possible. Butter, milk and other luxuries I ceased to use, and found that by living mainly on oatmeal and rice, with occasional variations, a very small sum was sufficient for my needs. In this way, I had more than two-thirds of my income available for other purposes. And my experience was that the less I spent on myself, and the more I gave to others, the fuller of happiness and blessing did my soul become." [2]

---

[1] Dr. and Mrs. J. Hudson Taylor, *J. Hudson Taylor, God's Man in China*, (Chicago, Moody Press, 1965) pp. 24-25.
[2] Ibid., p. 26.

Hudson Taylor's standard of living was the result of his stewardship goal. He was obsessed with giving God a good return on the assets God had entrusted to him. And therefore, **contentment came from good stewardship, not an increased standard of living**. His joy went up as his standard of living went down. He even changed his diet so he could increase his giving to the Lord. I wonder how many 21st century Christians have ever done anything like that.

Well then, should we adjust our standard of living to our income? No, not as Christians. We should let our standard of living adjust to our stewardship commitment. Let me ask you a question. Be on your guard for a curve ball here. Should we live within our *means*? Even a pagan world knows that living within one's means is a sound financial principle. But the Bible goes much further than that. The Bible says we should live within our *needs*, and use the rest to build the kingdom. That's the plan that brings fullness of life here on earth, and a fullness of reward in heaven.

Let's quit obsessing over our standard of living, and start concentrating on how we can make a maximum contribution to God's kingdom with the resources God has entrusted to us. Let's get still and quiet and submissive before God, and ask him to forgive us for past mismanagement, and let's ask Him to deliver us from pride and materialism lust. Let's sign the stewardship agreement, deed everything back to God, and hold everything with an open hand from this moment on. Let's ask the Holy Spirit to assist us in dying emotionally to all earthly wealth. (It won't happen any other way.)

HOW SHOULD I DETERMINE MY STEWARDSHIP?

The quick answer is, it depends entirely on how ambitious I am for eternal reward, and how willing I am to reduce my earthly standard of living. Unlike the Old Testament Israelite, I have complete freedom and latitude as I determine my giving, and in fact as I exercise all of my gifts and abilities.

The Old Testament Israelite had some latitude in his giving, the free will offerings, but most of his offerings were required. They were written in the law. But it's totally different now. We have complete latitude. There is no New Testament commandment to practice the principle of firstfruits. But we know God's mind about it from the Old Testament, and there's nothing wrong with developing a conviction from it as long as our heart is in it. Why not analyze our financial picture, pray and meditate in Scripture, then commit to a portion of our income today, and surrender it to God? Like Hudson Taylor did.

Analyze your own heart. Are you concentrating on what you are giving or on what you have left? Can you adjust it so as to get more into the kingdom? Let your standard of living here be a result of your fervent attention to your standard of living there (heaven). How much faith do you have that God will meet your needs if you give a substantial part of your income to Him? Do you worry about running out of money for food, clothing and shelter?

But let's not get out of the ditch on one side of the road only to run into the ditch on the other side. Let's not violate Jesus' command to not presume on the future (see Chapter 6). That command applies to giving as much as to going into debt, or any other financial stewardship decision. Let's not promise to give a certain percent of our income next year, or ten years from now. We have no idea whether we can make good on it.

> Do not boast about tomorrow, for you do not know what a day may bring forth [Proverbs 27:1].

> Instead, you ought to say, "If the Lord wills, we shall live and also do this or that." But as it is, you boast in your arrogance; all such boasting is evil. Therefore, to one who knows the right thing to do, and does not do it, to him it is sin [James 4:15-17].

It really comes down to a choice. What are you going to seek? What are you going to work for? What are you going to concentrate on? Which is more important to you, your standard of living in this life, or in the next life? Jesus told us which to concentrate on.

I close with a quote from the teacher of a businessmen's Bible class in which I was privileged to sit.

> "God makes you an incredible offer. You can give your life in exchange for the same thing for which Jesus spent His ......

67

people. People last forever. For good or bad they are eternal. Spend your life helping them prepare for their eternity. Don't give your life to mediocrity. Life is too short and the issues of eternity too significant. If you seek what the world deems great things, you will pass into eternity a pauper, but if you freely spend your life for others, you will 'receive a hundredfold, and inherit eternal life.' Those in the marketplace would tell you that that is a good return on investment!"[3]

So, how much should I give? And to whom should I give it? Should I tithe? These are some of the questions we'll be discussing in the next three chapters.

---

[3] Walter A. Henrichsen, *Thoughts from the Diary of a Desperate Man* (Ft. Washington: Christian Literature Crusade, 1977), p. 101.

CHAPTER 8

GIVING – OLD TESTAMENT SURVEY
(Handling Money God's Way – Where It Begins)

Just start reading through the Bible from page 1, and it won't be too long before your begin to realize that in God's mind the most important principle of handling money is giving. How do you react when the subject of giving comes up in the sermon on Sunday morning? ...... or during Bible study? If you have reacted negatively to teachings or sermons on giving in the past, my prayer is that the preceding chapters have already changed your reaction. That's what happened in my life, and that change was the most exciting part of the whole study for me. And it was the area in which my thinking changed the most. Because of the prominence God gives this subject in His Word, we want to try to give it adequate coverage in this study. We begin at the very beginning of human history.

> Adam lay with his wife, Eve, and she conceived and gave birth to Cain. She said, "With the help of the Lord, I have brought forth a man." Later she gave birth to his brother Abel. Now Abel kept flocks, and Cain worked the soil. In the course of time, Cain brought some of the fruits of the soil as an offering to the Lord. But Abel brought fat portions from some of the firstborn of his flock. The Lord looked with favor on Abel and his offering, but on Cain and his offering, He did not look with favor. So Cain was very angry, and his face was downcast [Genesis 4:1-5].

Here is the first mention in the Bible of an offering from man to God. Notice how early it is in human history. It's also the first mention in the Bible of what we might refer to as "the first portion." Here it is referred to as the "firstborn." In other Old Testament passages we see the term "firstlings," and the better known term, "firstfruits." All of these refer to that portion of our income which is taken out first and surrendered to God before any other expenditures are made. It is our stewardship commitment.

Since no other details are given, the question that occurs to me is, where did Abel get the idea of making the type of offering he made, and why was his offering more acceptable than Cain's? Here is a comment from the Pulpit Commentary which I found helpful.

> "We can only surmise that Abel's offering was in obedience to divine prescription and Cain's was not. The universal prevalence of sacrifice rather points to divine prescription than to man's invention as its proper source. Had sacrifices been of purely human origin, it's almost certain that greater diversity would have prevailed in its forms. Besides, the fact that the mode of worship was not left to human ingenuity under the law favors the presumption that it was divinely appointed from the first. From the beginning, God has required the consecration to Himself of the firstfruits of men's powers and callings."

The setting aside of the first part of our income, and the surrendering of it to God is written into God's plan from the beginning of human history. The scholars call this the "principle of firstfruits." I was able to find 23 passages in the Old Testament that teach it. Although it is consistent with New Testament teaching (see 1 Corinthians 16:1-2), it is not given as a specific command in the New Testament, probably because New Testament principles of stewardship are far more radical than Old Testament principles. For all intents and purposes, New Testament stewardship is stewardship of 100%. I believe God is pleased when we practice the principle of firstfruits if our hearts are in it, because by doing so we are acknowledging Him as the owner of all wealth and the provider of all our needs. Furthermore, it is an act of worship, and is so presented from the beginning of human history as Genesis 4 testifies.

A second principle of giving found in this first passage in the Bible on giving is that the offering from man to God should be voluntary. It should be given willingly from the heart. Here are two brothers, Cain and Abel, born into the same home, educated by the same parents, taught to worship the same God in the same way, and yet their worship is entirely different. Why is that? Free choice. God will not force any person to worship Him, or to make offerings to Him. It has to be by choice ...... voluntary. This truth runs through the Bible.

> Then Melchizedek, king of Salem, brought out bread and wine.
> He was priest of God Most High, and He blessed Abram, saying,
> "Blessed be Abram by God Most High, Creator of heaven and
> earth. And blessed be God Most High, who delivered your
> enemies into your hand." Then Abram gave him a tenth of
> everything [Genesis 14:18-20].

Here is the first mention in the Bible of the tithe, or tenth. And we find
it here 400 years before the tithe was incorporated into the Mosaic Law.
Abraham was practicing a form of firstfruits. He was surrendering
10% of the battle spoils. We do not know whether God instructed
Abraham to give 10% or not. If He did, there's no record of it in the
Bible that I've been able to find. But I think it's safe to say that
Abraham gave this tithe voluntarily, with a willing heart. That seems
implied. He gave it in recognition of God as owner and provider of
everything. This is bolstered by the fact that Abraham gave God the
title *Jehovah Jirah*, which means "the Lord provides." Further,
Hebrews 7:1-10, which is a New Testament commentary on Genesis
14, verifies the fact that Abraham considered his tithe an act of
worship.

> Then Jacob made a vow, saying, "If God will be with me and
> will watch over me on this journey I am taking, and will give me
> food to eat and clothes to wear so that I return safely to my
> father's house, then the Lord will be my God. This stone that I
> have set up as a pillar will be God's house, and of all that You
> give me, I will give You a tenth" [Genesis 28:20-22].

Here is the second mention of the tithe in the Bible. Again, this was
long before the giving of the Mosaic Law, and also appears to be a
voluntary offering by Jacob. But we see a progression here in the
principle of giving. We see the vow. A vow was a pledge, or promise
to give in a certain way. It was a firstfruits commitment. The use of
vows is seen in both Old and New Testaments, usually as pledges made
to God, but sometimes of vows made to fellow men.

Although God permitted the use of vows in the Old Testament, He did
not encourage them. And, He warned strongly against the failure to
keep them. The vow was not to be taken lightly. Once made it became
a binding contract which must be fulfilled. Thus, before making a vow

or promise to give in a certain way, a person should carefully consider all the potential consequences. We have already discussed this subject at length in Chapter 6, where we studied Jesus' command not to make any vow or promise which presumes on the future.

How then should we apply the principle of firstfruits to our giving? Practice the principle of firstfruits now, every day. Set aside and surrender the first portion of every dollar of income to God, but don't promise the specifics of what that will look like in an unknown future.

Surely the most prevalent violation of Jesus' teaching on vows in our culture today is the misuse of debt ...... that which involves the sin of presuming on the future. Because of its prominence, both inside and outside the church, we will deal with it in detail in Chapter 11 on the subject of borrowing and lending.

THE TITHE IS INCORPORATED INTO THE LAW OF MOSES

> A tithe of everything from the land, whether grain from the soil or fruit from the trees, belongs to the Lord. It is holy to the Lord [Leviticus 27:30].

Here it is clear that the tithe has been incorporated into the law that must be kept by the Old Testament Israelite. Notice how strong the wording is. "It belongs to the Lord. It is Holy to the Lord." It was not optional. It was *required*. Perhaps you are wondering as you read this, is the tithe binding today in the same way as it was under the Mosaic Law? We will deal in detail with that question in Chapter 10. It is far too important to hit lightly in passing. What we know from our survey thus far is that the giving of the tithe was practiced by Abraham and Jacob prior to the law, and it was required under the Law of Moses.

OTHER REQUIRED OFFERINGS UNDER THE LAW

The tithe was not the only giving required under the Mosaic Law. God prescribed many other offerings which were required. Most of the first seven chapters of Leviticus, and Chapters 16 and 23 give us the rules and regulations for these various offerings. There were burnt offerings, grain offerings, fellowship offerings, sin offerings, guilt offerings, heave offerings, drink offerings, and others. Certain of these offerings were to be given annually on certain feast days. Other offerings were to be given weekly, and even some were to be given daily. Some were to be given during harvest, and some were to be given following sin in the life. That is a brief sketch of this elaborate system of offerings. You can find the details of the frequencies for all these offerings in Numbers Chapters 28 and 29.

Then in addition to all of these, there was the tax of the firstborn. The first born male to open the womb was to be given to the Lord. Then there was the poll tax, or head tax, required of every member of the Jewish theocracy. Then, over and above all of these required offerings were the vows and the free will offerings. These could be called "discretionary offerings," because the amount was left to the discretion of each believer.

> These are the Lord's appointed feasts which you are to proclaim as sacred assemblies for bringing offerings made to the Lord by fire – the burnt offerings and grain offerings, sacrifices and drink offerings required for each day. These offerings are in addition to those for the Lord's Sabbaths, and in addition to your gifts and whatever you have vowed, and all the free will offerings you give to the Lord [Leviticus 23:37-38].

Just think about this. It is a partial list of both required and discretionary offerings.

> There (in Jerusalem) bring your burnt offerings and sacrifices, your tithes and special gifts, what you have vowed to give and your free will offerings, and the firstborn of your herds and flocks [Deuteronomy 12:6].

This is a different list of required and discretionary offerings. And the tithe is included in this list, but the tithe was only part of God's plan of giving for the Old Testament Jew.

THE PURPOSE OF GOD'S ELABORATE SYSTEM OF OFFERINGS

What does all this mean? God had a purpose in this elaborate system of required and voluntary offerings. I believe the main purpose of the required offerings was to teach the Israelite the owner-manager relationship, to teach him respect for God as owner of everything, and the provider of all his needs. Certainly a part of the purpose was to provide revenue for the operation of the theocracy. In other words, a part of the giving plan was in the nature of a tax. But other parts were to support the Levitical priesthood, and for charity. The purpose of the discretionary part of the offerings was to give latitude to the individual manager. Some would become good managers, some poor, by choice, and each would be accountable for his use of this latitude.

By the time we reach the Psalms in the Old Testament, God's elaborate plan of giving has become very well known, and is reaching its fullness.

> Sacrifice thank offerings to God, fulfill your vows to the Most High. And call on Me in the day of trouble. I will deliver you, and you will honor Me [Psalm 50:14-15].

This is a beautiful statement of the two sides of the giving transaction in the Old Testament, God's side and man's side. The duty of the believer was to glorify God, to honor God, to fear God and worship God. One of the ways he did that was to make good on his required offerings, as well as his vows and voluntary offerings. God's side was to deliver, to provide and to bless. This passage is saying if the Israelite will do his part, God will do His. It is stated in the form of a cause and effect axiom, clearly implying that if the believer fails to fulfill his side of the transaction, God will not bless him. There are many passages which express this cause and effect axiom.

> One man gives freely, yet gains even more; another withholds unduly, but comes to poverty. A generous man will prosper; he who refreshes others will himself be refreshed [Proverbs 11:24-25].

> He who is kind to the poor lends to the Lord, and He will reward him for what he has done [Proverbs 19:17].

> If a man shuts his ears to the cry of the poor, he too will cry out and not be answered [Proverbs 21:13].

He who gives to the poor will lack nothing, but he who closes his eyes to them receives many curses [Proverbs 28:27].

CAUTION – THIS IS AN OLD TESTAMENT PRINCIPLE

We should pause here and realize the cause and effect axiom we are discussing is Old Testament and may not be applied strictly to our day. Yes, Christians have many precious promises which may be claimed today, but they are different from those given to the Old Testament Israelite.

Here are the main differences in the Old and New Testaments in relation to giving. In the Old Testament, God promised temporal blessing, mainly material, for obedience, and temporal curses for disobedience (Deuteronomy 28). By contrast, Jesus promised to meet our material needs for obedience, but nothing beyond that in this life. (Matthew 6:33). He also promised spiritual blessings in this life, and reward in eternity (Matthew 6:19-20).

Paul added that we will be accountable for both obedience and disobedience. We will receive reward for our obedience and service to God. We will lose reward for disobedience. We may receive some rewards in this life, but our full rewards are guaranteed only in eternity. Likewise the poverty and curses suffered by the ungenerous giver described in the above Old Testament passages may at times happen to the New Testament believer, but there is no certainty that it will.

The full and complete balancing of the books occurs only in eternity. In Galatians 6:7 Paul tells us, "Do not be deceived: God cannot be mocked. A man reaps what he sows." Theologians call this "The Law of the Harvest." It applies to all men, lost and saved alike, but has nothing to do with salvation. Some of the reaping may occur in this life, but not necessarily. It will occur for certain in eternity. As believers, our sins are covered in full by the sacrifice Christ made on the cross. But forgiveness does not eliminate the consequences of our disobedience, for which we will be accountable at the Judgment Seat of Christ.

SUMMARY: OLD TESTAMENT PRINCIPLES OF GIVING

In this chapter we have studied God's earliest teachings on giving, beginning with the first people on earth and continuing through His instructions and commands to Israel. Today, in the church age, we are under the authority of the instructions and commands of Jesus and the apostles. That will be our study in Chapter 9. But before we leave the Old Testament, let's summarize its teachings on giving under six points, and ask ourselves some questions designed to help us understand what God wants us to learn from this earliest revelation.

• The believing Israelite was a manager of God's property and was accountable to God for his stewardship. **Question: Am I convinced that when I bring home a paycheck and deposit it to my account that all of it belongs to God?**

• The most important principle of managing money was giving money (offerings). **Question: If I went back through my tax returns with the objective of evaluating my giving, what would I find? Suppose I counted all the hours I spent in ministry as part of my giving, and deducted their value, using my hourly earnings rate, from my earnings, would the IRS be sympathetic at an audit?**

• The most important principle of giving was the principle of firstfruits: the setting aside and surrender of the first portion of one's income to be given as an offering to the Lord (see Proverbs 3:9-10). **Question: When God looks at my gift, does He see a mangy, crippled, animal that I culled out of my flock to improve my herd because I knew it was about to die anyway?**

• In order to teach His people the owner-manager relationship, God instituted an elaborate system of specific required offerings, the tithe being only one part. **Question: If it is my conviction that I should tithe, do I understand that God owns the other 90%?**

• God also instituted a program of voluntary or discretionary offerings to allow latitude in the believer's stewardship. **Do I**

understand that the discretionary offerings must be given willingly from the heart?

• God promised temporal blessings to the faithful steward, and withheld temporal blessings, and even sent curses upon, the unfaithful steward. **Question: Do I understand how this cause and effect law changes in the New Testament? We will answer this question in the next chapter.**

I close this chapter by asking this question: if we are accountable only for obeying the commandments and teachings of Jesus and the apostles on giving in the New Testament, why study the teachings on giving in the Old Testament? Answer: Because it gives us insight into the mind of God, which is valuable in molding our thinking. This can lead to the developing of convictions which will enhance our walk with God and our service to the kingdom. As long as we do not disobey a specific New Testament command, we are free to develop convictions from the Old Testament, such as the practice of the principle of firstfruits, but we are not free to impose such convictions on others.

In the next chapter we will study what the New Testament teaches, where God's revelation on giving reaches its fullness.

CHAPTER 9

GIVING – NEW TESTAMENT TEACHINGS

In Chapter 8, we surveyed the Old Testament on the subject of giving. We learned much about the mind of God, and what He commanded Israel to do. From that study, it seems clear to me that God considers giving to be the most important part of handling money. Some of that teaching is helpful to us in developing our own convictions about giving. But we are not under the commandments of the Old Testament. We are under the commandments of Jesus and the apostles. Jesus told us to obey, and teach others to obey, all He commanded. In this chapter we want to try to define and understand all that is commanded us on the subject of giving.

You might like to review the list of commandments in Chapter 3. Many of them concern giving. Here is a sampling of the giving commandments.

FROM JESUS

MATTHEW

5:42   Give to him who asks of you, and do not turn away from him who wants to borrow from you.

6:2-4   Do your giving in secret and your heavenly Father will reward you.

6:19-24   Do not store up for yourselves treasure on earth, where moth and rust destroy, and thieves break in and steal.

6:19-24   Store up for yourselves treasure in heaven, where moth and rust don't destroy, and thieves do not steal.

22:17-21 Render to Caesar the things that are Caesar's and to God the things that are God's.

LUKE

6:38   Give and it will be given to you, for by your standard of measure, it will be measured to you in return.

12:32-33 Don't be afraid. Sell your possessions and give to the poor, which will secure you treasure in heaven.

FROM THE APOSTLES

ACTS

4:34-35   Those with a surplus share with those in need that the work may go forward.

20:35   Work hard, helping the weak, remembering Jesus' words, "It is more blessed to give than to receive."

ROMANS

12:13   Contribute to the needs of the saints.

1 CORINTHIANS

9:1-14   Contribute to the financial support of those who minister the word to you.

16:1-2   As God prospers you, set aside each week your gift toward the offering for the saints in Jerusalem.

2 CORINTHIANS

8:7-8   Just as you abound in all other spiritual gifts, see that you also abound in giving.

8:11-15   Follow through and make good on your giving commitments. Those with a surplus share with those in need.

9:6-11   Give what you purpose in your heart to give, not grudgingly or under compulsion, for God loves a cheerful giver.

9:6-11   Understand those who sow sparingly will so reap, and those who sow abundantly will reap abundantly.

1 TIMOTHY

6:17-19   Instruct those who are rich to do good, to be rich in good works, to be generous and ready to share.

HEBREWS

13:16   Do not neglect doing good and sharing, for with such sacrifices God is pleased.

1 JOHN

3:16-18   Whoever sees his brother in need and closes his heart to him, how does the love of God abide in him?

Did you notice in these commands the recurrence of the word *need*? New Testament giving concentrates on the meeting of specific needs.

Paul instructed the Romans to "contribute to the **needs** of the saints," and in 2 Corinthians he wrote, "at the present time, your surplus will supply what they **need**," a reference to the saints in Jerusalem who were suffering financial hardship. To the Ephesians he wrote, "Let him who steals steal no more, but rather let him labor, performing with his own hands what is good, in order that he may have something to share with him who has **need**." In his first epistle, John wrote, "Whoever has the world's goods, and beholds his brother in **need** and closes his heart against him, how does the love of God abide in him?"

There is an interesting occurrence of the word "need" in the book of Acts.

> There were no needy persons among them. For from time to time those who owned lands or houses sold them, brought the money from the sales and put it at the apostles' feet, and it was distributed to anyone as he had **need** [Acts 4:34-35].

This is a description of what was happening in the Jerusalem church, but not a command. Many members with a surplus of wealth contributed money into the treasury of the church, and the church leaders made distribution to individual members to meet their needs.

In some passages, needs are implied though not specifically stated. Certainly, the commandments to support financially those who minister the word to us imply a need. Those who give full time to teaching and shepherding the local fellowship of believers are to be dependent on the members for their financial support.

And clearly the commandments Paul gives to Timothy concerning assistance for widows imply a financial need. So the New Testament commandments on giving pretty much boil down to giving to meet specific needs of individuals and ministries involved in building the kingdom.

But what are the legitimate needs referred to in these commands? Paul has left little doubt about the answer to this question, as he comments on Jesus' teachings.

> And if we have food and covering, with these we shall be content [1 Timothy 6:8 (NASB)].

We've already studied this passage in Chapter 5, but we note here in passing that "needs" are limited to the strict necessities ...... food, clothing and shelter, or as Paul states it, "food and covering." And before we are tempted to ask, what quality and quantity of food, clothing and shelter, let's remember Paul's next statement.

> People who want to get rich fall into temptation and a trap and into many foolish and harmful desires that plunge men into ruin and destruction [1 Timothy 6:9].

Here he contrasts the person content with the bare necessities with the person who is not. That person, Paul says, is a person who desires to get rich. Therefore he is defining rich as anyone who has more than the bare necessities. He's not saying it's a sin to be rich, just that it is a sin to **want** to be rich. That's made even clearer in the next verse. Notice how consistent this is with Jesus' command that we not store wealth for ourselves on earth, but in heaven.

But what we want to draw from this passage is the definition of "need" in the giving commandments. Those with a surplus above the bare necessities are to share with those who lack the bare necessities. But there's more than this to the definition of "need."

> ... if anyone will not work, neither let him eat [2 Thessalonians 3:10b (NASB)].

Food for a person who is able to work but refuses to do so does not fit the definition of "need" in the giving commands. To feed such a person would be a failure to love him with the "agape" kind of love we are commanded to exercise. As we have previously established, this love is unconditional and acts only in what is in the best interest of the one loved. That is the chief attribute of agape.

DESIGNATED GIVING BASED ON NEED

I have thought about the subject of giving for many years, and the best title to describe New Testament giving I have come up with is, "designated giving based on need." By this I mean giving designated to meet specific, known, legitimate, verifiable needs of individuals and/or ministries.

With that in mind, how then should we proceed to determine the details of our giving? How much should we give? To whom should we give it? What portion should go to our local church? Is the tithe binding on the Christian today? Should it be a guide or starting place for our giving? These are the questions we will seek to answer in this chapter and in Chapter 10, which will deal specifically with the tithe.

The answers to these questions are found in a single passage of Scripture. This passage, combined with only three or four cross references and the list of commands constitute the sum total of New Testament teaching on giving. The passage is 2 Corinthians Chapters 8 and 9. It is the longest passage in the New Testament on giving, 39 verses, and is an almost complete commentary on the list of giving commands of Jesus and the apostles, a fact I had overlooked for many years. To me, it is an amazing passage, and so important that it deserves a close verse by verse study. The following is my attempt to communicate its truth. I believe you would find it profitable to turn to this passage in your Bible and follow along as we study it.

HISTORICAL BACKGROUND – THE JERUSALEM RELIEF FUND

The background to this passage is an actual historical event, one which is both interesting and important to understand. The Jerusalem church of the first century was suffering extreme financial hardship, probably for two main reasons; a drought which was occurring, and persecution because of its identification with Jesus Christ. If you were a Jewish person in the first century who converted to Christ and bore witness to that fact, chances are you lost your job. And you were also ostracized in other ways in that society. Things got so bad in that church the members who had assets with value sold them, some even their homes, and brought the money to the apostles, who then distributed it to those in poverty according to their need.

The wording of Acts 4:34-35 suggests a rather extreme degree of financial hardship. Paul apparently became burdened for this financial need, and organized a fund raising effort among many of the other churches he had visited and helped start. The apostle mentioned this project in his first letter to the Corinthians.

> Now about the collection for God's people: Do what I told the Galatian churches to do. On the first day of every week, each one of you set aside a sum of money in keeping with his income, saving it up, so that when I come no collections will have to be made. Then, when I arrive, I will give letters of introduction to the men you approve and send them with your gift to Jerusalem [1 Corinthians 16:1-3].

Paul did not want this to be an incidental or impulsive offering. He wanted them to give thought, and no doubt prayer, and actually set the money aside in advance, so that he would not have to create the pressure of taking an offering when he got there.

Sometime after the writing of 1 Corinthians and before the writing of 2 Corinthians, Titus apparently went to Corinth and began this fund raising project at Paul's instructions. This seems apparent from 2 Corinthians 8:6.

> So we urged Titus, since he had earlier made a beginning, to bring also to completion this act of grace on your part [2 Corinthians 8:6].

But it's also likely that between the writing of the two letters, Titus, having gone to Corinth to begin this project, returned and reported to Paul that the Corinthians had not followed through on their initial commitment. And thus Paul felt compelled to devote this entire section of the second Corinthian letter to this subject. That is the interesting background to this passage. With this background in mind let's read the first 5 verses of the passage.

> And now, brothers, we want you to know about the grace that God has given the Macedonian churches. Out of the most severe trial, their overflowing joy and their extreme poverty welled up in rich generosity. For I testify that they gave as much as they

were able, and even beyond their ability. Entirely on their own, they urgently pleaded with us for the privilege of sharing in this service to the saints. And they did not do as we expected, but they gave themselves first to the Lord and then to us in keeping with God's will [2 Corinthians 8:1-5].

Macedonia was the northern part of the nation of Greece, and Achaia was the southern part, very much like two states in that nation. The Macedonian churches referred to here are generally believed to be the churches in Philippi, Thessalonica and Berea. Paul begins this part of his letter by citing these churches as examples of the grace of giving …… even, as we read, sacrificial giving. Here were a group of people over in Macedonia, not just willing to help another group of people in Jerusalem, but actually going to Paul and begging him for the right to have a part in the offering. That's a little unusual, isn't it? As he put it in verse 4, "They urgently pleaded with us for the privilege of sharing in this service to the saints." This surely must have delighted Paul. Perhaps he responded with something like, "That's wonderful." But then they surprised Paul and gave beyond what he expected …… they gave sacrificially.

This is certainly atypical to say the least, and the question came to me, why would a group of people like this, who probably had never even seen the people in Jerusalem, do this? The answer is found in these verses, and from it we learn important principles of the theology of giving. Notice again verse 1. "And now brothers, we want you to know about the **grace** that God has **given** to the Macedonian churches." Scriptural giving is a grace, or we might prefer the term "spiritual gift," which God bestows upon certain members of the body of Christ. And God selects who gets which gift and how much of it. But God gives this kind of a grace to a believer with a willing, dedicated heart. Look again at verse 5. "And they did not do as we expected, but they **gave themselves** first to the Lord and then to us in keeping with God's will. You have to want to be a disciple of Jesus Christ with all your heart before God will give you this kind of a grace or spiritual gift.

In trying to understand this, I think that this is a case of the sovereignty of God cooperating with the responsible choice of man. We must accept and act upon the fact that we have responsible choice in determining our stewardship, and yet God is sovereign in His bestowal of the graces and gifts among us. That's the best I can do with it.

But why is Paul telling this to the Corinthians? He wants to motivate them to the same kind of commitment that he saw in the Macedonians. He didn't see the grace of giving in evidence in Corinth. And that's interesting, because the Corinthian church was much more affluent than the Macedonian churches. The Corinthians didn't need any more money in the bank. They needed more grace in the heart. I believe that's still the problem today. I am convinced we don't need any more money in the bank accounts of Christians today to do God's perfect will. I think we need more grace in the heart. The message behind Paul's words here seems to be, "You Corinthians need a revival ...... which will lead to a heart commitment concerning your stewardship. You need to respond to the truth the apostles have taught you, and to the promptings of the Holy Spirit in your hearts, and then God will give you the grace of giving."

> So we urged Titus, since he had earlier made a beginning, to bring also to completion this act of grace on your part. But just as you excel in everything ... in faith, in speech, in knowledge, in complete earnestness in your love for us ... see that you also excel in this grace of giving [2 Corinthians 8:6-7].

Paul is complimenting the Corinthians on some of the gifts and graces at which they did excel ...... faith, knowledge, love. By highlighting their strong points, he wanted them to realize their weak areas ...... "see that you also excel in this grace of giving."

> I am not commanding you, but I do want to test the sincerity of your love by comparing it with the earnestness of others [2 Corinthians 8:8].

Paul wants them to understand that he is not telling them how much to give. He's not setting a quota, or the expectation of a certain minimum amount. I would note in passing that nowhere in the New Testament do I find any instruction to the believer as to how much or what percent to give. As we have previously noted, New Testament stewardship is stewardship of 100%. The believer has complete latitude in determining his giving, and then must give complete accountability for his decisions at the Judgment Seat of Christ. His reward and station in eternity will be based on how well he executed Jesus' command to store his wealth in heaven rather than on earth. In this we see that in no way does God "need" our gift. Giving is a system God has set up for *our* benefit, not His. It seems easier for us to enjoy the other spiritual gifts, and encourage others to excel in them. Today we miss out on the great blessing from giving, which is really for the giver.

Now look at the first phrase of verse 10.

> And here is my advice about what is best for you in this matter ... [2 Corinthians 8:10a].

In verse 8 Paul said, "I'm not telling you how much to give." Then verse 10, "but I do have some counsel ...... some advice." And then do we read something like this, "We need $100,000 for this offering, and if you folks in Corinth could give $20,000 as your part, it would be wonderful?" No, we don't read anything like that. He goes right back to the problem ...... a lack of willingness or commitment in the heart.

> Last year you were the first not only to give but also to have the desire to do so. Now finish the work, so that your eager willingness to do it may be matched by your completion of it, according to your means [2 Corinthians 8:10b, 11].

Paul's saying to them, "You've lost your willingness." Initially they made a commitment, but then did not follow up on it. I don't know of a better statement of this truth than what we read in verse 12. I think Paul really gets to the bottom line of the burden that is in his heart in verse 12.

> **For if the willingness is there,** the gift is acceptable according to what one has, not according to what he does not have [2 Corinthians 8:12].

That strikes me as a great statement ...... one which should relax us on this matter of giving. God does not expect us to give that which we do not have, or do not have control over. The problem is never a lack of money. The problem is a lack of willingness, or heart commitment ... thinking of ourselves as owners of wealth instead of managers of God's property. All true scriptural giving begins by dealing with that spiritual problem in the heart.

THE DIVINE SEQUENCE IN GIVING

Let me pause here and insert a summary or analysis of what I believe Paul is teaching in this passage. I have given it the title *The Divine Sequence in Giving*. It presents the giving transaction as a four step process when it is done according to the New Testament.

STEP ONE

The believer makes a decision to become a good manager of God's property. He makes a heart commitment to become a good steward. This is the point at which he turns his assets back over to God. He signs the stewardship agreement. Paul has called that "willingness" in the verses we have just studied. This is the first step in all true scriptural giving. Let me say to all of our hearts, don't wait until you have money to make this decision. Giving starts in the heart, not in the pocketbook.

When God reads willingness in the heart, then He takes over and performs the other three steps. Our only responsibility is to take the first step, then God takes it from there.

STEP TWO

God sovereignly bestows the grace of giving when He reads willingness in the heart. He gives the believer the spiritual gift of giving.

STEP THREE

God supplies the financial means of expressing the grace that He has put in the heart. Wouldn't it be unthinkable for God to give a person the grace of giving and nothing to give? Notice that the sequence is critical. You may not have any money today, but if you take step one, then the money will be there when the time for giving it comes. Or, perhaps when we decide to be a good manager, God removes the blindness that has prevented our seeing what He has already provided for us to give.

STEP FOUR

God lays a specific need of His kingdom's work on the heart of the willing steward, who then gives to meet that specific need, and that completes the process.

God is in control and has our best interest at heart. He is the sovereign engineer of the circumstances of our life. He will lay a specific need of an individual, or a ministry, on the heart of a willing steward. He has an unlimited number of ways of doing it. It might come from printed material. It might come from a sermon, a Bible study, a missionary report, contact with someone who is poor, or any number of other ways. Here Paul discloses the need in the Jerusalem church by letter, no doubt with the expectation and prayer that some of the Corinthians would make a commitment of heart, and thus go through these four steps.

When I first taught this subject in my church in 1980, our board of elders decided to add a section in our church bulletin entitled "Prayer and Giving Guide." It simply lists legitimate financial needs of our congregation and ministries, so that our members may be aware of them, pray for them, and give as God leads them. They are rarely mentioned verbally, and remain on the list until the need is met. At times this section is blank. It is a disclosure of need, not an appeal for money. After thirty years it's still a part of our bulletin. I have seen it greatly blessed over the years.

Keep this four step process in mind as we continue through this passage. You will note further references to the steps.

Our desire is not that others might be relieved while you are hard pressed, but that there might be equality [2 Corinthians 8:13].

Here we come to an area of the theology of giving in which it is very important to have the balance of Scripture, that is, all of the truth that bears upon it, else we are in danger of slipping off into error. There are times when God will lead us to give sacrificially ...... to give beyond our normal ability. There are other times when He will not. There are even times when He will lead us to give everything that we have. He does not usually lead in that way. But if He does He will give us the grace to give in that fashion. Remember the example of the widow who gave all that she had. God gave her the grace to do that. And as I have said, I doubt that she missed a meal following that incident, because God takes care of His good stewards.

I trust you can see from this the importance of holding all of the truth on a given doctrine in balance. Suppose we decided to formulate the theology of giving as found in the Bible, but read just this one verse. Our conclusion would be that God does not ever intend for us to be hard pressed as a result of our giving. Paul has just cited the Macedonian churches who gave to the point of being hard pressed, and he commended them for their sacrifice. Jesus commended the widow when she gave all she had. But here Paul is saying something to the effect of, "It is not my desire that you Corinthians on this occasion be hard pressed." Perhaps Paul did not think they had the grace to give sacrificially. God bestows grace for the occasion when He reads willingness in the heart. That is the principle. That's step two in the process.

I once heard an illustration which has helped me to understand this. We've all heard about dying grace. When a Christian who's in fellowship with God dies, God supplies dying grace. We don't want to die. We resist death with all the strength we have. And yet, when it comes time to die, a believer, walking in fellowship with God, will be supernaturally given the grace needed to step through the veil of death easily. And God bestows that grace when it is needed, not before. Someone once asked the great evangelist, Dwight L. Moody if he had dying grace. Perhaps it had come up in one of his messages. And Mr. Moody said, "No, I don't." The surprised enquirer asked, "Why don't you, Mr. Moody?" And he replied, "Because I'm not dying." You see, God supplies grace when it is needed, and not before.

So also with the grace of giving. If someone asked me today, do you have the grace to give 100% of all you have?, I would answer, "No, I do not, and I really don't think it's God's will for me today." But I think that the day could come when God would lead me, and some of you, to give sacrificially. One reason I think this is that I believe we could live to experience a world wide economic crisis and find ourselves doing the same thing these first century Christians did. And if so, I take comfort in the fact that the grace we will need will be there, as well as the financial resources needed to express that grace.

> Our desire is not that others might be relieved while you are hard pressed, but that there might be equality. At the present time your plenty will supply what they need, so that in turn their plenty will supply what you need. Then there will be equality [2 Corinthians 8:13-14].

We must be careful here with this word "equality," which Paul uses twice. He is not speaking of equal ownership of property. That's communism, and I do not see support for communism in the Bible. This equality to which he refers is equal relief from the burden of want. This is not a redistribution of wealth. This is a meeting of needs, which seems to be the clear intent of the giving commands. There is a big difference in the two approaches. One is welfare administered by the state. The other is a meeting of needs administered through the treasury of the local fellowship of believers. And one of the ways that we know this is the illustration with which Paul follows, the giving of the manna in the wilderness. He quotes Exodus 16:18 in verse 15.

> As it is written: "He that gathered much did not have too much, and he that gathered little did not have too little" [2 Corinthians 8:15].

Have you ever studied that story of the manna in the wilderness? You remember that God gave only enough for each day's need. And some people gathered a little bit more than they needed while others didn't get enough. So they shared. And that's a perfect illustration of God's plan. It is essentially a plan of those with a surplus sharing with those with a need. But it is not a wealth redistribution plan.

> I thank God, who put it into the heart of Titus the same concern I have for you. For Titus not only welcomed our appeal, but he is coming to you with much enthusiasm and on his own initiative [2 Corinthians 8:16-17].

We see here that Titus is going to go back to Corinth, some scholars think for the third time, to encourage the Corinthians to finally make good on their commitment. And, incidentally, they probably did, because it is mentioned in Romans 15:26-27 that they gave an offering.

> And we are sending along with him the brother who is praised by all the churches for his service to the gospel [2 Corinthians 8:18].

We do not know who this brother is. The important thing is not his name but his character ...... "the brother who is praised by all the churches."

> What is more, he was chosen by the churches to accompany us as we carry the offering, which we administer in order to honor the Lord Himself and to show our eagerness to help [2 Corinthians 8:19].

Paul is describing the appointment of some men as trustees to handle the money, describing their character and abilities which qualify them as being worthy of this trust.

> We want to avoid any criticism of the way we administer this liberal gift. For we are taking pains to do what is right, not only in the eyes of the Lord but also in the eyes of men [2 Corinthians 8:20-21].

Here we find a very important principle of handling the Lord's money. The conduct of the Lord's financial affairs should be handled with scrupulous honesty, integrity, accountability and disclosure. Having said that, I cannot help thinking about some of the television ministries which have been in the news in recent years. If they had been accountable and had fully disclosed what the money was used for, we wouldn't have had some of the scandals that occurred. So let this be a lesson to all of us in the church today. We must be accountable for the use of God's money in our ministries.

> In addition, we are sending with them our brother who has often proved to us in many ways that he is zealous, and now even more so because of his great confidence in you. As for Titus, he is my partner and fellow worker among you. As for our

brothers, they are representatives of the churches and an honor to Christ. Therefore show these men the proof of your love and the reason for our pride in you, so that the churches can see it [2 Corinthians 8:22-24].

Now we come to Chapter 9, and there is no break in the flow of the passage at all. Even though the King James translation put a break here, in most of the later translations there is no paragraph break at this point, so we go right on reading.

There is no need for me to write to you about this service to the saints [2 Corinthians 9:1].

This is an interesting statement because Paul is writing to them. And I think what Paul is intimating here is something like, "You are the kind of people that don't really need to be reminded about this. You're going to do the right thing." I think he's using a little psychology.

For I know your eagerness to help, and I have been boasting about it to the Macedonians, telling them that since last year you in Achaia were ready to give, and your enthusiasm has stirred most of them to action [2 Corinthians 9:2].

This is humorous. Apparently Corinth was the first to make a commitment toward this offering, so Paul cited the enthusiasm of the Corinthians to the Macedonians, which motivated them, and they gave that great sacrificial offering. Now Paul comes back and cites the example of the Macedonians to motivate the Corinthians. He's got a little friendly competition going between the churches. Paul was a great theologian. He was also a great fund raiser. And we can learn from him.

But I am sending the brothers in order that our boasting about you in this matter should not prove hollow, but that you may be ready as I said you would be. For if any Macedonians come with me and find you unprepared, we … not to say anything about you … would be ashamed of having been so confident [2 Corinthians 9:3-4].

This is almost a little bit sneaky of Paul. He is saying I've been bragging about you to the Macedonians, and wouldn't it be terrible if one of those Macedonians just happened to come with me to Corinth, and you had fallen down on your offering ...... that would be a terrible embarrassment ...... not only to you but to me.

> So I thought it necessary to urge the brothers to visit you in advance and finish the arrangements for the generous gift you had promised. Then it will be ready as a generous gift, not as one grudgingly given [2 Corinthians 9:5].

I think we would all agree that Paul is applying a little bit of psychological pressure here. He used the word "generous" twice. He doesn't want anything other than that in their minds. But he does this without ever violating any of the basic New Testament principles of giving. That will become even clearer as we read the next six verses. And his whole objective is to motivate the Corinthians to a change of heart, because he knows that if they make a heart commitment, God will give them the grace, and lead them to give as they should.

Now we come to the heart of this two-chapter passage. In verses 6-11 Paul repeats and re-expresses the four steps in the giving process. I think these six verses are the greatest expression of the theology of giving to be found in the entire Bible. If you are one who likes to memorize Scripture, I would encourage you to include these verses. Here is the heart of financial stewardship.

> Remember this: Whoever sows sparingly shall also reap sparingly, and whoever sows generously will also reap generously [2 Corinthians 9:6].

In verse 7, Paul will press the Corinthians for a decision about their part in the offering. But before he does that, he begins with the words "Remember this." It's as if he were saying to these people, "As you Corinthians consider your part in this offering, there is something I want you to remember ...... I want you to bear something in mind. I want you to be aware of the consequences of your decision. There is a cause and effect law that operates in the giving transaction." And Paul uses sowing and reaping, or planting and harvesting, to illustrate this cause and effect law. He is explaining that there are some ways in which farming and giving are alike. The way that a farmer sows his seeds in the ground ...... the amount of seeds, the amount of labor, the amount of water and fertilizer he puts into a crop will determine to a large extent what he harvests. And unless a farmer keeps back some of the seeds and some of the profit from a crop and invests it in the next crop, then there won't be a next crop. The same law applies to giving. This is divine viewpoint on giving. And like most major issues of life, it is opposite to human viewpoint or logic. Human logic says giving results in a loss to the giver, or a loss of security. Scripture teaches the opposite. Money given to the Lord's work should never be looked at as lost any more than a farmer would look at the seeds and water and labor he puts into a crop as lost. He looks at it as an investment with the expectation of a greater gain. That is Paul's point, "Whoever sows generously will also reap generously." But that is only half of the truth. Did you notice that Paul stated the negative side of the truth first, "Whoever sows sparingly will also reap sparingly." Not only will an ungenerous giver fail to get the blessings that could be his, he will actually suffer loss.

I remind us that the cause and effect axiom Paul is expressing here is what theologians call "The Law of the Harvest." It is also stated in passages like Galatians 6:7, "Do not be deceived, God cannot be mocked. A man reaps what he sows." But a law is not a law unless it is true 100% of the time. The Law of the Harvest is a law only in eternity.

The ungenerous giver may or may not suffer financial loss in this life, but he will suffer loss of reward in eternity 100% of the time. The books will be balanced perfectly in eternity. **It is very important to understand this, because many people believe this axiom is true only in this life**.

STEP ONE RESTATED

Each man should give what he has decided in his heart to give, not reluctantly or under compulsion, for God loves a cheerful giver [2 Corinthians 9:7].

Here Paul re-expresses step one of the giving process, and presses the Corinthians for a decision, a heart commitment. Stewardship is individual. Each one of us is responsible to make a decision of the will. One commentary I read translated, "Each person should give as he determines with the consent of his heart." Giving must be voluntary to be acceptable to God. Then Paul states it negatively after having stated it positively. He says, "not reluctantly or under compulsion." The word "reluctantly" means literally "out of pain, grief or regret." The King James translates "not grudgingly." That means wishing you hadn't given it.

Then he says, "not under compulsion," which means not under pressure. Have you ever given under pressure? It's not acceptable to God. It's giving motivated by your circumstances rather than your will. Sometimes we give because somebody twisted our arm. Sometimes we give because we want to make an impression on someone. Or we give perhaps with the idea of receiving something in return. Giving under compulsion is not acceptable to God.

So, scriptural giving is voluntary, willing, not painful, not pressured giving. And just to put the capstone on this verse Paul concludes with a phrase very well known to most Christians, "God loves a cheerful giver." Most of you have probably been taught that cheerful is a translation of the Greek word *hilaros*, from which we get our English word "hilarious." Scriptural giving is hilarious giving ...... joyous giving. The cheerful giver is one who does not hurt. He does not sorrow. He does not grieve. He does not regret.

He gives joyously, and he gives easily ...... it just flows out. And once he experiences *hilaros* giving, he wants to experience it again. It's almost intoxicating, if I can use that term in a good sense. As an example, a cheerful giver gets more joy and fun out of buying a car for a missionary than buying a car for himself.

NOTICE THAT VERSE 7 HAS ENTIRELY TO DO WITH ATTITUDE.

And until the heart attitude has been changed to that described by Paul in verse 7, step one has not been taken, and the giving process has not even begun as far as God is concerned. Once step one has been taken, then the other steps follow as he explains in the next verse.

STEPS TWO, THREE AND FOUR RESTATED

> And God is able to make all grace abound to you, so that in all things at all times, having all that you need, you will abound in every good work [2 Corinthians 9:8].

This is one of the great promises of the Bible, the reassurance that acting contrary to our natural instincts will not result in our harm. The world says that giving is a way of reducing your wealth and your security. The Bible says it's a way of increasing it. Which is right? We must decide. We have a choice between human and divine viewpoint. Either we trust in our natural instincts and logic, or we trust in the eternal sovereign God of this universe and His Word.

Paul says, "God is able." God is able to do what according to verse 8? Answer: Supply two things, the grace of giving, and the material resources necessary to express that grace. Notice Paul's four uses of the word "all." "All grace," meaning the full measure of the spiritual gift of giving which you will need. "In all things," meaning all the circumstances of life. "At all times," meaning it will always be there when needed. And "all that you need," meaning all the money which you will need to exercise the grace. What an incredible promise.

> As it is written: "He has scattered abroad his gifts to the poor.
> His righteousness endures forever" [2 Corinthians 9:9].

Here Paul quotes Psalm 112:9. Psalm 112 is a description of the God-fearing man, and one of the characteristics of the God-fearing man is that he consistently gives to people in need. If you read all of Psalm 112, you read how God keeps supplying the God-fearing man with resources to give, not resources to hoard, or spend selfishly ...... resources to give.

> Now He who supplies seed to the sower and bread for food will also supply and increase your store of seed and will enlarge the harvest of your righteousness [2 Corinthians 9:10].

Here is another interesting way of stating the truth he has just stated in verse 8. God will supply seed to the **sower.** Who is the sower? The one willing to put the seed into the ground. God does not multiply grain in the granary. He only multiplies it when it is sown into the ground. The message is clear. The sower is the one with the willing heart. The sower is the cheerful giver. That takes us right back to the thesis of the passage. Our job is to be willing and cheerful (that's step one), and God takes it from there and supplies the grace and the necessary resources (steps two and three). Then Paul states it in yet another way in the next verse.

> You will be made rich in every way so that you can be generous on every occasion, and through us your generosity will result in thanksgiving to God [2 Corinthians 9:11].

Here is a verse to let sink in. "Made rich" is passive voice both in the original and in the English translation. And the passive voice means that the subject, *you,* receives the action of the verb, *made rich.* You and I don't have anything to do with it other than a willing heart. God decides to make us rich - and how rich - financially, so that we can be generous on every occasion.

There are many ways a Christian can be made rich besides materially. But this entire context demands that the primary emphasis here is on material wealth. Having said that, we must be careful how we interpret this verse. The verse clearly states God's reason for making us "rich" is so that we can be generous ...... so that we'll have money to give. God does not make us rich for selfish purposes. Some Christians want to play this verse like the stock market. That's a misapplication, and it's always good to look at other verses which give counterbalancing truth.

> People who want to get rich fall into temptation and a trap and into many foolish and harmful desires that plunge men into ruin and destruction [1 Timothy 6:9].

The "made rich" of this verse is not a bonus for service. It's not so that we can heap up wealth on this earth. It's for kingdom purposes. It's so that we'll have more in order to keep the giving process going.

I consider 2 Corinthians 9:6-11 to be the greatest statement of the theology of giving to be found in the Bible. They are great verses to memorize and meditate on and pray about.

This service that you perform is not only supplying the needs of God's people but is also overflowing in many expressions of thanks to God. Because of the service by which you have proved yourselves, men will praise God for the obedience that accompanies your confession of the gospel of Christ, and for your generosity in sharing with them and with everyone else. And in their prayers for you their hearts will go out to you, because of the surpassing grace God has given you [2 Corinthians 9:12-14].

In verse 13, notice that obedience accompanies a true confession of the Gospel. I love verse 14, where Paul mentions one of the great benefits and blessings which we receive when we give. Those whom we support will pray for us. They will intercede before God on our behalf. Thus we will receive benefits in this life, then eternal reward in heaven. I cannot imagine a better deal than this.

Thanks be to God for His indescribable gift! [2 Corinthians 9:15].

Paul ends this great two-chapter passage with these familiar words. How appropriate to end a long discourse on giving by citing the greatest gift the world has ever known, Jesus Christ and His redemptive act, the full, final, all sufficient and only payment for our sins.

As we think back over this chapter, I would challenge each of us to ask ourselves some questions. Where am I in the giving process? ...... the four step sequence Paul lays out in 2 Corinthians 8 and 9? Have I taken the first step? Have I signed the stewardship agreement and deeded all my assets back to God? Do I hold them with an open hand as His manager, willing to give as He directs? Until I have taken this step, nothing of eternal value will occur.

Has God given me the grace of giving? Am I cheerful and joyous as I give? Is it easy? Or, am I reluctant? Do I wish I hadn't parted with the money? Do I feel pressured to give? Answering these questions will help confirm in my heart whether I have the spiritual gift of giving. I can have tangible evidence that I have a willing heart for giving.

Has God given me the grace to give sacrificially? That is a special gift He gives to some, as Paul explains in Romans 12:3, where he mentions that God gives us differing measures of faith along with the spiritual gifts. If I have this gift (sacrificial), giving is sometimes going to hurt, else it would not be sacrificial. That is not to say I will be grieved that I gave, but it still could be painful. Has God laid a specific need or needs of His kingdom's work on my heart ...... to the point that I feel a compelling burden to meet that need? Has God given me the material resources to meet that need? The willing steward is constantly looking for opportunities to meet needs, while being dependent on God to provide the resources for those needs.

Can you see how God's control and His best for you (Square One) apply to giving? Do you recognize the importance of constantly defeating autonomy-lust in your life if you are going to be effective in your giving commitments? The first few chapters of this book have more practical application than you thought they did when you first read them. This is the area where you will make your stand in your fight with the world. Will you add to your net worth here ...... or in eternity?

CHAPTER 10

THE TITHE

Sixty years ago, the church in which I was growing up taught me that I was required to give a tithe (10%) of my income to the Lord, and that it was to be given to the local church of which I was a member. This was referred to as "storehouse tithing." It was all right to give to other charities or ministries outside the local church, but the first 10% must be given to the local church. Over the years since then, I have heard less of this teaching from Bible-believing churches and teachers, but some still teach it and believe it. And I still receive questions about the tithe fairly often. Questions like, is the tithe binding on the church-age Christian? Is it a minimum standard for our giving today, or a suggested starting place for our giving? And, am I to bring the whole tithe to my local church?

As mentioned in Chapter 9, I really believe all these questions are answered by Paul's long passage on giving in 2 Corinthians 8 and 9, along with the giving commandments of Jesus and the apostles. But in some sense the answer could be looked at as an answer from silence. Nowhere in the New Testament have I found a single specific statement instructing a Christian how much to give - what percent, what amount, or how to determine it. Yet the tithe is mentioned three times in the New Testament, and the issue is still debated in the church. This was especially true the last time I taught this subject 25 years ago. So I think it is a worthwhile issue to examine biblically.

Let's begin with a verse we studied in Chapter 9.

> Each man should give what he has decided in his heart to give …
> [2 Corinthians 9:7a].

That verse taken alone would seem to settle the question. But there are many other verses in the Bible on giving, which scholars who believe the tithe is binding call upon to support their position, so the debate continues, and in some circles it has become quite emotional. The two sides have chosen up and are fighting it out, and it seems to me that the devil is getting most of the mileage from this.

Over the years I have likely spent at least 200 hours researching this debate, studying both sides, studying all the Scriptures I could find. In the early years of my study I vacillated from one side of this debate to the other. I admit to having been on both sides. And at times I got emotional about it, and that was a mistake.

This is not a major point of doctrine, such as the Deity of Jesus Christ, the virgin birth, salvation by faith alone - non-negotiable doctrines which we must defend. I do not think we should break fellowship over the tithe. In fact, I would say that probably the best way of resolving the issue is to agree that it is not wrong to have a personal conviction about the tithe, as long as we don't try to impose that conviction on others, and as long as we acknowledge we are stewards of 100% of our financial resources, and will be accountable to God for that stewardship. Having so said, let me state the two sides of the debate, as best I can, and look at some of the relevant Scriptures.

THE CASE FOR THE TITHE BEING REQUIRED TODAY

There are Bible believing, God honoring scholars that believe the tithe is binding today on Christians. They believe it is a minimum standard required by God. When they come to 2 Corinthians 9:7, they say, Paul is not talking about the tithe in this verse. They say he's talking about a special offering, which is, therefore, over and above the tithe, and entirely voluntary with each individual Christian, as the verse clearly states. Certainly, that is a logical argument for their position. These scholars further believe that the principle of the tithe, and other principles of the Law of Moses apply today, even though the theocracy of Israel is no longer in existence. Furthermore, they would point out that 400 years before the law was given, both Abraham and Jacob tithed to the Lord. And this is true. And the tithe, they say, was merely incorporated into the Mosaic Law when the time came, but it was God's plan from the beginning. They also point out that Jesus commended the tithe when He discussed it with the Pharisees. That is true also.

THE CASE AGAINST THE TITHE BEING REQUIRED TODAY

The other group of scholars, also Bible believing, and God honoring, believe the tithe is not binding today, nor is it intended to be a standard for our giving. They lean rather heavily on 2 Corinthians 9:7, taking the position that Paul intended for his statement to be taken as a general principle applying to all giving, which is consistent with the commandments of Jesus and the apostles, which replaced the Law of Moses when Jesus died. We discussed this at some length in Chapter 3. Let's begin by looking at the three references to the tithe in the New Testament.

> Woe to you, scribes and Pharisees, hypocrites! For you tithe mint and dill and cummin, and have neglected the weightier provisions of the law: justice and mercy and faithfulness; but these are the things you should have done without neglecting the others [Matthew 23:23 (NASB)]. (A parallel passage to this one is found in Luke 11:42.)

Note here that Jesus is addressing the scribes and Pharisees, who were still under the Law of Moses since Jesus had not yet died. Therefore, this verse has no application to the church. Even so, Jesus is not complimenting them for keeping the law of the tithe, which they should have done, but rather rebuking them for failing to keep more important provisions, justice, mercy and faithfulness.

> .I fast twice a week; I pay tithes of all I get [Luke 18:12 (NASB)].

This is a quotation of a Pharisee in the story which contrasts the prayers of the Pharisee and tax collector who both went up to the temple to pray. Again, this verse would have no application to the church-age Christian.

> For this Melchizedek, king of Salem, priest of the Most High God, who met Abraham as he was returning from the slaughter of the kings and blessed him, to whom also Abraham apportioned a tenth part of all the spoils ... [Hebrews 7:1-2 (NASB)].

This is a reference to the tithe Abraham paid to Melchizedek following his victory over several kings in battle. As previously mentioned in Chapter 8, there is no textual reason to assume this was other than a voluntary offering on Abraham's part. Four hundred years later, the tithe was incorporated into the Law of Moses and became part of the required offerings the Old Testament Israelite had to give. The historical incident recorded in Hebrews 7 may have played a part in the tithe becoming a part of the Law of Moses, but the reference here in Hebrews contains no command, instruction or suggestion relating to the New Testament Christian's giving.

Therefore, I conclude that the three New Testament references to the tithe can in no sense be taken as an instruction concerning our giving. In fact to so interpret them would put them in conflict with the whole New Testament concept of stewardship, which we presented in Chapter 9.

AN EXAMINATION OF THE TITHE UNDER THE LAW OF MOSES

I found it both interesting and instructive to study some of the key passages on the tithe found in the Law of Moses.

> A tithe of everything from the land, whether grain from the soil or fruit from the trees, belongs to the Lord; it is holy to the Lord [Leviticus 27:30].

> And to the sons of Levi, behold, I have given all the tithe in Israel for an inheritance, in return for their service which they perform, the service of the tent of meeting [Numbers 18:21(NASB)].

The second of these passages seems clearly to command the giving of the whole tithe to the Levites. It was the sole means of supporting their priestly ministry.

THE SECOND TITHE

As we continue to study through the Law of Moses, we find passages indicating there was more than one tithe required. In Deuteronomy 14 we read about what appears to be a *second* tithe, not given to the Levites, but used in an entirely different way. Once a year the tithes, which were in the form of grain and animals, were transported to Jerusalem and stored there in a barn or storehouse until needed. The second tithe was used to underwrite the expenses of transporting the tithes, as well as the cost of a banquet and celebration of the Lord's blessing upon the land (lasting seven days according to Deuteronomy 16:15). This is what is meant by "eating the tithe." Thus this second tithe is referred to variously as the *expense* tithe, the *festal* tithe, or the *celebration* tithe.

> Be sure to set aside a tenth of all that your fields produce each year. Eat the tithe of your grain, new wine and oil, and the firstborn of your herds and flocks in the presence of the Lord your God at the place He will choose as a dwelling for His Name, so that you may learn to revere the Lord your God always. But if that place is too distant and you have been blessed by the Lord your God, and cannot carry your tithe (because the place where the Lord will choose to put His Name is so far away), then exchange your tithe for silver, and take the silver with you and go to the place the Lord your God will choose. Use the silver to buy whatever you like: cattle, sheep, wine or other fermented drink, or anything you wish. Then you and your household shall eat there in the presence of the Lord your God and rejoice. And do not neglect the Levites living in your towns, for they have no allotment or inheritance of their own [Deuteronomy 14:22-27].

One translation of the first part of verse 26 reads, "Spend the money for whatever you desire, oxen, or sheep, or wine or strong drink, whatever your appetite craves."

I like the following quote about the second tithe and Deuteronomy 14:22-27. It comes from a devotional book entitled, *Thoughts from the Diary of a Desperate Man.*

> "Each year God's people took ten percent of their yearly wage and spent it in the presence of the Lord on whatever they 'craved.' Moses gave God's rationale for commanding the people to do this, 'that you may learn to fear the Lord your God always' (Deuteronomy 14:26).

> "What you spend you do not have, and what you do not have you must trust God to provide. Many people spend money they do not have and go into debt. This is not what Moses is talking

about. Rather you are yearly to take ten percent of what you do have and spend it on yourself. The desire to accumulate can easily become an expression of unbelief. You save for uncertain times because you do not wish to trust God to provide for you during those times. This does not mean that if you save you are living in unbelief. Only you and God know the difference.

"God does not carry the command to spend a second tithe over into the New Testament, so you are not obligated to follow Israel's lead in this matter. But you should be instructed. When Israel sought to accumulate and hoard the manna, it turned to rot. Liberality delights God when expressed in gratitude for His provision. You can trust God in a variety of ways. A second tithe is one of them." [1]

THE THIRD TITHE

But wait, there's more. Some scholars see a *third* tithe, but only every third year. This third tithe, which would average 3 1/3% per year, was given exclusively to the poor.

> At the end of every three years, bring all the tithes of that year's produce and store it in your towns, so that the Levites (who have no allotment or inheritance of their own) and the aliens, the fatherless and the widows who live in your towns may come and eat and be satisfied, and so that the Lord your God may bless you in all the work of your hands [Deuteronomy 14:28-29].

So, if in fact this tithe every third year is over and above the other two tithes, the average per year could be as high as 23 1/3%. Some scholars see only one tithe used for all three of these purposes. Some see three separate tithes. I read a number of scholars on each side, and I don't know who is right. And some of the scholars I read said they didn't know.

---

[1] Walter A. Henrichsen, *Thoughts from the Diary of a Desperate Man* (Ft. Washington: Christian Literature Crusade, 1977), p. 241.

The scholars who argue that the tithe does not apply today point out that the Levitical priesthood no longer exists, so there is no way you can follow the law on that tithe. They also point out that the storehouse (a barn appended to the temple, in which the tithes were stored) is no longer in existence, so there is no way you can take your tithe to the storehouse.

The scholars who take the other side of the debate (e.g., the tithe does apply today) have a counter argument for this. They point out that both Abraham and Jacob tithed before there was a Levitical priesthood or a storehouse. Therefore they say it's not fair to use that argument to prove that the tithe is not for the church.

So go the arguments. And there are other arguments on both sides, and I probably haven't fairly represented whichever side you may be on, if you have a side of the debate. Which is right? I find nothing in the New Testament that suggests the tithe is binding on the church today, nor any other percent or amount. And I think I know the reason why. It is because New Testament giving is stewardship of *all*. 100%.

God will hold us accountable for how we manage 100%. I personally believe the New Testament principles of stewardship are far more demanding than are those in the Old Testament, just as the New Testament concept of adultery or murder is far more demanding than those under the Law. Jesus raised the bar of difficulty for keeping many of the laws of Moses when He restated them in His teachings.

One of the best comments I have ever read on the tithe was that of Richard Foster, a professor of theology at Friends University in Wichita, Kansas. In his book entitled *Freedom of Simplicity*, page 50, he said,

> "The tithe simply is not a sufficiently radical concept to embody the carefree unconcern for possessions that marks life in the kingdom of God. Jesus Christ is Lord of all our goods, not just 10%. It is quite possible to obey the law of the tithe without ever dealing with our mammon lust. We can feel that our monthly check to the church meets the new law of Jesus, and never once root out reigning covetousness and greed. It is possible to tithe and at the same time oppress the poor and needy. Jesus

thundered against the Pharisees, 'woe to you, scribes and Pharisees, hypocrites, for you tithe mint, dill and cummin, and have neglected the weightier matters of the law, justice and mercy and faith. These you ought to have done without neglecting the others'.

"No doubt you noticed that Jesus did not condemn the tithe as such. The tithe is not necessarily evil. It simply cannot provide a sufficient base for Jesus' call for carefree unconcern over provision. It fails to dethrone the rival god of materialism .... perhaps the tithe can be a beginning way to acknowledge God as the owner of all things, but it is only a beginning and not an ending."

I want to comment on the last statement in the above quote. I found it intriguing. In studying the lives of several of the great disciples of history, I noticed that some of them came to exactly that conviction ...... that the tithe was the beginning or starting point for their giving to the Lord. I would imagine some of them struggled with it just as you and I have. But as they prayed, searched and meditated in the Scriptures, they came to this conviction. But they did not come to it because of a command, or an instruction, or a requirement. Nor was it a limit or cap on their giving. It was a starting place.

So, let's ask the question, is it all right to tithe? My answer is yes, as long as two conditions are met. First, it must be given from a willing, cheerful heart, as Paul instructed us. I believe this is the overriding principle of giving found throughout the Bible. It must be voluntary giving from a willing heart. Second, you must understand that *you are a steward of the other 90%*, and will be accountable to God for your management of it.

In the middle 1980s, I taught a seminar on Biblical Economics in a church in Tucson. The teaching sessions were at the regular Sunday services, then each night for a week. The pastor had scheduled one-on -one counseling sessions during the weekdays, about every hour. I was busy.

One morning a young man in his early 20s came for counseling, and he was different from all the rest. He didn't want to know how to get out of debt, or how to budget, or how to invest his savings ...... he didn't have any of the usual questions. He wanted to talk about giving. And he didn't have anything to give. He was going to school and had a part time job which paid a very low income. He told me that a year earlier he had committed to giving God a tithe of his income, and up to that point he had faithfully done so. Then he said something I will never forget as long as I live. He said, "I feel like I'm just tipping God."

For a few moments I was taken aback by his statement, and I pondered it. I thought to myself, that is good theology. I don't suppose he knew about all the complexities of the tithe ...... some of the things we've discussed in this chapter. But his theology was good. He wanted to get to the point where he could far exceed the tithe in his giving. You could detect that he was impatient and frustrated because he couldn't do it. He showed every evidence of a willing committed heart. I commended him, and told him that if he continued to have that kind of objective in his heart, God would make a great steward of him some day.

As Paul taught us, it all starts with a decision of the heart. Then God bestows the grace of giving, the financial resources necessary to express the grace in the heart, and then leads us to specific needs of His kingdom's work.

> For if the willingness is there, the gift is acceptable according to what one has, not according to what he does not have [2 Corinthians 8:12].

That is the verse I should have quoted to that young man. I don't remember whether I did or not.

CONCLUDING COMMENTS

Struggling with the concept of a tithe, and its application to stewardship, is evidence of the "willingness to give" that is necessary in the life of a believer. Adherence to "all that Jesus commanded" must certainly include the lifestyle of giving, and yet one hundred percent, not ten percent, must be available to the Lord any time He asks it.

Citizenship confers rights and responsibilities on all citizens. A believer's citizenship is in heaven. He has voluntarily recognized ownership by the Lord of his entire stewardship. He may live in a country that protects property rights, but he has already forfeited those rights. Instead, he has the privilege of managing God's assets in this world. In God's economic system, as in all else, God is in control, and He has set it up with our best interests in mind, and not the way any of us would have arranged it. He claims it is in our interest that we manage His property, and not claim ownership of it. Our well being is tied to adherence to this system. God's ownership doesn't include ten or twenty-three percent, but all that comes our way. The responsibilities included in this system will not allow the sentiment "I own the other ninety percent free and clear, and I have total autonomy over that portion, because I have given the tenth."

This in essence is the temptation with the tithe. "You are not your own, you have been bought with a price." If the Lord owns my time, my thoughts, my energy, and my labor, how do I reconcile the percentage of income that belongs to me?

God's whole management system can be summarized in these few words. *God owns it all.* I surrender my autonomy and submit to His authority (obey His commandments). I manage the portion He assigns to me. My needs are met by Him.

CHAPTER 11

PAY YOUR TAXES

In Chapters 8 and 9 I said, "It seems clear to me that in the mind of God, giving is the most important principle of handling money." Those two chapters survey the Old and New Testaments on the subject of giving. If you can read those two chapters, or better still read through the Bible, and not come to that conclusion, I would be surprised. Assuming I am correct in this conclusion, a logical question is, "What is the second most important principle of handling money?" Jesus Christ, the apostle Paul and the apostle Peter all answered this question, and did so in the form of clear, direct commands.

THE SECOND MOST IMPORTANT PRINCIPLE OF HANDLING MONEY

Jesus was first to command us to pay our taxes, and it seems obvious to me that Paul's and Peter's teachings are simply commentary and application of Jesus' command.

> And the scribes and the chief priests tried to lay hands on Him that very hour, and they feared the people, for they understood that He spoke this parable against them. And they watched Him, and sent spies who pretended to be righteous, in order that they might catch Him in some statement, so as to deliver Him up to the rule and the authority of the governor. And they questioned Him saying, "Teacher, we know that You speak and teach correctly, and You are not partial to any, but teach the way of God in truth. Is it lawful for us to pay taxes to Caesar, or not?" But He detected their trickery and said to them, "Show Me a denarius. Whose likeness and inscription does it have?" And they said, "Caesar's." And He said to them, "Then render to Caesar the things that are Caesar's, and to God the things that are God's" [Luke 20:19-25 (NASB)].

Here Jesus commands paying taxes to the Roman government of His day, even though it was one of the most godless and pagan governments in the history of mankind. In Matthew 17:24-27, we learn that Jesus and His disciples paid a tax to Rome. But what is more interesting to me is that Jesus here puts paying taxes on an equal level with paying God what is due Him. "Render to Caesar the things that are Caesar's and to God the things that are God's." By the way this is worded, one is no more important than the other. But we get more insight and understanding as we examine Paul's commentary on Jesus' command.

> Everyone must submit himself to the governing authorities, for there is no authority except that which God has established. The authorities that exist have been established by God [Romans 13:1].

This verse tells us that God has ordained human government for the good of mankind. We have human governments because God intended for us to have them. And even though a particular government may be godless and pagan, God has delegated certain authority to that government.

> Consequently, he who rebels against the authority is rebelling against what God has instituted, and those who do so will bring judgment on themselves [Romans 13:2].

To violate a law of the government to which you answer is equivalent to violating a law of God. It is actually an act of disobedience against God Himself.

> For rulers hold no terror to those who do right, but for those who do wrong. Do you want to be free from fear of the one in authority? Then do what is right and he will commend you [Romans 13:3].

I think you could boil verse 3 down to one simple statement ...... keep the law and you'll get along all right.

> For he (the one in a position of authority in the government) is God's servant to do you good. But if you do wrong, be afraid, for he does not bear the sword for nothing. He is God's servant, an agent of wrath to bring punishment on the wrongdoer [Romans 13:4].

Not only has God ordained human government for the good of man, but He has delegated the government the right to punish people who violate the law.

> Therefore, it is necessary to submit to the authorities, not only because of possible punishment, but also because of conscience [Romans 13:5].

As Christians, we don't obey the law just to avoid being punished. We obey the law because it's the right thing to do, or as Paul states it, because of conscience.

> This is also why you pay taxes, for the authorities are God's servants, who give their full time to governing [Romans 13:6].

The Roman government which Paul refers to here was a godless and pagan government. The Caesar in charge actually claimed to be God.

So against that background, would we not expect the apostle Paul to advise those early Christians to withhold taxes from this ungodly government? Or perhaps to support a tax revolt, or join the underground economy? Paul does exactly the opposite, having given us his reasons in the first five verses. Now it may be very difficult for you and I to think of the tax collector as a servant of God. But he is, because he's carrying out a God ordained function.

> Give everyone what you owe him. If you owe taxes, pay taxes;
> if revenue, then revenue; if respect, then respect; if honor, then
> honor [Romans 13:7].

This passage is saying in very simple language that God has ordained government for the good of mankind, and it costs money to operate the government. Therefore, God has also ordained the payment of taxes to underwrite the cost of government. And to withhold taxes is an act of disobedience directly against God. Robbing the government of taxes is equivalent to robbing God. That means that any believer who cheats on his income tax in any way, is robbing God, and will be accountable to God for his sin.

Even though we may disagree with a lot of the things the government does with our taxes, and we have the right to register our disagreements, we can certainly feel more comfortable about paying taxes to the United States of America than these early Christians must have felt about paying taxes to Rome.

The apostle Peter also commanded us to submit to the governing authorities.

> Submit yourselves for the Lord's sake to every authority instituted among men: whether to the king, as the supreme authority, or to governors, who are sent by him to punish those who do wrong and to commend those who do right [1 Peter 2:13-14].

SQUARE ONE, OUR AUTONOMY-LUST AND PAYING TAXES

The Bible is clear in what it says about paying taxes. It is my personal conviction that as far as the disbursement of money is concerned, God assigns the highest priorities to giving and paying taxes, and they should be so considered in any financial plan based on the Bible. And both have to do with the respect for authority. Every Christian is a citizen of two kingdoms, an earthly kingdom, or nation, and a heavenly kingdom. We're under the authority of two different regimes, and we must pay our share of the cost of operating each.

Notice the vital link with the foundational truths taught in the first two chapters. It's difficult enough to surrender our autonomy-lust to God, and submit to His authority over us. It is more difficult and nearly impossible for some Christians to submit to the government, and yet that is what we are commanded to do.

Many Christians believe we are no longer a "Christian nation," and to a large extent they are correct. Remember that the Roman government that Jesus and Paul commanded submission to was totally pagan. But that's not the point. For us to be able to humbly submit to our government today, we must draw heavily on the truth of Square One, that is, God is in control and He has our best interest at heart. We must remember that no person, government nor circumstance can touch our lives without the permission of God, and any which do are His agents in our lives, placed there by Him to accomplish His purposes. As Paul stated it in Romans 13:4, "For he is God's servant to do you good. But if you do wrong, be afraid, for he does not bear the sword for nothing."

So, unless we invest our faith in Square One, and surrender our autonomy-lust and submit to God, no financial plan will succeed. If we can get this settled in our hearts, and put giving and paying taxes as the highest priorities for our spending, we will have taken a giant step toward financial success as the Bible defines it. And let me just note in passing, paying taxes does not violate the command to not presume on the future. We are not asked to pay taxes on money we have not yet earned.

Yes, this is one of the most difficult areas in which we are asked to surrender our thirst for control. May God give us the conviction, the strength and the humility to do it.

CHAPTER 12

BORROWING AND LENDING

In the last few chapters we have made the assertion that giving and paying our taxes are the two highest priority principles for managing money. Jesus' simple command, "Give to Caesar what is Caesar's, and to God what is God's," would seem to support this assertion. Notice, we are talking here about the actual handling of money. Certainly the heart attitude comes ahead in importance ...... accepting that God is the owner of all wealth, and we are merely His stewards.

As I was preparing the original seminar on this subject, I asked myself the question: If giving and paying taxes are first in priority for managing money, what is the third most important principle? And I finally concluded there is no specific answer. That is, it depends on the individual situation. It varies from person to person and situation to situation. But I would guess that among a typical group of Christians today, getting out of debt would most often be the next highest priority. Thus, in this chapter we take up the subject of debt, or borrowing and lending. We seek biblical answers to two questions. Is it a violation of the Bible to borrow money? Is it a violation of the Bible to lend money?

BORROWING AND LENDING – OLD TESTAMENT

As we did with the subject of giving, we want to examine some passages in the Old Testament in order to gain insight from the mind of God on borrowing and lending. This can be very useful to us in forming our personal convictions, but we will look to the commandments of Jesus and the apostles as our authority over this area of our finances.

We begin by looking at a concept which you may never have associated with borrowing and lending money, but which the Old Testament does. That concept is the master-slave relationship.

> However, there should be no poor among you, for in the land the
> Lord your God is giving you to possess as your inheritance, He

will richly bless you, if only you fully obey the Lord your God and are careful to follow all these commands I am giving you today. For the Lord your God will bless you as He has promised, and you will lend to many nations but will borrow from none. You will rule over many nations, but none will rule over you [Deuteronomy 15:4-6].

Here we find wonderful insight into the mind of God as He instituted this cause-and-effect law with Israel. And we can be instructed and develop convictions from this insight, even though we are not under the Law of Moses. Here we learn that God favors lending over borrowing. He was saying to Israel, if you obey Me, I'll bless you, and one of the ways I'll bless you is that you will be a lender, and not be a borrower. In other words, you'll be an investor instead of a borrower. You can invest your capital, your savings, for purposes of earning a return on it.

But there was more to it than simply earning a return on it. Verse 6 goes on to say, "You will rule over many nations, but none will rule over you." In other words, lending tends to put you in a position of authority over the borrower. Borrowing tends to put you in a position of servitude to the lender. Lending was a sign of God's favor. Borrowing was a sign of God's judgment. One of the clearest statements of this truth is found in Proverbs 22:7.

The rich rule over the poor, and the borrower is servant to the lender [Proverbs 22:7].

Some translations use the word "slave." "The borrower is slave to the lender." This is a legitimate translation.

CAUTION – THIS IS OLD TESTAMENT

From the passages we've studied thus far, it seems clear that God intended for Israel to be in a position of dominion over other nations, not a position of servitude. Jesus and the apostles have not commanded us to rule over other nations. But we can be instructed by how God dealt with Israel. And we can be instructed by "the borrower is slave to the lender."

118

Consider this simple question. Are we Christians today lenders, in the main? I suggest the answer is no, we are *net borrowers*. And that, I believe, is part of the problem in the 21st century church. Think with me. If faithful stewards are the lenders in society, they will use their capital and their control for kingdom purposes, for godly purposes, for righteous purposes ...... to carry out the great commission, and other ministries to which God has called us. Not only that, but their righteous use of money, and their control, will provide some stability to society, and some restraint against evil in society.

On the other hand, if ungodly people are the lenders, and thus rulers, in society, how will they use their capital and control? Obviously for ungodly purposes, for selfish purposes, for materialistic purposes. Unbelievers do not see themselves as managers of God's property.

Lenders often establish rules and regulations that the borrowers must follow. If the lenders are godly people, then debt under these circumstances can be a restraint against sin in society, and thus a blessing of God.

Therefore, God provided under the Mosaic Law that the Israelite could charge interest to the non-Israelite, and demand repayment of the debt. But he could neither charge interest nor demand repayment from his brother in need. Let's look at other verses in Deuteronomy 15.

> At the end of every seven years you must cancel debts. This is how it is to be done: Every creditor shall cancel the loan he has made to his fellow Israelite. He shall not require payment from his fellow Israelite or brother, because the Lord's time for canceling debts has been proclaimed [Deuteronomy 15:1-2].

Let's pause and understand what we're dealing with here. This has to do with lending money to a brother who has an emergency need, who has become poor for one reason or another. I would suggest a title for this kind of lending. Let's call it, "the charity loan." That's what it is. It's much more charity than it is lending, and must be distinguished from debt in the usual sense, that is, commercial debt.

> If there is a poor man among your brothers in any of the towns of the land that the Lord your God is giving you, do not be

hardhearted or tightfisted toward your poor brother. Rather be openhanded and freely lend him whatever he needs [Deuteronomy 15:7-8].

The following parallel passage gives additional details of the charity loan plan.

Do not charge your brother interest, whether on money or food or any thing else that may earn interest. You may charge a foreigner interest, but not a brother Israelite, so that the Lord your God may bless you in everything you put your hand to in the land you are entering to possess [Deuteronomy 23:19-20].

LEARNING FROM THE CHARITY LOAN PLAN

The charity loan plan which God prescribed for Israel helps us understand His mind. We can learn and develop convictions from it. The church of which I am a member has a benevolence fund which operates essentially the same as the plan given to Israel. It has been a blessing in our church. Even though there is no New Testament command to follow the plan which God gave Israel, Jesus gave commands to give and lend. His commands are broader and less specific than Israel's charity loan plan, but not inconsistent with it. We discuss His and the apostles' commands below.

QUESTION: DOES THE OLD TESTAMENT CALL BORROWING A SIN?

While stopping short of classifying all borrowing as sin, the Old Testament does classify some borrowing as sin. An example is debt which you know in advance you are unlikely to be able to repay, or debt which you have no intention of repaying. This is called "wicked debt" in the following passage.

The wicked borrow and do not repay, but the righteous give generously [Psalm 37:21].

Additionally, I find no passages in the Old Testament which speak favorably of borrowing, with the single exception of the legitimate use of the charity loan. And this is not borrowing in the sense in which we understand it today. It was actually a form of charity or giving.

It's obvious that God favored lending over borrowing. I found no instance in which borrowed money was used to accomplish God's purposes for Israel, but there are instances in which all the money needed was raised in advance of beginning the project. An illustration is the building of the tabernacle.

> Then the whole Israelite community withdrew from Moses' presence, and everyone who was willing and whose heart moved him came and brought an offering to the Lord for the work on the Tent of Meeting, for all its service, and for the sacred garments [Exodus 35:20-21].

The passage continues with further instructions concerning all the resources needed for the project.

Don't miss the impact of the phrase "everyone who was willing and whose heart moved him." Money not given with the consent of the heart is not acceptable to God. It is better kept than given.

And then we read a most interesting comment a few verses later.

> So all the skilled craftsmen who were doing all the work on the sanctuary left their work, and said to Moses, "The people are bringing more than enough for doing the work the Lord commanded to be done." Then Moses gave an order and they sent this word throughout the camp: "No man or woman is to make anything else as an offering for the sanctuary." And so the people were restrained from bringing more, because what they already had was more than enough to do all the work [Exodus 36:4-7].

When is the last time your pastor told the congregation not to bring any more offerings?

Forty years ago when our church was founded we were led to the conviction that we would not use any borrowed money to build our building, or underwrite any of our ministries. That conviction was developed from study of the Scriptures. While we found no specific commandment against borrowing, we found nothing favorable about borrowing, and no instances of the use of borrowed money to do the

Lord's work. This is one of the passages which led to that conviction. We have remained faithful to that commitment until this day. During many of those years, interest rates were very high. The money which would have been spent on interest has gone into the kingdom, and we believe God has greatly blessed it.

OLD TESTAMENT WARNINGS OF THE DANGER OF DEBT

As already stated, although the Old Testament stops short of classifying all debt as sin, it has nothing favorable to say about it, and it sounds two primary warnings of the danger of incurring debt. First, it tends to put you in a position of slavery or servitude, and second, it presumes on the future.

THE ENSLAVING POWER OF DEBT

The rich rule over the poor, and the borrower is servant (slave) to the lender [Proverbs 22:7].

The alien who lives among you will rise above you higher and higher, but you will sink lower and lower. He will lend to you, but you will not lend to him. He will be the head, but you will be the tail [Deuteronomy 28:43-44].

The first quote applies to the individual, the second to Israel as a nation. In Deuteronomy Chapter 28, God lists curses which will come upon the nation for disobedience, and one of them was being in debt and servitude to a foreign nation. One instance in which this occurred was the Babylonian captivity.

Obviously, a primary reason debt leads to slavery is because of the interest which must be paid. The Hebrew word for interest is *nashak*. The literal definition of this word from the Hebrew dictionary is the phrase, "to strike with a sting like a snake." Synonyms include, "to bite," and "to oppress." The very word itself sounds a warning of danger. Interest is like the bite of a poisonous snake. I wonder if the average person in our culture today appreciates the destructive power of *compound interest*. Interest allowed to compound over time becomes oppressive. I never think about this without thinking about our own nation. Do you think there is any way our national debt can ever be repaid? Do you think we or the government even intend to ever repay it?

Sometimes a person I am seeking to give financial counsel will say something to this effect. "Well, I don't feel like a slave to my bank or lending institution." To which I usually reply, "just continue on the path of borrowing which you are on and one day you will know what a slave feels like." I am ashamed to admit I have been there and I know that feeling. It was the essence of stress and depression. There is a prayer in my heart that every person who reads these words would heed the warning and avoid this experience.

DEBT ALMOST ALWAYS PRESUMES ON THE FUTURE

The second Old Testament warning of the danger of debt is that it **presumes on the future**. This subject was dealt with in depth in chapter 6, so we will not repeat that information here. You might wish to review Chapter 6. Here we simply list some of the key Old Testament passages which sound this warning.

It is a trap for a man to dedicate something rashly and only later to consider his vows [Proverbs 20:25].

A prudent man sees danger and takes refuge, but the simple keep going and suffer for it [Proverbs 22:3].

Do not be a man who strikes hands in pledge or puts up security for debts. If you lack the means to pay, your very bed will be snatched from under you [Proverbs 22:26-27].

Do not boast about tomorrow, for you do not know what a day may bring forth [Proverbs 27:1].

Consider what God has done: Who can straighten what He has made crooked? When times are good, be happy, but when times are bad, consider: God has made the one as well as the other. Therefore, a man cannot discover anything about his future [Ecclesiastes 7:13-14].

BORROWING AND LENDING – OLD TESTAMENT SUMMARY

We summarize the Old Testament teachings on borrowing and lending under 5 points.

• The Old Testament stops short of classifying all debt as sin, but *never encourages* the use of debt. It is clear that God favors lending over borrowing. Lending puts you in a position of dominion or authority over the borrower, while borrowing puts you in a position of servitude to the lender.

• The only exception to the first point was the charity loan provision under the Mosaic Law, which was actually a form of charity, not borrowing and lending in the commercial or investment sense.

• Under the charity loan plan, the Israelite was commanded to lend to his poor brother. He could not charge any interest, and the loan was canceled in the sabbatical year if the brother was unable to repay it. By contrast, the Israelite could lend to a foreigner, charge interest and demand repayment.

• The Old Testament warned of the danger of debt as it tends to lead to slavery or servitude. This applied both to the individual and the nation.

• It also warned of the danger of debt as it involves presuming on the future.

BORROWING AND LENDING – NEW TESTAMENT TEACHINGS

There are very few passages in the New Testament which deal specifically with borrowing and lending, and I was able to find only three that were in the form of commands, two spoken by Jesus and one by the apostle Paul. None of the three commands are a clear prohibition of borrowing. We will examine each of these three.

WHAT DOES ROMANS 13:8 TEACH?

I believe it will be profitable to take a very careful look at this verse, as there are some scholars who take this verse as a proof text prohibiting all borrowing. And if there is such a proof text, this would have to be it in my opinion. We will read it in three different translations.

- King James Version: Owe no man any thing, but to love one another ...

- New American Standard Bible: Owe nothing to anyone except to love one another ...

- New International Version: Let no debt remain outstanding, except the continuing debt to love one another ...

Those scholars who believe the Bible prohibits all debt would likely lean on the first two of these translations. But the original Greek allows a different translation which produces a different meaning. Dr. Kenneth Wuest, late professor of New Testament Greek at Moody Bible Institute, on page 227 of his commentary, *Romans in the Greek New Testament*, says, "The original is saying, 'Stop owing to anyone even one thing,' that is, do not continue owing a person. Pay your debts.

"The language of the King James Version prohibits the Christian from contracting legal debts such as mortgages and business loans. But that is not Paul's thought here."

The New International Version has taken this interpretation of the original.

In view of the fact that neither Jesus nor any other apostle gave a command prohibiting borrowing, I would lean heavily toward this interpretation.

Let's look at what Jesus said about borrowing and lending. First, this command from the Sermon on the Mount.

Settle matters quickly with your adversary who is taking you to court. Do it while you are still with him on the way, or he may hand you over to the judge, and the judge may hand you over to the officer, and you may be thrown into prison. I tell you the truth, you will not get out until you have paid the last penny [Matthew 5:25-26].

Here Jesus is saying, pay or settle your debts, or you could wind up in debtor's prison, where you will have to work the debt off until the last cent has been paid. This is the way unpaid debt was handled at the time Jesus spoke these words. Notice that this is consistent with the NIV translation, and Dr. Wuest's interpretation of Romans 13:8, which may be Paul's commentary on Jesus' command. Don't let your debts remain unpaid.

As far as I know, Jesus gave no command prohibiting borrowing, just the command to pay or settle your debts. But He did command us to lend.

Give to the one who asks you, and do not turn away from one who wants to borrow from you [Matthew 5:42].

Jesus gives some further commentary on this in Luke's gospel.

Give to everyone who asks you, and if anyone takes what belongs to you, do not demand it back …… And if you lend to those from whom you expect repayment, what credit is that to you? Even sinners lend to sinners, expecting to be repaid in full. But love your enemies, do good to them, and lend to them without expecting to get anything back. Then your reward will be great … [Luke 6:30, 34-35].

There is a lot to chew on in these verses. I've heard a lot of different theories on the interpretation of this command. I doubt that I will make much of a contribution to the understanding of it. But here are my thoughts. First, these verses are in sympathy with the charity loan provision in the Old Testament, except that they are not restricted to fellow believers or fellow countrymen.

But what kind of parameters are we to use in applying the command to give or lend? Are there any limits on the amount? Are there no circumstances under which we would make an exception? Jesus gives us no qualifications or guidelines for obeying this command …… or does He?

THE PRINCIPLE OF ETHICAL HIERARCHY

As we obey a command of Jesus, or an apostle, we must not simultaneously disobey another command. If we are placed in a circumstance which calls for obedience to two commands, and the two are in conflict with one another, then we must choose which to obey and which to disobey. This is known as the principle of ethical hierarchy, which teaches us to obey the higher, more important law, and suspend the lower law.

One of the best examples of this is the arrest of Peter and John for preaching in the name of Jesus. Peter and John were under the command to submit to the governing authorities. At the same time they were under the command of Jesus to spread the gospel. When commanded by the authorities to stop speaking and teaching in the name of Jesus, they refused, citing their allegiance to Jesus' higher law (see Acts Chapter 4).

It just happens that Jesus gave us two commands which are higher than all other commands, sometimes called the "two great commandments." They are, love God with all you heart, soul and mind, and love your neighbor as yourself. As we seek to obey Jesus' command to give or lend to those who ask us, we must not disobey the higher law to love them.

In the two great biblical commands, the Greek word for love is *agape*. There are two main Greek words for love in the New Testament, *agape* and *philos*. From a study of these two words, we conclude that actions which proceed from agape are centered in the will, not the emotions. Unlike philos, when we exercise agape, it may or may not feel good. We may or may not enjoy the person loved. We may or may not please the person loved. He may even hate us. It may or may not involve sacrifice on our part. But we must act in a way which we perceive to be in the best interest of the person loved. **Acting in the best interest of the other person is the highest criteria of agape**. **It is the essence of agape**.

Thus, when we obey Jesus' command to give or lend, we must not disobey His command to love (agape). We do not give an alcoholic money to buy alcohol. When a five year old asks us for a loaded gun, we do not honor his request. As we respond to Jesus' command, we must always and only respond in a way that we perceive to be in the best interest of the other person.

SQUARE ONE AND JESUS' COMMAND TO GIVE AND LEND

Before we leave this command, let's not overlook the application of Square One (see Chapter 1) to it. When I read this command, and frankly several others as difficult as it in the Sermon on the Mount, my first tendency is to begin thinking hypothetically. I start asking myself the "what if" questions. What if he asks for $100,000? What if he hits my cheek really hard? And on and on. Soon I have built seemingly insurmountable obstacles in my mind. My first tendency should rather have been to go to Square One and realize, if the person is there, it's no accident. He's there by God's permission, under His control, and with my best interest at heart.

He is God's agent in my life. Yes, he may sin against me. He may borrow from me and not repay, but he will not alter my destiny. He's merely participating negatively in God's plan for my life, decided in eternity past. By understanding and believing in the truth of Square One, we can spare ourselves the torture of worrying about what could happen.

DON'T PRESUME ON THE FUTURE

Jesus' second command concerning borrowing and lending touches the subject by application. It is His command against making vows, found in Matthew 5:33-37.

As you know, I have interpreted the essence of this command as stated by the following "one-liner."

Fulfill your promises. Do not make any vows which presume on the future. Such vows are evil.

We have studied this command in detail in Chapter 6, so we will not repeat that material here.

THE SIN WHICH LIES BEHIND THE MISUSE OF DEBT

As stated previously, neither Jesus nor the apostles gave us any specific commands prohibiting borrowing. But like the Old Testament, there is nothing in the New Testament which encourages borrowing. And both testaments sound warnings of the danger of going into debt. Thus, we are free to borrow, but we must be prepared to accept the consequences which follow.

The problem is not the use of debt, but the misuse of debt. And the sin which most often leads to the misuse of debt is the sin of materialism. Jesus and the apostles also refer to it as greed, the love of money, the desire to get rich, dissatisfaction with what we have, and the envy of what others have. Chapter 5 was a biblical study of this sin, including its definition, its consequences in our lives, and the way of victory over it. You might wish to review that chapter. Here we will limit our discussion of this sin to its role in the misuse of debt.

Let's look at the two most common ways of misusing debt.

BORROWING MOTIVATED BY THE DESIRE TO GET RICH

> People who want to get rich fall into temptation and a trap and into many foolish and harmful desires that plunge men into ruin and destruction [I Timothy 6:9].

In this passage the desire to get rich is defined as a sin. And remember that Paul defined the desire to get rich as wanting more than the strict essentials of survival (1 Timothy 6:8). Having fallen into this sin, we often borrow money in an attempt to speed up the accumulation of wealth.

This is called using leverage, the idea being that by borrowing a portion of the cost of a business or investment, you can get a greater return, assuming, of course, that the investment becomes profitable enough to cover the cost of the interest you pay plus enough more to provide the greater return. Again, the sin is not the use of leverage, but rather the desire to get rich, which usually leads to going into debt, which presumes on the future (another sin), and almost always ends badly. Read 1 Timothy 6:9 again and meditate on it.

Because the Law of the Harvest applies to the eternal, one might "beat the system" using leverage time and time again. He might perceive his actions as almost never ending badly. The *desire* to get rich is what he will be accountable for in eternity, not whether it worked out well here.

BORROWING MOTIVATED BY DISCONTENT

> Keep your lives free from the love of money and be content with what you have, because God has said, "Never will I leave you; never will I forsake you" [Hebrews 13:5].

The sin of discontentment in the heart of a believer can manifest itself in many ways. A partial list of symptoms of this sin includes overspending, compulsive buying, reducing or suspending our giving, and cheating on our income tax. But surely the most prevalent symptom of this sin today is borrowing in an attempt to increase our standard of living, borrowing in order to pay for consumer goods and services, such as cars, furniture, appliances, entertainment, and vacations. Before we do this, we should face the stark truth that it is tantamount to telling God He doesn't know what He's doing. By that I mean we are inferring that God has not provided sufficiently for our needs, thus we are forced to borrow to make up for His failure. Think about this very carefully. God has promised to meet our needs (not necessarily our wants) if we seek first His kingdom and righteousness (Matthew 6:33). We may actually be calling God a liar if we borrow in an attempt to increase our standard of living beyond what He has provided.

Standard-of-living borrowing by a Christian is a misguided attempt to satisfy a dissatisfied heart, a heart which can never find satisfaction in the things that borrowed money can buy. Isn't that a perverse thought? When a Christian gets caught up in this kind of borrowing, he is literally on a spiritual treadmill. He doesn't find satisfaction, he finds *bondage*.

Follow the logic. When you use borrowed money to pay living expenses, you are *lowering* your standard of living, not raising it. Obviously, there is a momentary illusion of an increased standard of living right after you buy something, but it soon wears off. As time passes the standard of living will decrease because of the interest paid on the debt. **You must see this and believe it or you will never become a good manager of God's property**.

Select any period of time, say the next ten years. During those ten years you will earn a certain amount of income. You don't know how much it will be, but whatever it is, that amount of money will buy less goods and services if you use borrowed money than if you pay cash. That is a simple mathematical certainty. If we let borrowing for consumer goods and services become a way of life, we will *lower our standard of living.* Our lenders dictate to us a lower standard of living, and I submit that that's a form of slavery. The lender has gotten some of our money and therefore some of God's money, reducing our standard of living and our stewardship of God's assets. The apostle Paul commands us not to place ourselves into bondage to men.

> You were bought at a price. Do not become slaves of men [1 Corinthians 7:23].

Again, the sin is not in *borrowing*. The sin is *a discontented heart*. Emergencies and catastrophes may come at any time. I may be unable to handle them without seeking help. But if I am not guilty of the sin of discontentment, if I am seeking first the kingdom of God and His righteousness, then God will meet my need in His own way and in His own time (Matthew 6:33). He may use a gift or loan from a loved one, or the church. This is very different from standard-of-living borrowing that arises from a discontented heart.

NEW TESTAMENT SUMMARY – BORROWING AND LENDING

Jesus and the apostles give us no commands prohibiting borrowing, but they do command repayment of all debts, and they never encourage borrowing. Like giving, we have complete latitude in the use or non-use of debt, but we are accountable to God for our decisions. Further, they give us specific commands against materialism lust, the desire to get rich, the love of money, and presuming on the future. All these sins often lead to borrowing. The use of debt is not a sin. The misuse is.

DEBT AND OUR LUST FOR AUTONOMY

In Chapter 2, we established that our problem with God is that we want to decide what is in our best interest rather than submit to what God says in our best interest. I believe that probably the best way God communicates to us what is in our best interest is through His commandments. It is always in our best interest to obey all His commandments. We will one day regret every time we were disobedient, but never regret obeying His commandments.

One of the commandments is, "Keep your lives free from the love of money and **be content with what you have**, because God has said, 'Never will I leave you; never will I forsake you' " (Hebrews 13:5).

The following is repeated from Chapter 6.

Our culture is full of young couples with two, three or more children. By design, God has entrusted them with differing amounts of material wealth and income. Think of the couple with the heavy responsibility of raising three children, but whose income is near the bottom of the middle class income spectrum. They are under the same command as those at the top: *be content with what you have*. God is telling them it is in their best interest to be content with their income … to live within the means He has provided.

They look around. They see the house and car their peers have. They see the entertainment they participate in. They see where they travel, the clubs they belong to, and on and on. And of course everything they see or hear in the media is designed to make them feel dissatisfied with their standard of living. They have no difficulty getting one or more credit cards, and begin buying the things they feel they should have.

They are disobeying the commandment. They are presuming on the future. They do not know the future. They do not know whether the husband will have a job in a year or two, whether he will be disabled, or even whether he will be alive.

If we believe that God is in control and has our best interest at heart, and if we take seriously Jesus' and James' commands, and if we take to heart all the wisdom quoted above from the Proverbs and Ecclesiastes, why would we ever want to presume on the future? Answer, because it is in our nature to do so. The lust for autonomy is born into us. Add to that the sin nature, and the marvelous intellect God has given us, and soon enough we begin to believe we can predict the future ... well, not really, but we think we can analyze our world well enough to know much of what is likely to unfold. Or perhaps we feel we're smart enough or skillful enough to plan and take actions which will cause to happen in the future what we want to happen. Re-read the following verses quoted in Chapter 6, and notice how starkly and bluntly God's Word refutes all such notions.

It is a trap for a man to dedicate something rashly and only later to consider his vows [Proverbs 20:25].

A prudent man sees danger and takes refuge, but the simple keep going and suffer for it [Proverbs 22:3].

Do not be a man who strikes hands in pledge or puts up security for debts. If you lack the means to pay, your very bed will be snatched from under you [Proverbs 22:26-27].

Do not boast about tomorrow, for you do not know what a day may bring forth [Proverbs 27:1].

Consider what God has done: Who can straighten what He has made crooked? When times are good, be happy, but when times are bad, consider: God has made the one as well as the other. Therefore a man cannot discover anything about his future. [Ecclesiastes 7:13-14].

Come now, you who say, "Today or tomorrow, we shall go to such and such a city, and spend a year there and engage in business and make a profit." Yet you do not know what your life will be like tomorrow. You are just a vapor that appears for a little while and then vanishes away. Instead, you ought to say, "If the Lord wills, we shall live and also do this or that." But as it is, you boast in your arrogance; all such boasting is evil. Therefore, to one who knows the right thing to do, and does not do it, to him it is sin [James 4:13-17 (NASB)].

If you have already misused debt, then the next chapter is for you.

CHAPTER 13

HOW TO GET OUT OF DEBT

The rich rule over the poor, and the borrower is servant (slave) to the lender [Proverbs 22:7].

This chapter is dedicated to those who are experiencing the reality of Proverbs 22:7, as well as those who may be on a course leading in that direction. I will suggest a seven step plan for getting out of debt.

STEP 1 – IDENTIFY THE REAL PROBLEM

The first step in the solution to any problem is to understand the problem. If you are in debt, and have reached a point where you are unable to repay the debt as you promised when you contracted it, you will in all likelihood ask yourself the question, "What is my problem?" And answers may begin coming to your mind, such as, I lost my job, or I had unexpected medical expenses, or car expenses, or I had an accident, or I haven't been able to build an emergency fund, or ...... Thus, you conclude, I was unable to pay my debt as agreed because of these unpredictable events, and that is my problem.

If this is the way you are reasoning, I want to suggest that you have merely identified one or more symptoms of the problem, but not the root problem. Let me state the root problem in simplified, general terms, and then apply it to our subject, the inability to repay debt. The root problem can be stated in two simple propositions. First, a lack of understanding of, or belief in, what Scripture reveals about God. And, second, a lack of understanding of, or belief in, what Scripture reveals about man (myself). The details of the root problem are given in the first two chapters of this book.

I must understand and believe that God is in control and that He has my best interest at heart. For the believer, that is true at all times and under all circumstances, including being hopelessly in debt. Only God knows what is in my best interest. He always has me exactly where He wants me, and if I am unable to repay my debts, then that is in my best interest at the moment.

135

I must also understand that, even though saved, I have a sin nature, and the essence of that sin nature is my lust for autonomy, my desire to decide what is in my best interest, rather than submit to what God says is in my best interest. In other words, I want to be God. This predisposes me to disobey one or more of the commandments. When I do, I must accept responsibility for my disobedience, and the consequences which result from it. Whatever God does will always be in my best interest, and will be designed to move me toward surrender of my lust for autonomy, and submission to His authority.

Thus, if I am in debt, and unable to repay it, I may have disobeyed one or more of the commands outlined in Chapter 12. I may have desired to get rich, and gone into debt to seek to realize that desire. Almost certainly I presumed on the future, ignoring the clear commands of Jesus and James. I may have been dissatisfied with the financial assets which God has entrusted to me, and borrowed money in an attempt to increase my standard of living.

All of this we must understand as the root problem behind the symptom of being in financial bondage. The issues raised in Chapters 1 and 2 must be understood and accepted before there can be any lasting solution. But having understood and accepted them, we are ready for Step 2.

STEP 2 – STOP ALL BORROWING

Getting out of debt is always difficult at best, because it involves facing up to the consequences of our past mistakes. Please memorize this statement: **Consumer debt is money we have already spent but not yet earned**. (If we were sitting in a fifth grade school classroom, the teacher might have us write that sentence 100 times.) It can also be expressed this way: When we borrow for consumer goods and services, we are spending future income. We are mortgaging the future to some extent, and since no one can forecast the future, we are presuming on the future, which is dangerous. Thus when we stop borrowing and begin repaying our debt, we will have less money to spend. It will involve sacrifice.

But this step must be taken sooner or later, and usually, the sooner the better. Step 2, therefore, is to **stop** all borrowing. Pay **cash** only.

Destroy all credit cards unless you can use them without paying any interest and without overspending your budget.

A WORD ABOUT CREDIT CARDS

There is nothing intrinsically evil about a credit card, nor is its use a violation of any commandment. It can be used in such a way that you pay no interest, and spend only what you plan to spend. It can be a convenience device. But this requires discipline and careful budgeting because credit cards facilitate impulse buying, or unplanned, unbudgeted buying. And unless you have the discipline and commitment to not overspend, you may be better off discontinuing the use of credit cards, at least until you are out of debt.

Here's another statement I suggest you memorize. It is a quote from a book entitled *You Can Be Financially Free*, by George Fooshee, a book I recommend.

"A credit card is a device which creates the ability to buy without creating the ability to repay." Think about that. We should ask ourselves, have these credit card companies invented some ingenious way for us to spend more than we make? Of course not. What they have done is induce us into a trap which *lowers* our standard of living rather than *raising* it.

If you do decide to use a credit card, I recommend that you follow Larry Burkett's three rules for using them. (1) Never buy anything which is not budgeted. (2) Pay your full balance every month, thus avoiding the payment of any interest. (3) Destroy your cards the first month you are unable to pay the full balance.

A WORD ABOUT CONSOLIDATION LOANS

There is another pitfall which is gaining wider use in our day, and that is the "consolidation loan", sometimes referred to as "refinancing your debt". As the name implies, the consolidation loan combines all of your debts into one big loan, which is then stretched out for a longer period of time than the average duration of your loans, thus reducing your total monthly payment, and theoretically making it easier to repay your debt. You might ask,"what's wrong with that"? In a word, a consolidation loan makes the problem **worse**, not better, because it results in more interest being paid and more time being required to get out of debt.

Please memorize this statement: **You cannot borrow your way out of debt. You can only pay your way out.** The consolidation loan treats the symptom of the problem but not the problem. The symptom is a lack of money to meet living expenses. The problem is *overspending*. And unless the overspending is stopped, the symptom will return, and when it does, the disease will be worse. Right after you do a consolidation loan, there is a feeling of temporary relief, but it soon wears off. Then things get worse, inevitably putting pressure on your marriage. Let me say this to you husbands. It is not fair to put your wife through this kind of pressure. Financial bondage takes a terrible toll on the marriage. So, almost always the consolidation loan aggravates the problem.

A word of balance. There can be some rare instances in which some refinancing can help. Occasionally you can reduce your rate of interest by refinancing, and not lengthen the repayment period. And in extreme situations, a counselor might suggest some consolidation of debt. It's often good to seek counsel, but make sure your counselor approaches your problem from a biblical perspective. Most likely, God's best for you will be to get out of debt at the earliest possible date. He probably wants the solution made harder, not easier.

IS IT SCRIPTURAL TO TAKE PERSONAL BANKRUPTCY?

This is an important question because today we have a personal bankruptcy law. It is legal to use bankruptcy as a means for getting out of debt. As this is written, the number of personal bankruptcies is setting record highs. It is a difficult question because of the many complexities and different situations to which the law applies. Those who believe that it is not a sin to take personal bankruptcy argue that the Christian is instructed to follow the laws of the government which is in authority over him, and one such law is the law allowing personal bankruptcy. They would cite Romans 13 in defense of this position. But I believe it is not that simple, because there are clear commands to repay debt, and no provision for avoiding repayment. All of the passages were covered in Chapter 12.

Larry Burkett had this to say in his discussion on bankruptcy: "I believe a principle that has been greatly overlooked in our generation is that of making a vow. A vow is literally a promise. When someone borrows money, he makes a promise to repay according to the agreed upon conditions of the loan. It's not an option once an agreement is reached. It's an absolute as far as God is concerned. The rights all fall to the lender, and the borrower literally becomes the lender's servant. Once a Christian borrows, it's a vow to repay. Bankruptcy is a legal remedy, not a scriptural remedy."

It is my personal conviction that taking personal bankruptcy, or any other system of avoiding repayment of debt, is not a biblical principle, even though it is a legal remedy under our laws today. Obviously a Christian can be forced into bankruptcy. If he is, then his debts are under the control of the court. But to voluntarily take bankruptcy with the intent of avoiding debt repayment, I believe, is to disobey the clear commands of Jesus and the apostles.

For those who are in a position of not being able to pay their debts as agreed, but have not yet elected, or been forced into, bankruptcy, I suggest the seven step plan of this chapter. We have already established Steps One (identify the problem) and Two (stop all borrowing).

STEP 3 – REDUCE SPENDING

Make a list of all current expenditures in the order of importance, listing the expenses with the highest priority at the top, etc. Then discontinue (or reduce) any expense which is not absolutely essential for survival. That would include any service you can do without, or perform yourself rather than pay someone else.

STEP 4 – SELL ASSETS

Sell any asset which is marketable at a reasonable value, and if absolutely necessary, replace it with a similar asset at a lower cost. In other words, you are downsizing from higher cost to lower cost necessities, releasing the cash difference to apply on your debts. The most readily obvious choices for such downsizing would be your house, or second house, one or more of your cars, or any other big-ticket item which is in the nature of a luxury ...... a non-necessity. For example, for someone in financial difficulty, buying a new car makes no sense. Not only that, if you cannot afford to buy a $10,000 used car for cash, then buy a $5,000 car. If you cannot afford a $5,000 car, then buy a $2,000 or $3,000 car, and if you cannot afford that, you might ask God to give you a car. I've seen Him do it a number of times. He might use the charity loan approach to provide you a car. If the spiritual problem in the heart has been dealt with (Step 1), then you have the power of God working for you, and anything is possible.

Consider the following mathematical proposition. If you will commit to paying cash only for your cars for the rest of your life, then you will buy a greater number of cars, or more expensive cars, with the same number of dollars than if you continue to finance your cars. When you stop buying on credit, you raise your standard of living.

Depending on your situation, you may have to sell a long term non-liquid asset, such as a piece of land, a building, or even your home. Any of these can be perfectly good investments in and of themselves, but they can be wrong in your picture if you are in financial bondage. You cannot buy groceries, pay doctor bills and educate children with the equity in a home. You can only pay these expenses with cash. And think about this. If the value of the asset drops while you are sitting there with it, you have lost part or all of your equity, and that asset can no longer be used to repay debt, or meet your family's needs.

Please memorize this statement: **Never allow any material asset on this earth to become an idol**. All earthly assets are temporary ...... transitory. All of them will one day wind up in the city dump. It is crazy for a Christian to become attached to them. Owning a home or any other earthly asset is not nearly as important as obeying God's commandments. Therefore, you may have to sell your home or any other material asset in order to get out of debt.

STEP 5 – CONSTRUCT A BUDGET BASED ON STEPS 1 THRU 4

If you have taken steps 1 thru 4, you have identified the spiritual problem. You have stopped all borrowing. You have stopped all unnecessary expenditures, and you have sold everything you can to raise cash. Next, sit down and construct a budget based on those first four steps. If the budget is in balance at this point, including the required payments on your debts, then thank the Lord, for that budget will take you out of debt.

A WORD ABOUT BUDGETING

One of the greatest enemies of financial success is ignorance. I'm not referring to a low IQ. I'm talking about ignorance of your true financial condition and ignorance of where you are headed financially.

> Be sure you know the condition of your flocks. Give careful attention to your herds, for riches do not endure forever, and a crown is not secure for all generations [Proverbs 27:23].

Few of us today have flocks and herds, but the verse was directed to an agrarian culture, and thus used language appropriate for it. In our language today, the verse is saying that unless you know where you are headed financially, you will fail. And the illustration the verse gives is very interesting, "riches do not endure forever, and a crown is not secure for all generations." In other words, even the king will go broke if he violates sound financial principles. Therefore, to follow the wisdom of this verse, you must have some kind of budget and financial system which accurately tracks your financial condition at regular time intervals. I recommend at least monthly, especially while you are seeking to get out of financial difficulty.

NOTE: This will tell you where you are and where you are headed financially, but will not tell you why. That's where the seven-step plan of this chapter and the simple stewardship plan to be explained in the next chapter come in. They tell you what to do. If you feel you need help with your budget, I recommend Howard Dayton's web site, www.crown.org, which has some excellent material.

As stated above, if step 5 produces a budget which will take you out of debt, then you are blessed, and in fact untypical. Step 5 does not usually produce a balanced budget. If, after step 5, you are still paying out more than you are taking in, then you must proceed to step 6.

STEP 6 – FIND EXTRA WORK UNTIL YOUR DEBTS ARE REPAID

This may mean that the husband has to take a second job. It may mean that the wife has to work part time if she's not already working. I do not advocate the latter as a normal or usual practice. It would likely not be God's best, especially if there are children in the home. But when you are hopelessly in debt, it could be the will of God. Consider it divine discipline, part of the price you must pay for having disobeyed God. The best thing to do is get it over with as quickly as possible, so that you can return to God's best for your family.

Let's suppose you are able to find additional work. Then at that point, revise your budget to reflect the additional income, as well as any additional expense, such as taxes, childcare expense, car expense, meal expense, or others. If the revised budget is then in balance, thank the Lord, because in time it will lead you out of debt.

But what if even after these six steps your budget is not in balance? What if your debt is not declining fast enough to get you out of debt in a reasonable period of time? And I must interject that that is the case I have often found in counseling Christian couples. There is one last step.

STEP 7 – FOLLOW PROVERBS 22:7 TO ITS LOGICAL CONCLUSION

...the borrower is servant (slave) to the lender [Proverbs 22:7].

As you meditate on that verse, what thoughts come to your mind? What does the verse imply? What does it suggest? Here are some of my thoughts when I was first awakened by its truth many years ago. Why not accept the fact that I am a slave if I am hopelessly in debt? And why not act like a slave? Why not act like a good slave, a submissive slave? A submissive slave does not avoid his master (in this case, his lender). He doesn't refuse his phone calls. He doesn't wait for him to sue him. He goes to his lender, humbles and submits himself, and asks his lender to tell him what to do. That would be acting like a good slave. And that in fact is what the wisdom of Proverbs 6:1-5 suggests. Let's look at this passage.

My son, if you have put up security for your neighbor, if you have struck hands in pledge for another, if you have been trapped by what you said, ensnared by the words of your mouth, then do this, my son, to free yourself [Proverbs 6:1-3a].

Before continuing, let's understand that this is referring to someone who has cosigned or guaranteed another person's debt. Of course, the same thing would apply to our own debts. We are personally liable for our own debts. So the advice given in this passage applies to any situation in which you have made yourself personally liable for a debt which you later find that you are unable to pay. In the words of the text, you were trapped by your words (your promise or your signature). What should you do?

Then do this, my son, to free yourself. Since you have fallen into your neighbor's hands: go and humble yourself. Press your plea with your neighbor! Allow no sleep to your eyes, no slumber to your eyelids. Free yourself like a gazelle from the hand of the hunter, like a bird from the snare of the fowler [Proverbs 6:3-5].

Notice that this counsel is consistent with Proverbs 22:7. More importantly, notice that it is consistent with Jesus' command.

Settle matters quickly with your adversary who is taking you to court ... [Matthew 5:25].

So the counsel contained in these verses is, at the moment you realize that you have committed to a promise you can't make good on, go to your creditor, humble yourself and submit to him, and work out a plan of repayment. I remind you that when you follow God's counsel you have the power of God working for you instead of against you, and that's what makes the difference. Often the situation appears hopeless, but God is omnipotent. He can change the heart of your lender. There's nothing wrong with a lender reducing a debt, or rearranging the repayment terms, or even forgiving the debt. There's nothing wrong with God supernaturally supplying resources to repay a debt. He can and has done so.

I have been amazed and disappointed to watch believers shun this biblical advice, and seek an unbiblical solution to their problem ...... bankruptcy, or a consolidation loan, or letting a lender repossess property and take a loss on it, avoiding a lender, refusing his calls. Doing these things is actually seeking to avoid repayment of debt rather than doing what Scripture instructs. "The borrower is slave to the lender." That is a statement of eternal truth which will not change while the earth stands. So the best thing to do is get in step with it rather than resist it.

A SUGGESTED PLAN FOR FOLLOWING PROVERBS 6:1-5

Proverbs 6 counsels "press your plea with your lender." That means to go to him and negotiate a repayment plan. Usually there is more than one lender involved. Therefore you must go to **all** your lenders, and I stress the word "all." My counsel is to do your best to treat all your lenders alike, and let all of them know you intend to do that. It is true that repaying your highest interest rate debt first is to your advantage financially, and that is certainly the thing to do **if you are able to meet the agreed upon payments on all your debts**. But if you can't make full payments on all debts, which is usually the case, then, I consider it unethical to discriminate between creditors.

It is also true that those lenders which hold collateral against your debt (such as a mortgage on your house or other property) have the right to take that collateral as payment, or partial payment, of the debt. But often they will go along with an overall plan of repayment which treats all lenders alike.

So here is the plan I suggest. Go to **all** your lenders and explain your debt situation fully. Tell them it is your intention to repay all of your debts in full including interest. Tell them you have cut your expenses to the bone. Tell them you have sold everything of value which is not absolutely essential to survival. Tell them you have taken a second job, if you have. Tell them your wife has taken a job, if she has. Give them the full picture. And tell them exactly how much money you have to pay every month on all your debts. Give them the exact figure.

Let's suppose this figure is 50% of all the regular payments on all your debts. Then tell every lender that if he will accept 50% of his normal payment, then by the grace of God it will be there every month, and be there on time. And then tell him that any additional funds which become available for debt repayment will be paid proportionately to all lenders. I have seen this plan work. If all your lenders understand the whole truth of your situation, and sense that your intention is to repay your debts, they will usually go along with such a plan. And, of course, if the intention of your heart is to do as Scripture counsels, you have the power of God working for you. Nothing could be better than that. As a bonus you have the opportunity of bearing witness to your lenders, for they will see something in you which they do not see in the typical borrower. And trust me when I say, there is no feeling which can match the feeling of being debt free after having been in financial bondage.

THOUGHTS ON OUR NATIONAL DEBT

In Chapter 12 we studied Deuteronomy 15. In that passage God told Israel if they would obey His commandments, He would bless them. And one of the ways He promised to bless them was that they would lend to other nations, but not borrow from them. And they would rule over other nations rather than be in servitude to them. Although the people promised to obey all God commanded, they in fact disobeyed Him. The result was that they became borrowers instead of lenders, and they lived in bondage to other nations.

As this is being written, our nation has run up debt which exceeds the debt of any nation in all of human history. In addition to this we are accumulating unfunded future liabilities at an unprecedented rate. There are currently five programs responsible for this. I call them "The Big Five" - Social Security, Medicare, Medicaid, Pension Guaranty, and at this writing, the "War Against Terror." A study done in 2003 concluded that the total unfunded liabilities of the nation stand at approximately $42 trillion. I almost hesitate to mention that number as it is almost impossible for our minds to grasp its significance. And besides that, it's already out of date, and will only get worse if things continue as they are.

How will we meet those liabilities? You might answer, "Certainly not by levying additional taxes. There's no way the American people can pay any more taxes." But the truth is there is no other source of funding except the taxpayers. So the government will do what it has been doing for many years, borrow more money and print more paper currency.

This will reduce the value of our currency, therefore, we are paying the additional taxes required by losing purchasing power of our money. The inflation tax is by far the easiest way out for the government. They don't even have to legislate a tax increase to effect it.

Why do I bring this up? Because the citizens of this country, including, sad to say, most Christians, are following their government deeper and deeper into debt. And when the debt pyramid one day collapses, or run-away inflation destroys most of the value of our currency, those Christians in debt will go down with the rest of the country. God does not intend it to be that way. He intends for us to be part of the solution, not part of the problem. Therefore my purpose for this discussion is to motivate those who read this to get out of debt at the earliest date possible. May God use the 7-step plan to help you do so.

WHEN YOU GET OUT OF DEBT, THEN WHAT?

Start thinking and planning what you will do with the money you are now using to make debt payments. While in debt, have you disobeyed Jesus' command to store treasure for yourself in heaven? Don't make the mistake of continuing to disobey that command. And don't add another broken commandment, the command to *not store treasure for yourself on earth*. If you don't start planning now, you know how the devil is going to influence you, not to mention, sad to say, most financial counselors. Push it out of your mind now, and when the day arrives, you'll either start attempting to raise your standard of living, or you'll begin trying to hoard earthly wealth, or both. It will be as natural as breathing. The choice is yours. Make your commitment now, not later.

This concept is the subject of the Epilogue of this book (see p. 229). It could be in your best interest to read it now, before continuing with the next chapter.

CHAPTER 14

OWNING A HOME – THE AMERICAN DREAM

Even though owning a home is not the only thing the average American would consider as "the American dream," it would surely be a high priority for most Americans. The house is, of course, a major economic asset. I have seen studies which show that it constitutes a major portion of the wealth of a large segment of the population. That being the case, the question came to my mind, does the Bible give us any specific wisdom or commandments relating to buying or owning a home? Is there economic wisdom in the Bible which bears upon buying or owning a home? The purpose of this chapter is to answer these questions, and be true to the Scriptures as we do so.

A secondary purpose of this chapter is to share with you my suggested rule for purchasing a home, based on my personal convictions developed from studying the Bible. That will lead naturally to a third purpose for the chapter, which is to briefly pull together all of the principles and truths we have studied in the preceding chapters and begin to formulate a stewardship plan.

WHAT DOES THE BIBLE SAY ABOUT THE HOUSE?

The word "house" appears several hundred times in the Bible, but I was able to find only six passages that speak of the house in a financial way, that is, from the standpoint of our financial stewardship. I was amazed at how these passages present truth that bears directly upon the question, how do I buy a house in the will of God? We will look at four of the six passages before I give you my rule. The reason is … that my rule is so strict, so hard, that I want a firm foundation from Scripture to back me up, else I fear that some will discontinue this study. In fact, the contents of this chapter will be too strong for some. I understand this very well, because not too many years ago it was too strong for me.

Understand that my rule is not your command. Like giving, under the New Testament teachings on stewardship, you have complete latitude in selecting the home you buy or build, whether or not you have a mortgage, and so forth. Just keep in mind that you will be accountable to Jesus on how well you obeyed His command to store treasure in heaven rather than on earth.

Well, let's look at the four passages which are the foundation for my rule for buying a home. There is a common thread which runs through these passages, and it has to do with financial priorities.

PASSAGE 1 – ECCLESIASTES 2:1-11

First, a word of background. Most scholars believe the book of Ecclesiastes was written by King Solomon. In this book, Solomon confesses his sin of materialism. We've been learning that one of the forms of idolatry mentioned in the Bible is materialism lust, and since Solomon was the richest man that had ever lived, it was a natural trap for him, and he fell into it. Apparently, later in his life, he realized his sin and he wrote about his materialism and other sins in the book of Ecclesiastes. We can profit from Solomon's mistakes and his testimony.

> I thought in my heart, "Come now, I will test you with pleasure to find out what is good." But that also proved to be meaningless. "Laughter," I said, "is foolish. And what does pleasure accomplish?" I tried cheering myself with wine, and embracing folly – my mind still guiding me with wisdom. I wanted to see what was worthwhile for men to do under heaven during the few days of their lives [Ecclesiastes 2:1-3].

Solomon embarked upon a series of experiments in search of happiness, or meaning in life. In these opening verses he mentions three of these experiments, pleasure, wine and folly. In verse 4 he mentions another.

> I undertook great projects ... [Ecclesiastes 2:4].

I think that one of the best interpretations of this statement for our day would be, "I undertook the accumulation of status symbols." I think that communicates to us what Solomon was getting involved in. He bought every status symbol that money could buy. And notice which one he mentions first.

I undertook great projects: I built houses for myself and planted vineyards [Ecclesiastes 2:4].

I would imagine that the most universal, time-tested status symbol in human history is the house. It's not the only one, of course. Today we have many others ... cars, clothing, jewelry, club memberships, sun tans, boats, condominiums, and on and on the list would go. But surely the most time-honored of all the status symbols has been the house. And Solomon puts the house first in his list. His list continues.

I made gardens and parks and planted all kinds of fruit trees in them. I made reservoirs to water groves of flourishing trees [Ecclesiastes 2:5-6].

He had to put in an irrigation system to water all of his orchards and groves.

I bought male and female slaves and had other slaves who were born in my house [Ecclesiastes 2:7a].

All down through history, servants have been a status symbol.

I also owned more herds and flocks than anyone in Jerusalem before me. I amassed silver and gold for myself, and the treasure of kings and provinces. I acquired men and women singers, and a harem as well, the delights of the heart of man. I became greater by far than anyone in Jerusalem before me. In all this my wisdom stayed with me [Ecclesiastes 2:7b-9].

Solomon broke the record for possessing status symbols. His statement, "In all this my wisdom stayed with me," could mislead us if we did not learn from the Hebrew scholars that this is a Hebrew idiom, which we would interpret today something like, "I stuck with my experiment to the bitter end." Or we might say, "I gave it all I had." And this is consistent with what he says in verse 10.

I denied myself nothing my eyes desired. I refused my heart no pleasure. My heart took delight in all my work, and this was the reward for all my labor [Ecclesiastes 2:10].

Think about this. Solomon probably had as close to an unlimited supply of money as anyone has ever had in history. And he could pay cash for anything he wanted. But when we get to the first word of verse 11, there is a definite turn in the argument. He's going to tell us what all these status symbols did for him. Surely they brought him happiness and joy and fulfillment in life, didn't they?

> Yet when I surveyed all that my hands had done and what I had toiled to achieve, everything was meaningless, a chasing after the wind; nothing was gained under the sun [Ecclesiastes 2:11].

Did Solomon enjoy his houses and other status symbols? The answer is clear: "All is meaningless and a chasing after the wind." It's like grabbing for a fist full of wind. Why?, we might ask. Because *his priorities were wrong*. Instead of using wealth to glorify God and build the kingdom, Solomon used wealth in an attempt to satisfy his own lust. **He tried to buy happiness with money**. But God did not give him wealth for that purpose. Thus, when he mismanaged it, God sent him sorrow and misery and restlessness. Is it possible that we could some day find ourselves saying the same thing about our house that Solomon said about his houses?

PASSAGE 2 – HAGGAI 1: 1-11

> In the second year of King Darius, on the first day of the sixth month, the word of the Lord came through the prophet Haggai to Zerubbabel son of Shealtiel, governor of Judah, and to Joshua son of Jehozadak, the high priest: This is what the Lord Almighty says: "These people say, 'The time has not yet come for the Lord's house to be built' " [Haggai 1:1-2].

A word of historical background will help our understanding of this passage. The year is approximately 520 BC. It's after the Babylonian captivity. The remnant had returned to Jerusalem. The feasts had been reinstituted, and a foundation for a new temple had been laid. But that foundation sat there with no building on it for fifteen years. And the people's excuse? We read it in verse 2, "These people say, the time has not yet come for the Lord's house to be built." They were saying something like this, "Economic conditions are not right for us to build this temple. We're in a recession. We're in a drought. Besides that, we're in a hostile political climate." There were foreigners surrounding them, putting pressure on them. "Oh yes, we intend to finish building the temple, but the time is just not right. We have to wait for conditions to improve." That's basically what they were saying, and they had been saying this for fifteen years. Well, God had a word for them through the prophet.

> Then the word of the Lord came through the prophet Haggai: "Is it a time for you yourselves to be living in your paneled houses, while this house (the temple) remains a ruin?" [Haggai 1:3-4].

The word "paneled" in verse 4 is the translation of a Hebrew word which meant ceiling material. That's the reason in the King James translation we read "your ceiled houses." But this ceiling material was also used as paneling in the more expensive, luxurious homes of that day. It was a status symbol. Today we have a perfect word to interpret this word "paneled". It is the word "plush." And he's saying in verse 4, "Is it time for you yourselves to be living in your plush houses while this house remains a ruin?" There's a good bit of sarcasm here. God through the prophet is saying in so many words, "I notice that the economic conditions and drought didn't keep you folks from building plush houses. Somehow you got the money to do that. But you haven't been able to get My house, the temple of God, built. And your only excuse is that the time is not right. Conditions are not right." Well, God had a further word for them.

> Now this is what the Lord Almighty says: "Give careful thought to your ways" [Haggai 1:5].

Do you know what that's saying? Consider your priorities. Put first things first in your life. Put the work of God in first place.

> You have planted much but have harvested little. You eat, but never have enough. You drink, but never have your fill. You put on clothes, but are not warm. You earn wages, only to put them in a purse with holes in it [Haggai 1:6].

Isn't that an interesting description of inflation? A purse with holes in it! We're not the only culture in history that has suffered from inflation. Throughout history, inflation has been a natural consequence

151

of men violating financial principles. I believe God uses inflation to judge the sin of materialism. These people were suffering inflation and drought because they had their priorities wrong. This passage also indicates the presence of medical problems. Food did not satisfy. Clothing did not warm. In other words, God stopped providing their basic needs. That was the consequence of their wrong financial priorities.

> This is what the Lord Almighty says: "Give careful thought to your ways. Go up into the mountains and bring down timber and build the house, so that I may take pleasure in it and be honored," says the Lord [Haggai 1:7-8].

It is interesting to me what God does *not* say in verse 8. He does not say, "As soon as the economy recovers from recession, build that temple." He does not say, "As soon as inflation drops to 3%, build My house." He does not say, "As soon as the political situation stabilizes, build the house." He does not say, "As soon as you finish your house, your office, your condominium, or whatever else you're working on, then build My temple." He said, "Do it now ...... immediately." He did not even say, "As soon as you are able to arrange a mortgage, or financing, build My house." This is one of 16 passages in the Bible that mentions buildings in relation to God's work. And as I have said previously, there's not a single illustration in the Bible of the use of borrowed money to do God's work.

Let me ask you a question to meditate on. If most of the members of a local church are poorly managing God's money, how likely is that church to raise sufficient cash to underwrite the cost of a building? So what they usually do is take out a mortgage. Then they begin to waste some of God's money by paying the interest on the mortgage. During my lifetime I have seen many churches default on their mortgages, damaging God's reputation, and hurting the cause of Christ.

The value of studying this Old Testament passage in Haggai is to better understand the mind of God. Here is what I believe God wants us to understand about Him from this passage. He expects us to carefully consider our priorities, and put our stewardship of His property in first place. If a work of God needs to be done (spreading the Gospel, feeding the poor, supporting the local church and its ministries), it shouldn't go wanting while God's people build plush houses and accumulate other status symbols for themselves. We are free to choose our priorities, but our choices will determine our reward and standing in eternity. I once heard a preacher state it in a way that has stayed with me. He said, "**Every Christian is the product of his priorities.**" That is worth meditating on.

PASSAGE 3 – ACTS 4:34-35

> There were no needy persons among them. For from time to time those who owned lands or houses sold them, brought the money from the sales and put it at the apostles' feet, and it was distributed to anyone as he had need [Acts 4:34-35].

This was the Jerusalem church which was suffering from a drought, as well as extreme persecution. Their financial condition became so critical that in order to survive, they had to begin selling their assets, even their homes, and bringing the money to the local church treasury, from which distribution was made as people had need.

As I studied this, I wondered, could we do this today? Is it possible that we could do today what these first century Christians did? I am inclined to think we could, but I think things would have to get much, much worse before we could. If economic conditions became extremely hard, I think we might rise to this kind of action. Notice that this passage conveys the same message as the other two passages cited above, and that is that houses are not the priority that we have been conditioned to think they are.

I believe we have been deceived by the world concerning the priority of houses. Owning a home, or a particular home, should never take priority over doing the work of God. **Beware lest a house become an idol to you or me.**

Any time we come to believe we have to have some material asset … a certain car, a certain house, a vacation, a certain investment … watch out! It can easily become an idol. I encourage you to memorize and meditate on the following proposition: **When any material asset becomes an idol to us, then it becomes a liability instead of an asset, and sooner or later it will bring sorrow.** Yes, God intends for us to enjoy earthly assets … but only if those assets are dedicated to Him … only if they are not idols to us … only if our priorities are right. Re-study 1 Timothy 6:6-19, where both sides of this truth are taught in balance.

I have profited from studying the lives of some of the great heroes of the faith of the past 300 years, men like Hudson Taylor, George Mueller, John Wesley and others. I remember reading that on one occasion John Wesley was told that while he was away on a preaching assignment his house burned down. His response was, "It's not my house. It's God house, and it's one less responsibility for me."

This was the kind of emotional detachment to material things that these great men of the faith had. They were not attached to earthly treasure. If you and I can begin to develop this kind of attitude toward material possessions, guess what will happen? We will learn to enjoy material wealth. This truth is counter cultural and counter intuitive. The true enjoyment of material wealth comes from being unattached to it.

PASSAGE 4 – PROVERBS 24:27

Finish your outdoor work and get your fields ready; after that, build your house [Proverbs 24:27].

It is immediately obvious in this verse, like the others, that the verse sets a priority. And guess what it's not? It's *not* the house. This verse uses a farming illustration because it is set in an agrarian culture. Here, in my opinion, is a good 21st century interpretation of this verse. "Get your financial affairs in proper order; after that, build your house." This little sentence sermon is pregnant with wisdom, and contains one of the most important principles of financial management to be found in the Bible. I want to state the principle in as many ways as I can think of, so that we can learn it and learn it well. In its simplest form, this verse is saying: **Secure a source of income before starting your home**. The word "house" in this verse is broader than four walls and a roof. That's included, but it is really saying something like this: Before taking on the obligation of marriage and a family, secure a source of income.

Generalizing the truth a little more, we might state it like this: **Don't begin any task until the necessary resources are assured**.

Here is a third way of expressing the wisdom of this verse: **Wealth must be acquired before it is consumed**. That is almost so simple that we can miss it. We have become a nation of consumers ... I mean *expert* consumers. Our children are growing up automatically being expert consumers, but not being expert producers and savers. We are majoring on consumption and minoring on production and saving, and as this trend intensifies, we will decline as a nation. At this writing we are declining as a nation. Nations like China, Japan and other Asian nations that major on producing and saving are buying us out. They are buying our land, our businesses ... they are buying us out a piece at a time. The citizens of those countries save 15% to 30% of their income. As this is written, the US savings rate is essentially zero. We are consuming all our income, then borrowing to increase it further, and we will decline economically if this trend continues.

Let me suggest one last way of expressing the wisdom of this verse, in the form of an instruction, designed to give us a practical application to financial management: **Allocate your resources instead of attempting to pay for your desires**. Please let that sink in. Think about it long and hard. If you go through life attempting to pay for your desires, you will crash and burn financially.

Biblical financial management is the allocation of your resources according to the will of God, not the satisfaction of your desires. This is true for a very simple reason, because the property belongs to God, and we are His managers, not owners in our own right. If we ignore this wisdom, we will never find satisfaction or contentment. But if we accept it and follow it, our desires will be realized. "Delight yourself in the Lord, and He will give you the desires of your heart" (Psalm 37:4).

THE BEGINNING OF A FINANCIAL PLAN

There is a common truth in the four passages we have just discussed. It is very clear. That truth is that the house is not a top financial priority. And if the house is not, then what are the top financial priorities which we glean from studying the Bible? We have discussed them in preceding chapters. Let me list four priorities which come ahead of the house, in my opinion.

• I believe a God-honoring plan of giving is more important than owning a home, or owning a particular home.

• I believe that paying taxes according to the law is more important than owning a house, that is, it has a higher priority. The reason I mention this is because Jesus puts paying taxes on an equal level with giving God what is due Him. It's a higher priority than the house.

• I believe that the elimination of consumer debt is more important than buying a house. This is almost too simple. If I have consumer debt, I am lowering my standard of living, and making it harder to pay for a house. That is just common sense. Do the math.

• I believe that establishing a systematic savings program to meet future known needs and emergencies is more important than owning a house, or a particular house that I might wish to buy. This will be the subject of the next chapter, and I believe it is a higher priority than buying a house. In other words, if I couldn't do both, I would set up a systematic savings program and delay the purchase of a house.

MY RULE FOR BUYING A HOUSE

Having established four priorities which come ahead of buying a house, I would like to give you my rule for buying a house. It is based on the wisdom derived from Proverbs 24:27, which implies that a set of conditions should exist before you build your house. **RULE**: Never buy a house, that is, a particular house you may be considering, until **all** of the following five conditions exist.

• You are honoring God in your giving.

• You are paying taxes to the government according to the law.

• You are out of consumer debt and paying cash for all living expenses.

• You have a systematic savings program in place with an agreed-upon amount going in each month.

• You have a balanced budget with sufficient income to pay all the costs involved in owning your proposed house.

The first four of these conditions are clear. They need no further explanation. But number five needs a little more explanation. Here's what it means. After paying the Lord, the government, your savings and all living expenses, you have sufficient funds remaining to cover all the costs required to own the house. What are they? The mortgage payment, insurance, taxes, utilities, upkeep and repair. And be careful not to underestimate upkeep and repair, which must be included in the budget.

By following this rule, you are *allocating resources* instead of *attempting to pay for desires*.

The five conditions fit together like the pieces of a puzzle, and note that when condition 5 is not met, sooner or later you will run out of cash to pay bills. When that happens, you either stop paying God and/or taxes, stop saving, or start borrowing. There are just no other alternatives. And at that point, you have stopped allocating resources, and started trying to pay for desires.

I admit to you that my rule is hard, and strict, especially when compared to the typical thinking in our culture today. Some of you, as you read this, may have been thinking, if I have to meet those conditions, there's no way I can buy a home. If that's what you are thinking, you are getting the message I wish to convey.

Many Christians cannot afford to buy a house, but they have not realized it. You cannot ignore the financial wisdom God gives us in the Bible and hope to prosper.

There is no wisdom, no insight, no plan that can succeed against the Lord [Proverbs 21:30].

The Congress of the United States cannot change that divine eternal truth. The Federal Reserve Board cannot fix it so that we can violate these financial principles and hope to prosper.

I want to be sure I am being understood. I am not saying that buying a house, or signing a mortgage to do so, is in and of itself a violation of Scripture. All I'm saying is that when these five conditions are not met, you are going counter to the wisdom of the Bible, and under those conditions the house becomes a liability, not an asset. And sooner or later, it will bring troubling times.

WHICH IS BETTER – BUYING OR RENTING?

Through the years I have often heard it argued that buying a house is always better than renting. Most of the time the reason given is that you are throwing your money away when you rent, and since houses always go up in value, you're better off buying than renting. I have no problem with this argument as long as the five conditions are met.

But I would add that houses do not always go up. In the twentieth century there were periods of several years during which houses went down in value. In my home town, there was a six year period in the 1980s when they went down. During that period the renters were the winners because they did not ride the house market down, losing their equities.

But even during times when houses are going up in value, you are not throwing your money away by renting. You are getting value received for your rent just as with all other goods and services you pay for. The market determines the value of all goods and services, including rent, and that can go up or down. As I write this today, it is very clear that overall, nationwide, renting is a better value than buying ... not just better, but much better in most cases. I will not argue for either approach. Much of the time buying would be better than renting. I'm saying, let the five conditions guide you to the right decision. If you can meet them by buying, then do it. If you can meet them easier by renting, then rent until you are in a position to buy.

GOD'S BEST MAY BE A DEBT FREE HOME

I cannot end this chapter without planting some seeds of truth from God's word which could bear fruit in your life. I cannot imagine even one in a hundred Christian couples ever asking God to make it possible for them to go through their entire married life without any debt whatsoever, not even a mortgage on their home.

That is such a foreign idea to our culture, it would rarely even be considered. But when I was born (1928), it was actually the norm. I may not be perfectly accurate with this figure, but I have read that at that time only 2% of all the homes in the United States had any debt against them.

There were no car loans in those days, and in fact it was many years later before people began to borrow to buy a car. So what I'm about to suggest to you would not have seemed unusual in those days. Today it is very unusual. That's the reason I'm suggesting it to you.

Since signing a mortgage involves a long term commitment, and no one knows the future, why not consider the possibility that signing a mortgage would not be God's best for you. Why not consider following all of God's wisdom which we are discussing in this book, and ask God for a house free of debt. He's been doing this for centuries. He owns all the houses. Please meditate on the following passages.

> You do not have because you do not ask God. When you ask, you do not receive, because you ask with wrong motives, that you may spend what you get on your pleasures [James 4:2b-3].

This passage suggests asking God with the right motive. And what is the right motive? I would suggest an all-out commitment to follow all of God's financial wisdom and obey all His commandments, along with the understanding that God is in control and His answer to your request will be in your best interest.

> This is what the Lord says – your redeemer, the Holy One of Israel: "I am the Lord your God who teaches you what is best for you, who directs you in the way you should go. If only you

had paid attention to my commands, your peace would have
been like a river, your righteousness like the waves of the sea
..." [Isaiah 48:17-18].

This has become a very special passage to me. And every time I read
this passage, I think back over my own life ... of all the heartache, all
the failure, all the stress ... which I could have avoided if only I had
paid attention to God's commandments and wisdom. Please meditate
on this passage.

Does having a house free of debt sound like more than you can
imagine?

Now to Him who is able to do exceeding abundantly above all
we ask or think, according to the power that worketh in us, unto
Him be glory in the church by Christ Jesus throughout all ages,
world without end. Amen [Ephesians 3:20-21 (KJV)].

How can you possibly estimate "exceeding abundantly above?"...... I
realize my next statement is to some extent foolish, for no one can
return to the past, but if I could start over as a young man with the
present knowledge and understanding of the information in this book,
this is the approach I would take with respect to a house. I would
commit to never signing a mortgage on a home, or going into debt for
living expenses, and I would ask God to give me a home free of debt,
when and if it was His will to do so. I would wait in faith and eager
anticipation for God to make good on His promise to do "exceeding
abundantly above all I could ask or imagine," whatever that turned out
to be. I believe that is God's highest and best approach to owning a
home.

FINAL THOUGHTS

Here is financial management based on biblical wisdom reduced to one
sentence: **Pay the Lord, the government and yourself (savings) first,
then live on the balance without borrowing**.

Memorize the four priorities of Proverbs 24:27.

- Secure a source of income before starting your home (family).

• Don't begin any task before the necessary resources are assured.

• Wealth must be acquired before it is consumed.

• Allocate your resources instead of attempting to pay for your desires.

QUESTIONS FOR MEDITATION (Take to the prayer chamber)

• Does your house (or the house you are considering) meet the five conditions of my rule (see page 156) for buying a house?

• Are you honoring God in your giving?

• Is your house a joy? Really? Or do you find yourself saying about it what Solomon said about his houses? ("All is meaningless and a chasing after the wind.")

• Are you allocating resources or attempting to pay for desires?

• Have you thought about asking God for a house free of debt?

• (The all encompassing question) Have you taken the steps necessary to determine whether your house is the perfect will of God? Don't buy a house until you have.

CHAPTER 15

STORING GOD'S PROPERTY

The question we seek to answer in this chapter is, should a Christian save money for the future? I mean by that, should we store any wealth on earth, in this life, for future consumption in this life? I am not aware of any specific command by Jesus or the apostles that we do so. But Paul gives us a command, the keeping of which all but requires it, and in another passage he puts his sanction on it for certain purposes. In addition, the Proverbs commend to us the wisdom of saving some wealth for an uncertain future, calling those who do so wise, and those who fail to do so foolish.

Having said that, Jesus devoted an entire section of the Sermon on the Mount to the subject, which He began with the clear command, "Do not store up for yourselves treasures on earth ..." There's no doubt which side of the issue Jesus intended to emphasize, though even He seemed to put His sanction on storing some wealth on earth for certain purposes. We learned this in Chapter 4 as we studied the Parable of the Talents. God entrusts differing amounts of His property to His stewards to manage for Him, and management presupposes some planned storage. Paul instructed those with a surplus to share with those in need (2 Corinthians 8:14). If no one had a surplus, the plan would not work.

All in all, it makes for an interesting, yet critically important, study from the Bible. Beyond any question in my mind, the key passage is Matthew 6:19-34. We will devote most of the chapter to it, but try not to neglect the balance of truth found in the rest of the Bible. We will seek to bring the balance which Scripture gives to this issue.

One of my heroes of the faith is George Mueller, who started a great orphanage ministry in England in the 19th century. In addition to this ministry, he was an accomplished Bible scholar, and wrote a lot of good Bible study material. He made a statement which has been very helpful to me. Here it is, quoted from page 371 of the biography of his life entitled *George Mueller of Bristol.*

"Whatever parts of truth are made too much of, though they were even the most precious truths connected with our being risen in Christ, or our heavenly calling, or prophecy, sooner or later those who lay an undue stress on these parts of truth, and thus make them too prominent, will be losers in their own souls. And if they are teachers, they will hurt those whom they teach."

The church is full of Christians who have been hurt by the kind of teaching which George Mueller despairs of in that quote.

I live with a holy fear of hurting someone as I teach or write, and I pray God would protect my readers, correct my errors, and give me greater understanding of the whole counsel of God as presented in His Word.

I'm sure people have been hurt by out of balance teaching on Jesus' command, "Do not store up for yourselves treasures on earth." And yet, we have illustrations in the Bible of people who gave all they had to God, and they did it in the will of God. There are circumstances under which it is proper to store nothing on earth, as long as other commands are not disobeyed. The key is the motive and purpose for which wealth is either stored, or not stored, on earth.

Let's look at both sides of the question, storing God's property on earth and storing His property in heaven, and seek to find the answer to the question posed at the beginning of this chapter. Jesus gives us full discretion to draw the line between storing God's property on earth, or storing it in heaven; then holds us accountable for where we draw it. Many passages give us help in making that choice, but I do not believe we will ever be totally free of the tension which comes with drawing the line. I don't think God intends for us to be free of that tension. Well, let's begin with storing wealth on earth.

STORING GOD'S PROPERTY ON EARTH

Go to the ant, you sluggard: consider its ways and be wise! It has no commander, no overseer or ruler, yet it stores its provisions in summer and gathers its food at harvest [Proverbs 6:6-8].

Here we are told to observe the activities of the ant and learn wisdom from it. What does the ant do that we can learn wisdom from? It stores food for future consumption. It saves for the future. The passage says that the ant has no commander, overseer or ruler, which I take to mean its actions are the result of instinct put into it by its Creator. God programmed the ant to do it. But He did not *program* us to do it. We are not forced to do it. We have to *choose* to do it. According to this passage, we are wise if we do it. We are foolish if we don't.

> Four things on earth are small, yet they are extremely wise: Ants are creatures of little strength, yet they store up their food in the summer [Proverbs 30:24-25].

> In the house of the wise are stores of choice food and oil, but a foolish man devours all he has [Proverbs 21:20].

A wise man doesn't spend all of his income as he earns it. He saves some for the future. In other words, he foregoes present desires and benefits to help assure the meeting of future needs. But the foolish man consumes all his income as he receives it, and takes no thought for the future.

Three times in the book of Proverbs we are told that it is wise to save for the future and foolish not to. We also have similar New Testament wisdom.

> But if any one does not provide for his own, and especially for those of his household, he has denied the faith and is worse than an unbeliever [1 Timothy 5:8 (NASB)].

The provision referred to in this passage is financial provision, as the context reveals. The word translated "provide" in this text is a very descriptive word. Dr. Kenneth Wuest, late professor of New Testament Greek at Moody Bible Institute, in his commentary on 1 Timothy, said this about that word, "At the time of the writing of the New Testament, the word translated 'provide' meant 'taking thought in advance.' " The word is *pronoeo*, literally "to think beforehand." Dr. Wuest translates this verse, "If anyone does not anticipate the needs of his own, and especially those of his own household, and provide for them, he has denied the faith and is worse than an unbeliever."

This verse is addressed to those who are responsible for providing for the needs of the family, and it is saying that any such person who fails to anticipate the future financial needs of the family, and provide for them, has denied the faith. What does he mean by "denied the faith?" He must mean that he has violated a principle of the Christian faith. "The faith" is the body of truth or doctrine which comprises the Christian faith. And Paul says that such a person is "worse than an unbeliever." How could such a believer be worse than an unbeliever? Obviously in a limited sense, that is, in the sense that even many unbelievers understand and practice this principle of saving for the future needs of their families.

It is clear what God thinks about a believer who squanders wealth which God has provided for the needs of that believer's family. How will the world view such a person? How credible will his profession of a relationship to Jesus Christ be?

Paul also made a statement to the Corinthians about saving money. He wanted to impress upon the members of that church his willingness to sacrifice himself for them. He chose the illustration of parents saving for the future needs of their children, sacrificing present desires in order to insure the meeting of those needs.

> Now I am ready to visit you for the third time, and I will not be a burden to you, because what I want is not your possessions but you. After all, children should not have to save up for their parents, but parents for their children. So I will very gladly spend for you everything I have and expend myself as well. If I love you more, will you love me less? [2 Corinthians 12:14-15].

A good parent will forego present benefits and desires in order to assure future financial needs of his children.

I conclude from these five passages that it is our responsibility to anticipate the future financial needs of our family, and to do our best to have the money there when the need arises. It seems clear that the apostle Paul considers this to be a tenet, or principle, of the Christian faith. I further conclude that there is only one way to practice this principle, and that is to save some of our income for the future. Financial needs do not come at the same time or rate that our income flows. The cost of raising a child will be different at different times of the child's life. Paul says you must anticipate those differences, and save for them.

Many of the future needs of our family are predictable, at least to a reasonable degree. For example, if it is your conviction that you want to provide all or a portion of a college education for your child, then you have about 18 years from the child's date of birth to accumulate the money for that need. With a hand calculator, and an assumed rate of interest which the money will earn, in five seconds you can know the amount of money which you need to save every month to meet that need. You know you will need to paint your house every five to ten years, and replace your car every five to ten years. These are the kinds of expenses that can wreck a budget unless they are planned for and anticipated in advance. And if we fail to prepare for such needs, then we usually wind up borrowing the money when the need arises, paying interest, thus lowering our standard of living.

In addition to the known, predictable needs in our future, there will always be unpredictable, emergency needs ...... sickness, accidents, premature deaths, disasters ...... we live in a fallen, uncertain, dangerous world. If you have largely escaped these emergencies in your life to this point, then thank and praise the Lord, but understand that it will not last. Some kind of emergency fund should be accumulated in addition to the predictable needs. Some of these can best be provided for through insurance. By paying premiums on insurance, you are setting money aside for future emergencies. But insurance will not cover all of your unpredictable needs, so it is well to have an emergency fund for those needs. More on that in the next chapter.

We have seen five passages which instruct us, or commend to us saving some money for the future. Now let's look at the other side of the issue, storing God's property in heaven, and then try to put both sides into balance which is faithful to the Bible.

STORING GOD'S PROPERTY IN HEAVEN

Beyond doubt, Matthew 6:19-34 is the key passage on this subject. Many, I'm confident, would consider it the most important passage in the Bible on the subject of managing money as a Christian. My prayer is that we will not miss its greatest lessons and truths.

> Do not store up for yourselves treasures on earth, where moth and rust destroy, and where thieves break in and steal. But store up for yourselves treasures in heaven, where moth and rust do not destroy, and where thieves do not break in and steal. For where your treasure is, there your heart will be also [Matthew 6:19-21].

There are many ways to store treasure in heaven that do not involve the use of money ...... visiting the sick, evangelizing, ministering to the elderly, and many others. Some of these involve little or no money. But in this passage, Jesus is speaking specifically of money, or material wealth. Anything that the moth and rust and thieves can get is material wealth. In a moment we will read in verse 24, "You cannot serve both God and money." It is clear that Jesus is talking about money here.

So when Jesus said, "Do not store up for yourselves treasures on earth," He had reference primarily to money. But we have just studied five passages which instruct us, or give us the wisdom of, saving here on earth for the future. So when we come to Matthew 6:19, we must seek to understand it without disregarding these other passages. After all, Jesus wrote them also.

When we do that, it seems to me that Jesus is presenting two different life goals, or objectives, in relation to managing money, the goal of storing treasure on earth, and the goal of storing treasure in heaven. And every Christian has the latitude to choose which he will give the higher priority, and where he will draw the line between the two.

It seems to me that Jesus is classifying all believers in two camps, the "store-on-earth camp," and the "store-in-heaven camp." My heart's desire, my passion, my priorities, and my resulting actions ...... all will reveal to me which camp I am in. Let's re-read verses 19-21 with that idea in mind.

> Do not store up for yourselves treasures on earth, where moth and rust destroy, and where thieves break in and steal [Matthew 6:19].

Do not make your goal in life, your focus, your passion, storing wealth on earth. In other words, do not hoard wealth. Hoarding differs from saving for known future needs and emergencies. Hoarding is saving for selfish purposes, rather than kingdom purposes. Notice that Jesus uses the phrase "for yourselves." By the way, the ant does not hoard food. It stores only what it needs to get through the winter ...... to the next summer.

> But store up for yourselves treasures in heaven, where moth and rust do not destroy, and where thieves do not break in and steal [Matthew 6:20].

Make that your higher priority. Build your life around that objective. Again Jesus uses the phrase "for yourselves." The profit motive is perfectly legitimate. In fact, it was put into us at creation. Here, Jesus instructs us to subordinate the desire for profit on earth to the desire for profit in heaven in the next life. As you give and as you save for your family's needs, your overall goal is storing treasure in heaven. Store on earth and in heaven for kingdom purposes.

> For where your treasure is, there your heart will be also [Matthew 6:21].

You cannot separate the physical handling of God's money from the purposes of your heart. You cannot separate the handling of your financial affairs from your goal in life. How you handle God's money will demonstrate which of these two camps you're in.

As He often did, Jesus stated a precept, then followed with an illustration. He selects the human eye, a physical organ, to illustrate a spiritual truth.

> The eye is the lamp of the body. If your eyes are good, your whole body will be full of light [Matthew 6:22].

If your eyes are healthy, you can see. That's a physical truth which is designed to convey a spiritual truth, which I think might be expressed something like this. If your goal in life is storing treasure in heaven, your soul will be full of light, or spiritual understanding. You'll be spiritually healthy.

But if your eyes are bad, your whole body will be full of darkness ... [Matthew 6:23b].

The physical illustration is, if you have unhealthy eyes, you will have poor vision. That is designed to teach the spiritual truth that if your goal in life is storing treasure on earth, it will blind you spiritually. The stark reality of that truth came as a shock to me the first time it penetrated my soul. My attitude toward money affects my ability to understand spiritual truth ... my ability to understand the Bible. That's spiritual blindness. How serious is it?

If then the light within you is darkness, how great is that darkness! [Matthew 6:23a].

There is simply nothing worse than spiritual blindness. It's far worse than physical blindness. If I'm in the store-on-earth camp, I will not see eternal profit associated with storing treasure in heaven. I will not see the futility of borrowing for consumer desires, nor the futility of hoarding.

Jesus first stated his precept (command), which could be paraphrased, "Make storing treasure in heaven, not on earth, your life goal." Next, He gave His illustration to teach the far reaching effects of your choice. At stake is the difference between spiritual understanding and spiritual blindness. Then He pressed for a decision.

No one can serve two masters. Either he will hate the one and love the other, or he will be devoted to the one and despise the other. You cannot serve both God and money [Matthew 6:24].

You can't have both goals in life. You can't be in both camps. Notice that Jesus did not say, "It is unwise to serve both masters." And He did not say, "It is difficult to serve both masters." He said, "It's impossible." "No one can serve both masters." In other words, you can't do the impossible. You must make a choice between the two.

I cannot judge any person's heart. But my observation of the actions of those of us who make up the body of Christ today suggests to me that the typical Christian is attempting to do the impossible. We will swear allegiance to Jesus Christ. We are not ashamed to name Him before men outwardly. We identify with the church and its ministries. We may teach a Sunday School class. We may give to missions, or serve on a church committee ... but inwardly our hearts are torn between allegiance to two masters. And according to Jesus Christ in this passage, that puts us in the store-on-earth camp.

JESUS ANSWERS THE BIG QUESTION

Here's a blessed thought. *Jesus came to this world to minister to the store-on-earth camp.* Aren't you glad? He came to minister to those of us who would accept Him as Savior, and then try to serve two masters. We all start out in the store-on-earth camp. Some of us are still in it. As Jesus preached that day on the mountain, some of His hearers were interested in changing their life goal. Some were not. I believe it's the same today.

I would ask anyone reading this (including myself), are you interested in changing camps? Are you interested in becoming an expert at storing treasure in heaven? If you are, you will be encouraged by what Jesus says next in His sermon. He will answer the question that probably is in your mind at this point in the sermon. He will answer the question in the mind of any interested disciple. What is that question? Here's how I would state it. "Lord, if I make my life goal storing treasure in heaven, what happens if I run out of money down here?"

Maybe you would say it like this. "Lord, if I put money in your kingdom that I could put in savings, what assurance do I have that my needs will be met?" That's the question Jesus proceeds to answer. He knew the thoughts in every mind. Jesus is God, and His answer is a theological masterpiece.

> Therefore I tell you, do not worry about your life, what you will eat or drink; or about your body, what you will wear. Is not life more important than food, and the body more important than clothes? [Matthew 6:25].

A word of caution is in order. We must *never* remove this verse from its context. I have heard this verse quoted out of its context in an attempt to teach something it does not teach. I believe this verse is a conditional promise, not a blanket promise. I have heard it used as an unconditional or blanket promise.

But the word "therefore" ties this promise to what has preceded. I believe this is a conditional promise that Jesus will meet the needs of any Christian whose goal in life is storing treasure in heaven. I believe the idea that He means to convey here is: Assuming that your goal is storing treasure in heaven, you need not worry about your earthly needs. That is the thrust of the remainder of this passage, all the way through verse 34.

> Look at the birds of the air; they do not sow or reap or store away in barns, and yet your heavenly Father feeds them. Are you not much more valuable than they? [Matthew 6:26].

If God supplies the needs of the birds, how much more certainly is He going to provide for a Christian whose goal in life is storing treasure in heaven?

> Who of you by worrying can add a single hour to his life? [Matthew 6:27].

The implied answer to this question is "Nobody." The point is that a believer whose goal is right doesn't have to worry.

> And why do you worry about clothes? See how the lilies of the field grow. They do not labor or spin. Yet I tell you that not even Solomon in all his splendor was dressed like one of these. If that is how God clothes the grass of the field, which is here today and tomorrow is thrown into the fire, will He not much more clothe you, O you of little faith? [Matthew 6:28-30].

If God clothes billions of flowers with a beauty which cannot be matched in the laboratory, or the textile mill, and then throws them all away and does it again the next day, don't you think such a God can clothe a Christian who is concentrating on storing treasure in heaven? You would have to be devoid of faith to think otherwise. "O you of little faith."

So do not worry, saying, "What shall we eat?" Or, "What shall we drink?" Or, "What shall we wear?" For the pagans run after all these things, and your heavenly Father knows that you need them [Matthew 6:31-32].

The life goal of the materialist is to be in control, in truth, to be his own god. To him, an important element of this control is the accumulation of earthly wealth. The goal of the Christian is to be the opposite, surrender of his natural lust for control, and submission to God's control. Don't miss what Jesus said here. God knows that a believer whose focus is on storing treasure in heaven has earthly needs. He has not overlooked that. And His next statement is that great summary verse which many of us learned in Sunday School when we were children.

But seek first His kingdom and His righteousness, and all these things (material needs) will be given to you as well [Matthew 6:33].

Is that not a conditional promise? I will never forget what my teacher in a businessmen's Bible class said when He came to this verse. As best I remember his words, he said, "It is so important to Jesus that His followers make their life goal storing treasure in heaven, and not on earth, that He has taken upon Himself the full responsibility for meeting the earthly needs of those who obey Him."

Therefore do not worry about tomorrow, for tomorrow will worry about itself. Each day has enough trouble of its own [Matthew 6:34].

Under what condition do we not worry about tomorrow? Under the condition that our goal in life is right. Under the condition that we are serving the right master. The promises of this passage are conditional, all the way from verse 25 through verse 34. I do not see a blanket promise in this passage. If my goal is accumulating earthly treasure for myself, then I'm on my own. I am meddling with and mismanaging God's property, putting my home and family at risk. I have no promise in this passage. The whole thrust of the passage is that storing treasure in heaven becomes the means of assuring the meeting of our earthly needs. Had you ever thought of it in that way? It's the only real security.

I'm convinced we have fallen into a major error of interpretation by thinking of treasure stored in heaven as being available to us "up there," after we get to heaven, rather than being of some benefit to us in this life. I don't think the Bible teaches that. By urging His followers to store treasure in heaven, Jesus had no thought of denying them their earthly needs, nor even earthly blessings and benefits derived from material wealth. Your heavenly Father knows you have earthly needs. What I think Jesus was saying is that your earthly store can fail you ... there is no guaranteed security in material wealth.

In verse 19, He said the moth and rust and thieves will get your earthly treasure. That language may sound a little strange to us. But we can understand it if we know what it meant to those who heard it 2000 years ago. In that day, three of the most common forms of wealth were clothing, food and money (gold and silver coins). If you had a good supply of clothing, food and coins, you were considered wealthy. But the moth could eat your clothing, and if it wasn't the moth with wings, it was the moth of style change. And, of course, that moth is still "eating" clothing today. If you had stores of food, you were considered wealthy, but the rust could destroy your food. The word "rust" is the translation of a Greek word which means "the eaters." Anything that eats or eats away, such as insects, rodents, bacteria, severe weather ... those are the eaters or rust that could destroy your food. Money existed as gold and silver coins in that day, and there were no bank vaults, so people hid their money in an attempt to keep it safe, but thieves could still get it. So that's the reason for the wording of verse 19.

If Jesus were preaching this sermon today, He might word it something like this, "Don't concentrate on accumulating earthly wealth for yourself, which inflation, bankruptcy, fraud, taxes, stock market crashes and depressions will consume."

However He would say it, He's saying the same thing; there is no security in earthly wealth in any period of history. In a manner of speaking, He's saying, you're better off storing wealth in My bank than in your own local bank. This is no criticism of the banks. They perform a good service. But I can tell you that there is a lot of wealth stored in the local banks that would be safer in God's bank in heaven. And, I think it would be more likely to be there when we need it.

Consider an illustration. Suppose you go to your local bank tomorrow and deposit $1,000. Then you go to the grocery store and buy a sack of groceries which cost $60. You give the grocer a check for $60. What do you expect to happen? You expect your bank to pay or credit your grocer $60 because you have plenty in your account to cover it. And you would be incensed if your banker refused to cash that check.

Now make the spiritual application. If I deposit money in God's bank in heaven, and then I have a legitimate earthly need, I can, in a manner of speaking, write a check on my account in God's bank, and God will "cash it," or meet the need.

And I do not have to worry about all these things that can destroy earthly wealth. I don't even have to worry about holidays on which my local bank is closed. God's bank is open every day, even on Sundays and holidays. I do not have to worry about my earthly needs as long as my priority in life is storing treasure in heaven. I think that's what Jesus is teaching in this passage.

DRAWING THE LINE

We have tried to present what Scripture teaches about storing wealth on earth and in heaven. We are instructed to do both. We are told it is wise to save for legitimate future needs. We are commanded to make storing wealth in heaven our highest priority, to "seek first the kingdom." Where do we draw the line between storing on earth and storing in heaven? The short answer is we draw it wherever we want to draw it. We draw it at the place which our heart approves (2 Corinthians 9:7). Just understand *we are accountable* for where we draw it. We determine our standard of living in heaven by where we draw it.

Why would Jesus give us specific instructions for where to draw the line? If He did that, it would destroy the whole accountability-reward system outlined in the Bible. There would be no opportunity to walk by faith. There would be no such thing as sacrificial giving which would earn greater reward. Unlike the Old Testament, in the New

Testament we are given complete latitude in our giving. But we're also told we will be accountable for where we draw the line. We are told, "To whom much is given, much is required." The real issue is never how much we give, but *how much we have left* after we give, i.e., what did it cost us to give. I don't think we will ever escape the tension that will accompany drawing the line.

A LESSON FROM THE LIFE OF JOHN WESLEY

Many years ago I read a biography of John Wesley's life. I also read many of his sermons. The financial stewardship theme runs prominently through his life and his preaching. Both his actions and his words conveyed the idea that he was emotionally detached from earthly wealth and had a passion for storing treasure in heaven. His three simple rules for managing money were, (1) Earn all you can. (2) Save all you can. (3) Give all you can. But you must understand the word "save" in rule 2 did not mean save up or store, as we have used it in this chapter. By "save," John Wesley meant keep your expenses as low as possible. Spend only what you have to in order to survive. He meant "save" in the sense we use it when we buy something on sale.

So his three rules were, (1) Earn all you can. (2) Keep your expenditures as low as you can. (3) Give all you can. He faithfully practiced his three rules. He believed in the practice of "capping his expenses," and "capping his accumulation of wealth," and giving away all above the caps. He was afraid of laying up treasures on earth, so the money went out to charity as quickly as it came in. He reports that he never had as much as 100 pounds at any one time. When he died in 1791 at the age of 87, his total remaining monetary assets were 28 pounds (probably equivalent to less than $500 today). Over his lifetime, he had earned a fortune, mostly from the books and tracts he wrote, but he lived on a very minimum amount, and gave away the rest. All his needs had been met. God enabled him to preach until a few days before he died.

MY OWN STRUGGLE WITH DRAWING THE LINE

Reading the biographies of men like John Wesley, Hudson Taylor, George Mueller, and others impacted my life as a young man. They influenced me in making life changing decisions concerning my stewardship. In the early years of our marriage, my wife and I tried to follow John Wesley's three rules. Our income was moderate. In our minds, we gave all we could, and we accumulated very little earthly wealth. Years passed, and because I did not remain vigilant and re-examine my own heart and life, my focus began slowly and insidiously changing from storing treasure in heaven to storing treasure for myself on earth. We continued to give, some would say generously, but the focus, the goal was not the same.

Then I began studying and preparing to write this book. About the time I completed the first draft, a copy of Randy Alcorn's book, *Money, Possessions and Eternity* (Tyndale House Publishers, Inc., Wheaton, Illinois, 2003) fell into my hands. It contains much of the material on John Wesley and others which I had studied years earlier. What happened to me in those early years began happening all over again. One section of the book had a particularly profound effect on my thinking. The author captioned it *Forty Questions To Ask God About Your Giving*. I think it is a powerful tool for use in self-examination, which Paul commands of us. For that reason, we have included the list of questions in the Appendix (see page 233), and we commend it to you. I'm sure there will be a wide range of reactions to these questions, but if your reaction is anything like ours was, you will never be the same again.

YOU MUST DRAW THE LINE FOR YOURSELF

What can I say that will help you to decide where to draw the line? Maybe very little, but I'll try. You are commanded to store treasure in heaven. What you store there is "for yourself" as Jesus clearly said. It will be waiting there for you when you get there, and be yours for all eternity if I am interpreting Scripture correctly. But you also have the right to store wealth on earth. If you fail to save for future known needs, and some unforeseen needs, you may be unwise.

You even have the right to store large quantities of earthly wealth, but if very little of it ever gets into God's estate, you will do so at great eternal loss to yourself. To fulfill your management agreement with God, your goal must be to increase His estate, not yours. As you attempt to increase your standard of living on earth (which you have the right to do), you are decreasing your standard of giving, and that will reduce your standard of living in heaven.

With these things in mind, I came up with a rule which I suggest when I teach this subject. And that rule is: **Never concentrate on storing treasure on earth apart from concentrating on storing treasure in heaven. Never let the two separate in your thinking.** In other words, evaluate every financial decision in the light of its effect on God's kingdom. Develop this as a practice, and over time you can become more efficient at it.

Every day when I awaken, the lust for autonomy awakens with me. I have to re-surrender my addiction to self-rule, and re-submit to obedience to Jesus every day. If I submit today, and He permits me to live another day, I'll get the chance to submit tomorrow.

CHAPTER 16

PRINCIPLES OF INVESTING

Having concluded in Chapter 15 that it is not a sin to store some of God's property on earth, for certain purposes and under certain conditions, we now consider the question, in what form should we store it? In other words, how should we invest the part of God's property stored here on earth? Does the Bible give us any wisdom or commands which answer these questions? We will seek to answer these questions in this chapter.

Before we can invest, of course, we must have something to invest. Some people overcome this obstacle by borrowing money to invest. Some already have a significant amount of consumer debt (usually credit card debt) which they are trying to service, yet they want to begin an investment program before that debt is paid. A lifetime of observation, both of my own financial management, and that of many others, has convinced me that this approach to investing almost always ends badly. I wonder if the average person realizes how nearly impossible it is to earn as much on borrowed money as the interest you are paying on it, especially over extended periods of time.

Before we begin the subject of investing, we must face two issues. First, is it the will of God for us to store any of His assets on earth at all? Remember the widow who put her last two coins in the temple offering. Jesus did not rebuke her for failing to save them for a rainy day. He commended her. Based on His promise (Matthew 6:33), I am confident He met her earthly needs until the day she died. And based on His comment to her, I would imagine her reward in eternity will be great.

Jesus calls some of His disciples to give up their income and possessions to further His cause full time. Others He calls to hold possessions and earn an income to generously support the same cause. (But He doesn't call any of us to hoard possessions to do with as we please.) The text we studied in Chapter 9 makes this point rather clearly.

> At the present time your plenty will supply what they need, so that in turn their plenty will supply what you need ... [2 Corinthians 8:14].

> Now he who supplies seed to the sower and bread for food will also supply and increase your store of seed and will enlarge the harvest of your righteousness. You will be made rich in every way so that you can be generous on every occasion ... [2 Corinthians 9:10-11].

If you feel your calling is to forego storing God's assets on earth, you won't need the information given in the rest of this chapter. This was the conviction reached by John Wesley. He said he was afraid to hold money ... fearing it would burn him, so when money came in, he quickly gave it out to charity, and committed to not holding more than 100 pounds at any time. There is a blessing which is enjoyed by those who choose this approach to stewardship. They never have to face the tension of deciding where to draw the line between storing on earth and storing in heaven.

But assuming you believe it is the will of God for you to store some of God's property on earth, there is a second issue which should be faced. Before it makes any real sense to begin investing money, the financial priorities discussed in the preceding chapters of this book should be met.

All of the following conditions should exist before we begin investing God's assets.

1. We should be giving generously to the Lord.

2. We should be paying our taxes according to the law.

3. We should have eliminated all consumer debt.

4. We should have a balanced budget in operation.

5. A designated portion of each dollar of income should be set aside in a savings plan.

Think for a few moments about these five conditions. Consider condition 3, for example. Consumer debt is inconsistent with savings. It is in fact *negative* savings. It is future income which you have already spent, instead of being current income set aside for future needs. And, as already mentioned, you are probably paying more interest on your consumer debt than you are earning on your savings, which suggests that until your consumer debt is eliminated, the best investment you can make is repaying it.

Think about condition 4. It is more important to have a balanced budget than to begin a savings program. If you don't have a balanced budget, you are automatically failing to meet one or more of the other conditions. The shortage has to come from somewhere. It may come from your giving commitment, and God will not bless that. If you're cheating on your taxes, God will surely not bless that. If you are borrowing to pay your living expenses, you are sinking deeper in debt and further away from the ability to begin a savings program.

So, until these five priorities have been achieved, the best counsel I can give is, take up a prayer vigil and work on achieving all five. Let me urge you to prayerfully work down through these conditions, making certain that all five are in place before you begin an investment program. It may take several months to know that you have achieved number 4 (a balanced budget). I also suggest that you meditate often on two of the rules given in previous chapters.

Allocate your resources rather than attempt to pay for your desires.

Never concentrate on storing treasure on earth apart from concentrating on storing treasure in heaven.

So, assuming the five conditions have been met, are we then ready to seek out God's wisdom on investing? Well not quite. I hate to bring it up again, but we need to re-think the message of Chapters 1 and 2 as it applies to saving and investing. I'll be brief, but you might want to re-read the chapters.

God is in control and He has my best interest at heart. One of the logical conclusions of this truth is that God decides who gets His wealth, how much and in what form. Before we undertake to invest our savings, we must understand and accept this truth.

No matter how diligent we are at learning the principles of investing, or how hard we work at it, we won't accumulate a cent more (or a cent less) than He has pre-determined. If you'd like to review some of the key verses which teach this, I suggest Jeremiah 10:23, Psalm 75:6-7, Proverbs 22:2, Ecclesiastes 7:13-14, Lamentations 3:37-40 and Proverbs 21:30. It will be good to have Proverbs 22:2 in our minds now.

> Rich and poor have this in common: The Lord is maker of them all [Proverbs 22:2].

What *we* can control is the amount of wealth we accumulate in heaven, and it has no relationship to the amount we have to work with here on earth. It is determined by how well we manage God's property for His glory ... by where we draw the line between what we store here and what we surrender here to be stored there. It depends on where our heart is. Until we reach **a state of perpetual surrender of our lust for autonomy**, we won't be satisfied with what God has chosen to entrust to us. We'll attempt to usurp God's role ...... to build our "fortune" to that level we think will make us secure, or happy, or able to do great things for God ...... a mythical level which does not exist. I suggest that you re-read the two "rules" (p. 181) and the five "conditions" (p. 180) which should precede investing, and see if you can find some measure of peace with them.

Having said all of that, are we now ready to study biblical wisdom on investing? I think so. I hope so. After all, God included such wisdom in His Word. We will now seek to answer the question, how should a Christian invest his savings?

BEGIN WITH AN EMERGENCY FUND

The first part of the answer to the question is easy, the rest, not so easy. Let's take the easy part first. Consider the first portion of savings which you build as an emergency fund. Its purpose is to meet unexpected and unpredictable needs which could arise. Some financial counselors suggest half of one year's income, but you must decide the amount, which will depend on your family situation. The important thing is to get started. Your emergency fund should be invested in a safe, liquid investment, from which you can easily withdraw funds when needed, without penalty or loss of interest. My favorite is an interest bearing money market account which allows checks to be written on it like a bank account.

Until you have built your emergency fund, you don't need to attempt other kinds of investing such as stocks, bonds, mutual funds, gold, etc. But once your emergency fund has reached its planned level, and all five of the conditions listed above have been met, including an agreed-upon amount going into savings every month, then you are ready to begin other forms of investing. Let's call these "second level savings."

HOW SHOULD WE INVEST OUR SECOND LEVEL SAVINGS?

The answer to this question is not easy. The Bible does not give us specific instructions. It doesn't tell us to invest 5% of our savings in a blue chip stock, or invest 15% of our savings in a balanced mutual fund, or 10% in gold coins. In the parable of the talents, the estate owner gave no instructions on how to invest the assets he entrusted to the three managers. He left it to the discretion of each manager. That's the position we're in. But we are not without biblical wisdom regarding this responsibility.

The Bible gives us a number of principles of investing, or wealth-building, which equip us to make these decisions. As we follow this wisdom, along with all the other financial principles and commands we are examining in this book, we'll be on the road to successful saving and investing.

We are now ready to consider actual strategies for investing our savings, which follow the wisdom God has given us in His Word. I will suggest three strategies. You may choose to divide your second level savings among any one, two or all three strategies, as you feel the Lord leads you.

STRATEGY 1 – SAFE, INTEREST-BEARING DEPOSITS

We've already suggested this strategy for your emergency fund. Its principal objective is to keep the money safe and easily available when needed without delay or penalty. Its secondary objective is to earn some interest. I believe this is the proper strategy for our emergency fund. But some believers will prefer it for all of their savings, especially some older believers. Or, you may want to use it until you develop confidence and skill in one or both of the other two strategies to be discussed next.

Let me be quick to add that when I say this strategy is safe, I mean risk free only in the sense that the money you invest, plus the interest it earns, will always be there. But it is not risk free in the sense that its purchasing power will be the same or greater than when you invested it. Since the Federal Reserve System was created in 1913, the U. S. dollar has lost more than 95% of its purchasing power due to the huge debts being taken on by the government, and the printing of ever-increasing amounts of paper currency to cover the deficit spending of the country.

History demonstrates that all paper currencies eventually become worthless, the only exception being those which by law may be converted into tangible wealth at a guaranteed rate (usually a weight in gold or silver). Thousands of paper currencies have become worthless throughout history, including two in our own nation during its short history. Despite these realities, I use this strategy for a part of my own second level savings, and as we move on to a discussion of strategy 2, you should get a clearer vision of the part it might play in yours.

STRATEGY 2 – SEEK INVESTMENT COUNSEL

The Bible commends to us the wisdom of seeking counsel.

> The way of a fool seems right to him, but a wise man listens to advice [Proverbs 12:15].

Here we sense the pathetic state of a fool, who knows no other standard than his own knowledge and opinion. He is contrasted with the person who seeks counsel. The first step toward solving any problem is to understand the problem. Understand that you are not an expert at investing money, but you are competing head-to-head with those who are.

> He who walks with the wise grows wise, but a companion of fools suffers harm [Proverbs 13:20].

This verse teaches us that we have to be very careful with our associations. Bad counsel is as bad, or worse, than no counsel. One of the things we must learn is how to distinguish between good and bad counsel. One of the ways we do that is to carefully examine the life and reputation, and in the case of investment counsel, the track record of the person from whom we seek counsel.

> Listen to advice and accept instruction, and in the end you will be wise [Proverbs 19:20].

The way to become an expert at anything is to go into training under one you believe to be an expert.

> Plans fail for lack of counsel, but with many advisors they succeed [Proverbs 15:22].

This key passage teaches us one of the ways of avoiding bad counsel. Get several opinions.

> There is no wisdom, no insight, no plan that can succeed against the Lord [Proverbs 21:30].

> Commit to the Lord whatever you do, and your plans will succeed [Proverbs 16:3].

Here are three observations about these five passages from the Proverbs. First, the first three have to do with counsel from other people. Note that the word "many" is used in Proverbs 15:22. I suggest taking its implication seriously. You may find counselors who are experts in certain areas of investing, but who might not look at things from a biblical perspective. Some may not be Christians. You can profit from their expertise and knowledge, but you will also want counselors who are believers, who will help keep you from failing to follow biblical financial wisdom. In short, learn to distinguish biblical advice from investment advice. Sometimes you get both from the same person. Sometimes you don't.

Second observation: The last two passages teach us that our main counselor is God Himself. We consult him through prayer, meditation and studying the Scriptures. Any financial plan which fails to follow that counsel will fail, as Proverbs 21:30 so clearly states.

Third observation: We must be careful not to misapply the use of counsel. The purpose of counsel is to prepare us to make the decisions. What we want from our counselor is data, ideas, suggestions ...... his knowledge of the value of certain assets. But *we* are God's managers, and He will hold *us* responsible for deciding how to invest His property.

A SUGGESTED RULE FOR THE USE OF INVESTMENT COUNSEL

Before making any investment, seek the counsel of at least three experts. Then pray for thirty days and ask God to impress upon you which, if any, are right. If He doesn't do that, then don't act.

This thirty-day rule can help in at least two ways. It helps prevent impulse investing, which very often turns out badly. If you've been investing for very long, you've probably learned this. Beware of any investment which has to be made *today* ...... immediately, or you will miss out on some great opportunity. If you hear that, take it as a danger signal.

The thirty-day rule also provides time to apply the principles of divine guidance, time in prayer, time in the Scriptures, time with other counselors, time to wait on God to convict us about what we should do. Our objectives are entirely different from those of the materialistic world. In the final analysis, if God is not in it, it will fail (Proverbs 21:30).

A PERSONAL TESTIMONY

Strategy 2, the use of counsel, is a strategy which I chose many years ago. Beginning around 1965 I began reading books and investment newsletters, which were proliferating rapidly around that time. I recall at one time subscribing to more than twenty different newsletters at the same time. Each had some good choices and some bad choices. Each had good years and bad years. The more I read and studied, the more confused I got.

It was also at this time that I was given the responsibility of managing the investment portfolio of the company I worked for, a life insurance company in Amarillo, Texas. Our company investments were regulated by the Texas Insurance Department for the protection of the policyholders. I studied the investments of the major insurance companies. I met with the investment officers of several of them, and learned how to make safe investments which complied with the regulations. Most of our policyholders' reserves were invested in high grade bonds and commercial mortgages secured by real estate land and buildings. It was permissible to invest a portion of the assets in common stocks. I had no confidence in my ability to invest in stocks, so we kept that portion small. Our investments did well during the years I managed them, from 1960 to 1986, the year I left the corporate world.

After this, I began managing investments for myself and a few friends and family as a ministry. By the late 1990s I was managing money for more than 30 people. It was at that time that I began to realize that I did not have the wisdom, knowledge and expertise to excel, even though I had had years of experience and research. I also realized that I needed to follow my own advice which I had given when I taught the seminar on which this book is based, the advice given in the paragraphs above. I committed the entire project to God, took up a prayer vigil, and asked Him to lead me to the experts whose knowledge, advice and counsel I should listen to in order to succeed.

God has answered my prayers. Today there are only about ten people in whom I have any real confidence. Some of them are no longer active, so I am reading only 5 or 6 on a consistent and regular basis. They are the basis of my investment strategy today. There are a few other people I consider worth reading, and I do read them, but my confidence is in the top 5 or 6. God has blessed this strategy.

I considered listing them here. But they are subject to change without notice. I would rather God lead you to those He knows are right for you, assuming you choose this strategy for investing your savings. So I felt it best to not include the list, with one exception, which I will mention for your consideration, with enthusiasm.

Harry Browne is one of the best investment minds of the twentieth century. His first book, *How You Can Profit from the Coming Devaluation,* was published around 1970, and has become a classic. He predicted the devaluation of the dollar, the continuing debasement of the dollar through monetary inflation, and the importance of including gold as part of a diversified investment portfolio.

His latest book, *Fail-safe Investing*, was published in 1999. It is short, very easy to read, and is presented in the form of "the 17 simple rules of financial safety," including rule 13, "How to establish a diversified portfolio which will protect your money in all economic environments." As this is written, the book is available in many book stores, or at www.amazon.com. It can also be downloaded from *www.libertyfree.com* for a small fee. I cannot imagine a better value.

In 1982 Mr. Browne started a mutual fund which follows the strategy outlined in the book. It is still in operation and has gained over 9% per year average return since its beginning. Information on the mutual fund is available at *www.permanentportfoliofunds.com*. This book could be the single most important book you will ever read on investing, an absolute must-read in my opinion.

THE IMPORTANCE OF DIVERSIFICATION

I had not realized that diversification was part of the wisdom of the Bible relating to investing until I studied the 11th chapter of Ecclesiastes.

> Cast your bread upon the waters, for after many days you will find it again [Ecclesiastes 11:1].

I have heard this verse interpreted as an instruction to give to those in need. But if you read it as part of the paragraph which includes verses 1 through 6, it seems clearly to teach the wisdom of spreading your risk in business or investing, and some commentaries point this out.

Give portions to seven, yes to eight, for you do not know what disaster may come upon the land [Ecclesiastes 11:2].

One commentary which I studied pointed out that in the day in which this was written, a common form of investing was to finance the cost of shipping goods across the ocean to other countries, sharing in the profit produced by this enterprise. This probably accounts for the phrase "Cast your bread upon the waters." There were many risks and hazards involved in this business … pirates, storms, mutinies, time delays, deterioration or damage to the cargos, and the like. So the writer counsels investors to divide their investment between seven or eight ships, so that if disaster strikes one of them, they won't lose all their investment.

If clouds are full of water, they pour rain upon the earth. Whether a tree falls to the south or the north, in the place where it falls, there will it lie [Ecclesiastes 11:3].

Here is a further illustration of the wisdom of spreading your risk. If you have all of your savings concentrated in one spot, and "the tree falls on that spot," you can be wiped out.

Whoever watches the wind will not plant. Whoever looks at the clouds will not reap [Ecclesiastes 11:4].

In this verse the writer brings in some balance, and he's describing the person who is afraid to take any risks of any kind. He watches the weather (or the news) and wonders where the storm is going to strike. He sees danger in all directions. The writer implies that you have to take risks. All of life involves risk; just spread your risk … diversify.

As you do not know the path of the wind, or how the body is formed in a mother's womb, so you cannot understand the work of God, the Maker of all things [Ecclesiastes 11:5].

This is one of many verses which teach that men cannot forecast the future, thus another good reason for diversifying.

Sow your seed in the morning, and at evening let not your hands be idle, for you do not know which will succeed, whether this or that, or whether both will do equally well [Ecclesiastes 11:6].

Here I believe he summarizes the thesis of the passage. Don't be afraid to take some risks. Go ahead and enter into business or make investments, but use the principle of diversification. It is an important principle of investing God's property. There are many ways of employing this principle, and diversification can be overdone, resulting in a lower average rate of return. But one of the best diversification strategies which I have found is that which is described by Harry Browne in his book, *Fail-safe Investing.*

STRATEGY 3 – BECOME AN EXPERT AT INVESTING

Don't dismiss this idea quickly. Don't say, "I can't do that." You can if God wants you to. Certainly not all, but some who read this should employ this strategy. Let's re-read two of the verses quoted earlier.

He who walks with the wise grows wise, but a companion of fools suffers harm [Proverbs 13:20].

Listen to advice and accept instruction, and in the end you will be wise [Proverbs 19:20].

I believe God intends some of us to become experts at investing His money. This is an extension of Strategy 2. We actually sit at the feet of the experts. We diligently study their methods and writings. For the past twenty years, I have sought to employ this strategy.

But I caution any who decide to pursue this strategy (including myself) that there is a major pitfall lying in our path. That pitfall is the temptation to get our eyes off of the main goal in the Christian life, *storing treasure in heaven.* We can easily fall into the trap of wanting to get rich. Many passages warn of this trap.

He who works his land will have abundant food. But he who chases fantasies lacks judgment [Proverbs 12:11].

This is one of many passages that warns against the sin of wanting to get rich. One of the results of a get-rich-quick mentality is impaired judgment, and impaired judgment leads to mistakes and problems.

Dishonest money dwindles away, but he who gathers money little by little makes it grow [Proverbs 13:11].

I believe this is one of the most important verses in the Bible on saving money. God's wisdom on building wealth is gathering money little by little. It is the opposite of chasing fantasies. The best way of storing God's wealth here on earth, assuming He intends for you to do it for kingdom purposes, is to become a collector of lasting values.

When I use the term "lasting values," I'm not referring to "eternal values." The only thing of eternal value is treasure stored in heaven. I'm referring to earthly assets which tend to hold their value or increase in value over periods of years here on earth. They would include the common stocks of companies which have produced a long record of growth in earnings and dividends. Land and buildings can be an example of lasting values.

Gold and silver have been a store of value since the beginning of human history. There are hundreds of references to gold and silver in the Bible, many of which say that gold is a store of wealth. These are examples of assets with lasting values. If you become a systematic collector, little by little, of things of lasting value, you are employing God's wealth-building system.

When you employ this plan, your savings can increase in three ways. First, your savings will increase by the amount you add to your plan each month. No plan will work unless you are adding regularly to it out of the fruits of your labor.

Second, your savings will increase by any income which your investments produce, such as dividends on stocks, interest on bonds or deposits, rent on real estate, and so forth. And note, by reinvesting this income you are harnessing the power of compounding. Someone has called compound interest the "eighth wonder of the world." Given enough time and patience, it truly can be.

Third, your savings can increase by the capital appreciation of certain assets, the increase in their market value. Stocks can go up in value. Bonds can go up. Real estate can go up.

Understand that there are no earthly assets which always go up, and none guaranteed not to go down. So combine the three strategies discussed in this section, that is, (1) Add to your savings faithfully, (2) Collect different things of lasting value (diversification), (3) Employ the power of compounding to the income produced by your investments. This is a plan based on the wisdom of Scripture. Never forget the phrase **"he who gathers money little by little makes it grow**." It implies patience. It implies waiting on God and trusting Him with the results. After all, He is in control and has our best interest at heart. Notice the contrast in this approach with the next two passages.

> Do not wear yourself out to get rich; have the wisdom to show restraint. Cast but a glance at riches, and they are gone, for they will surely sprout wings and fly off to the sky like an eagle [Proverbs 23:4-5].

> He who works his land will have abundant food, but the one who chases fantasies will have his fill of poverty. A faithful man will be richly blessed, but one eager to get rich will not go unpunished [Proverbs 28:19-20].

I suggest you spend some time meditating on these two passages. The same truth is stated from slightly different perspectives. In the first, the person striving to get rich sees his wealth sprout wings and fly off. He ends up broke. The second passage says the person who chases fantasies will have his fill of poverty.

One of the things that hastens the process of going into poverty is borrowed money. In my opinion, other than the sin of desiring to get rich, the number one contributing factor to the loss of wealth is borrowed money.

There is no commandment which prohibits borrowing, and the use of leverage is not, in and of itself, a sin. But when you borrow with a covetous heart, a get-rich-quick motive, it is a sin, and will lead to trouble. Here's why. If I borrow, invest and win, what will I do? I'll try again. Not only that, I'll take a bigger risk the next time, because I have some profit from my first investment. If I continue to win, I'll keep increasing my bets. The reason I do that is because the more I make the more I want. There is no amount which satisfies a get-rich-quick mentality. The Bible tells us that.

> Whoever loves money never has money enough; whoever loves wealth is never satisfied with his income. This too is meaningless [Ecclesiastes 5:10].

There is no amount which satisfies a covetous heart. Enough is not enough. You cannot live a victorious Christian life with these emotions controlling your life. Most often, it will eventually lead to poverty, and the Proverb is fulfilled: "The one who chases fantasies will have his fill of poverty" (Proverbs 28:19).

FINAL THOUGHTS

In view of the perils and temptations involved in the pursuit of earthly wealth, should we even try to become experts at investing? Are we "playing with fire" as we invest much of our time and energy in trying to get above average returns on the portion of God's property which remains under our stewardship in this life? Am I really able to know, as I accumulate and distribute assets, the difference between managing God's property and grasping it? Can I be trusted with God's property?

Why not just give most of it to ministries we judge to be contributing the greatest to the kingdom of God, and look to Him for the meeting of our needs? Then we won't be tempted to selfishly consume or hoard God's assets, at least that portion of them. They will be safely in our account in heaven, and be ours for all eternity.

On the other hand, we are given biblical wisdom for storing wealth on earth as well as in heaven. Isn't it possible that by wisely investing earthly wealth, and generously giving to the Lord from the income and gains on that wealth, we could make a greater contribution to the kingdom than if we simply gave most of it away now? But is that a reasonable possibility, in view of our depravity, and our inborn lust for independence?

These are all legitimate questions. As we discussed in Chapter 15, I believe there is wisdom in storing God's property both on earth and in heaven, and that based on the New Testament, God has given us the latitude of choosing where we will draw the line between the two. We will give account of where we draw it when we stand before Jesus at the Judgment Seat. But Scripture is also clear in teaching us that storing on earth is fraught with far more perils than storing in heaven, and we will live all the days of our lives under the tension of drawing the line. As you struggle with this tension, I suggest you prayerfully read the Appendix (see page 233) and ask God to use it to reveal His will for you.

I consider every dollar we give to the Lord as an investment, just as I consider every dollar we store on earth as an investment. I try to invest His earthly wealth in assets which are undervalued, which have a reasonable probability of going up in value or producing a good income. In the same way I try to be zealous in finding heavenly investments which will produce the best returns for God's kingdom. Besides our own local church, which has a great teaching heritage, a book publishing ministry, and individual commitments to service in the community, we look for those ministries we believe are spreading the Gospel and feeding the poor.

Several years ago I met a woman missionary who has given her life to one of the most incredible ministries I have ever seen. As a young woman, she went alone to downtown Tokyo, took up residence there, and notified the hospitals that she was prepared to take any unwanted babies born in those hospitals. Miraculously, the authorities let her begin adopting new born babies. At times she would have several babies in the bottle-feeding, diaper-changing phase.

She raised many of the children to and beyond school age, won most of them to Christ, eventually adopting them all out to Christian families. This year she finished her 50th year in that ministry, having adopted a total of more than 200 children.

Over the years many of her children have gone to Bible college and seminary in the US, then returned to Japan as missionaries. Most now have children of their own who are serving God. I cannot imagine a better investment than a ministry like this. Every time we send money to her, I tingle with excitement at the potential return on our investment. And I am reminded of the verse with which I began this book, "I tell you, use worldly wealth to gain friends for yourselves, so that when it is gone, you will be welcomed into eternal dwellings." (Luke 16:9). When we get to heaven, we may be met by a welcoming committee of Japanese Christians.

In the final analysis, success at investing is not to post a gain over a specified time period, but to spend longer and longer periods of time aware that the wealth of the nations all belongs to the Lord, and He is the One sufficient to bring an investor peace. To Him I say, "Lord, God Almighty, I long for that peace, and yet I know that as the accounts rise and fall, and the perceived responsibility increases or decreases, that peace may become more elusive. Who can abide the Day of Your coming? Even so, Lord Jesus, come quickly."

CHAPTER 17

RETIREMENT

In Chapter 14 we discussed owning a home, suggesting that for many Americans it best expresses "the American dream." If I were asked my opinion of what Americans would consider second in importance in their definition of "the American dream," I would answer without hesitation, "Retirement!" By that I mean the accumulation of a retirement fund, at some planned age, sufficient to permit one to quit working, and live out his remaining years in ease. Having myself already traversed well beyond the typical "planned age" for retirement, I am at least somewhat of an authority on this area, for I believe I was an average American during my earlier working years. And I confess to you that it was my dream to do just that. To be honest, it was a higher priority in my mind than owning a home.

In any case, I think we can agree that a study of Biblical Economics would surely be incomplete without seeking to answer the question, "What does the Bible say about retirement?" Before we research the Bible on this question, let me pose some questions for you to meditate on ... to prepare your thinking for the study. What is your concept of retirement? Are you looking forward to retirement? Are you making plans for it? What mental pictures come into your mind when you think about retired life? Do you think of a life of total leisure with no work in it? ... perhaps sleeping late every morning, or going to the golf course every day, or sitting out on the creek bank fishing, or traveling, or ...? Are you looking for a "little bit of heaven" this side of the grave?

If these are the kinds of pictures which come into your mind, and are the kinds of things you look forward to after you retire, then the Bible may change your mind completely. It did mine. Frankly, I was rather surprised when I studied this question from the Bible, the reason being that I found nothing in the Bible that supports retirement as it is practiced today in our culture. Possibly I have missed it. I certainly do not have exhaustive knowledge of the Bible, but in over 25 years of study, I have not found a single verse which encourages it, and among the many experts whom I have studied, not one of them has pointed out any passage which supports retirement as it is generally viewed today.

Some of you reading this may be young, in the early part of your working life. Perhaps you are thinking to yourself, "Retirement is years away for me. I probably don't even need to know this information today." Let me suggest to you that is not the case, and that the time to get straight on this subject is while you're young, so you don't waste half a lifetime on the wrong track. I wish I had known this as a much younger person.

Our objective is to view the concept of retirement from two perspectives: (1) as the world views it, and (2) as the Bible views it.

RETIREMENT DEFINED

Let's begin with the word "retire" itself. In the English dictionary, I found this definition, "To withdraw from office, business or active life." In other words, to bring your vocation, career or life's work to an end at an arbitrary, predetermined age. The most common such age is 65, probably because the founders of the Social Security system selected it as the age for benefits to begin. As far as I know there was nothing scientific involved in the selection of that age, other than the fact the legislators were aware that life expectancy at the time was in the low 70s. If 65 was a good choice at the time, it certainly doesn't make sense now, for life expectancy has increased by 5 to 10 years since.

Over the years since enactment of the law, many businesses, especially the large corporations, have instituted age 65 as a mandatory retirement age to dovetail with the Social Security system. The business world has long debated whether having a mandatory retirement age is a good thing or a bad thing. Apparently, many businesses have concluded that it is a good thing, or that at least the good outweighs the bad. I suppose from a business point of view that might be the case in some situations. But for a believer in Christ to stop functioning at some arbitrary age, an age at which he is still active, healthy, and able to work, is a concept that I find foreign to Scripture. Thus, if you are employed by a business which has a mandatory retirement age, I would suggest that long in advance of reaching that age you begin making plans for continuing in active service for the Lord. That could include starting a business, if that is your calling, or it could mean taking a salaried job with an employer that doesn't have a mandatory retirement age. The life of a disciple of Jesus Christ may involve one or more job changes, but never retirement as it is viewed in our culture.

A word of balance is in order here. The aging process is the plan of God. He intends for our bodies to wear out and die. Viewed biblically, this is a good thing, not a bad thing. The earthly life is not an end in itself, but rather a means to an end. After the body dies, the soul will live on forever, and the earthly life is a preparation for that eternal existence following this life. During this earthly life two things are determined: (1) where we will spend eternity, determined by whether or not we trust Christ as our Savior, and (2) for those who do trust Him, their reward and position in heaven, determined by their deeds in this life. For those who reject Him, their degree of punishment in hell will be determined by their deeds in this life. Clear passages which support this thesis are Romans 2:6-11, 2 Corinthians 5:10, and Revelation 20:11-12.

We are given very little specific information about our lives in eternity, but commanded to keep our hope and focus on the eternal rather than the temporal.

> Set your mind on things above, not on earthly things
> [Colossians 3:2].

The incentive for obeying this command is the knowledge that we can maximize our reward in eternity. We have the same opportunity for reward as the most gifted believers, as those given long years of life and health and material wealth, by simply making the most of what we are given to work with. That was the message of Chapter 4. Obviously, as the body slows down both mentally and physically, we may become unable to perform certain work. We may have to step down from certain duties, and we should have the wisdom to do that.

Incidentally, the word "retire" appears only one time in the New International Version of the Bible, in Numbers 8:25. It is an instruction to the Levites to retire from the hard manual labor of building the tabernacle, at age fifty. But they did not stop working, they merely took on lighter work. The very fact that the body is wearing out and will die adds to the incentive to make every moment count. The apostle Paul calls it "redeeming the time," in Ephesians 5:16. As long as there is life in our bodies, God has some ministry, some witness, some purpose for our being here, and our work is not finished. To withdraw ourselves arbitrarily from service is not His plan.

DID JESUS OR THE APOSTLES COMMAND US NOT TO RETIRE?

But wait. Is there a specific command which forbids retiring? As far as I am aware there is not. Why should there be? New Testament stewardship of all God's property, including energy, gifts, wealth and years of life, is entirely at the discretion of the individual believer. Clearly Jesus sets the goal as storing treasure in heaven rather than on earth. But we have complete latitude for determining what that will look like. We do this with the understanding that there will be full accountability of our stewardship at the Judgment Seat of Christ. If we want to spend a fourth or half of our lives doing things we enjoy which make no contribution to the kingdom, we have that right, just as we have the right to give as large or as small a percent of our money to the Lord as we choose. But our choices will determine our reward and position in eternity. Never think of things like long life, health, wealth, and intellect in terms of greater blessings. Always think of them in terms of greater accountability. As Jesus put it, "To whom much is given, much is required."

DOES BUILDING A RETIREMENT FUND VIOLATE SCRIPTURE?

I think, for the most part, we have answered this question in Chapter 15. You might want to review that chapter. We learned that the wise man saves a portion of his income for future needs, but the foolish man spends all his income as he receives it (Proverbs 21:20). The apostle Paul also puts his sanction on saving some of one's income for future needs, especially the needs of family members for whom we are responsible (1 Timothy 5:8 and 2 Corinthians 12:14-15). But I am not aware of any command of Jesus or the apostles to save specifically for old age. On the contrary, Jesus clearly commands us, "Do not store *for yourselves* treasure on earth." I interpret this to mean do not store earthly wealth for selfish purposes.

As we concluded in Chapter 15, we have the right and responsibility to draw the line between storing treasure on earth and in heaven, understanding that our choice will determine our reward and position in heaven. It's part of the stewardship latitude given to us in the New Testament. But I would hasten to add, it seems to me there is more risk involved in storing money for old age than storing it for other anticipated needs. Our culture has conditioned us to think in terms of building a retirement fund to secure our financial needs in old age from the time we stop working until the time we die, a concept never mentioned in Scripture as far as I can determine. Yet Jesus clearly tells us that if we make serving Him our priority, He will assume responsibility for meeting all our needs (see Matthew 6:33).

We must decide where to draw the line, and we can draw it anywhere we want to. Rest assured there will be tension as we draw it, and we will not know this side of the grave how well we did it. This logically leads me to simply suggest some ways we may examine ourselves as we make our financial decisions. Here are four tests we could use as we set aside money for old age.

THE HOARDING TEST

When Jesus commanded us not to store wealth on earth *for ourselves*, He was warning against the sin of hoarding. But how do I know when I cross the line between legitimate needs and hoarding? I must examine my heart. Do I love money? Do I want to get rich? These are clearly defined as sins, as we learned in Chapter 5, and, I might add, with frightening consequences (see 1 Timothy 6:9-10). Solomon also warned of the consequences of hoarding.

> Whoever loves money never has money enough; whoever loves wealth is never satisfied with his income. This too is meaningless. As goods increase, so do those who consume them. And what benefit are they to the owner except to feast his eyes on them? The sleep of a laborer is sweet, whether he eats little or much, but the abundance of a rich man permits him no sleep. I have seen a grievous evil under the sun: wealth **hoarded to the harm of its owner** [Ecclesiastes 5:10-13].

In His parable of the rich fool, Jesus also warned of the consequences of hoarding. He told the story of the man who accumulated so much wealth that he felt compelled to tear down his barns and build bigger ones so that he could store even more wealth with the intent of consuming it on his own desires at a future time.

> But God said to him, "You fool! This very night your life will be demanded from you. Then who will get what you have prepared for yourself?" This is how it will be with anyone who stores up things for himself, but is not rich toward God [Luke 12:20-21].

Hoarding flows naturally from the love of wealth, or the love of accumulating wealth. The person who hoards does so with a view toward consuming his hoard sometime later on his own selfish desires rather than meeting his true needs. The Christian who hoards is storing wealth on earth that should be stored in heaven. The hoarder's plans for future consumption most often never take place at all. It is a perverse truth, I think, that a committed hoarder really never intends to consume the wealth, but thinks he can continually amass wealth indefinitely. He never truly thinks he will use the money, but wants more and more just in case. And note Jesus' final statement in this parable. He's letting us know that the person with hoarded wealth is not more *blessed*. He is more *accountable*!

I cannot read these passages without being terrified. Every time I do, I am motivated to re-commit to a goal of storing treasure in heaven rather than on earth.

THE INACTIVITY TEST

If you are accumulating money to fund your needs during a *planned* period of inactivity at some selected age in the future, during which period you would quit working and live off of what you have accumulated, even though you are still active and able to work, I believe you risk violating Jesus' command to not store for yourself treasure on earth. This is retirement as the world views it, a concept I cannot find in Scripture. It is based on an unscriptural premise, the idea that God intends for us to live a portion of our lives inactively, or in recreation for our own enjoyment.

Of course, because the New Testament gives us latitude to determine our stewardship, we may choose this worldly approach to retirement. But let us never forget that God determines our standard of living on earth, and not for a part of our earthly life, but for all of it, including old age. If we serve Him faithfully ("seek first His kingdom ..."), He takes full responsibility for meeting our needs, including old age (Matthew 6:33). I'm not saying having some wealth in old age is a sin, in and of itself. I'm saying that if God doesn't intend for me to have a retirement fund, it won't be there no matter what I do. The moth, rust, and thieves (such as inflation, bankruptcy, unfunded pension plans) can take it away. If I fail the inactivity test, my old age could well end in despair.

THE CALAMITY TEST

Some of us are attempting to secure our future against total calamity, and to do it with money. Fear of the future has become so common in our culture today that even some Christians have been trapped into squirreling away large sums of money without any real plan for the future use of it. This is a violation of Jesus' clear command.

> Therefore I tell you, do not worry about your life, what you will eat or drink, or about your body, what you will wear ... [Matthew 6:25].

As we learned in Chapter 15, this is a conditional promise that if our life goal is storing treasure in heaven, we have no reason to worry about our needs. Jesus taught us that financial security comes from having the right goal in life, not from having wealth. He made it clear that there is no security in having earthly wealth if the goal is wrong. If you want to know where to place your fear, the One to fear is the Lord of Hosts. He wants you to fear Him so much that there is no calamity that could possibly compare to fear of Him.

THE STEWARDSHIP TEST

This is a very simple test. If I am setting aside money for old age at the expense of giving God a good offering today, that is, at the expense of giving God a good increase on His estate, I am running the risk of disobeying His command to not store for myself treasure on earth. That's the reason we suggested this rule to memorize: **Never** concentrate on storing wealth on earth apart from concentrating on storing wealth in heaven. Never let the two separate in your mind.

Having examined our hearts using these four tests, the question then arises, how should we determine the amount we should set aside for old age? No one can answer this question for you. What I can say on the authority of Jesus' promise is, if we are faithful stewards of all the wealth He has entrusted to us, and if our goal is increasing God's estate, not our own, we will arrive at old age with just the right amount for our needs. And we don't even need to know today what that amount is.

A PERSONAL TESTIMONY

I am ashamed to admit to you that when I was a young businessman I used to dream of retiring. I was obsessed with the idea, and I had a goal of accumulating a certain amount of money by a certain age, so that I could live out the rest of my life in ease. I won't tell you what that age or amount was, because I scrapped the whole plan many years ago. I came to realize that it was an unscriptural goal. I got a new goal after studying this subject in the 1980s. That goal is to do the best job managing whatever God entrusts to me, to give Him a good return on it every year as long as I live, and let Him decide what amount to give me and when to give it to me. I have no set goal for earthly treasure, and no intention of retiring. I want to remain active and productive as long as God is pleased to allow it.

FINAL THOUGHTS

The concept of retirement as practiced in our culture is not supported by the Bible. The scriptural concept of retirement is death of the body, therefore a planned withdrawal from active life at some predetermined age does not square with Scripture. There are a few bumper stickers that present good theology. I saw one which said, "A Christian's retirement benefits are out of this world." How true, because Christians do not retire in this world. They retire in the next world! There they get their retirement benefits. Service continues in eternity. The work will be a pleasure then.

I wonder how many Christians retire here on earth, begin drawing their retirement benefits, only to die in a few months or years and get a cut in retirement pay? I wonder how many of us would be better off storing more in heaven while on earth? Heaven is where we will receive our real retirement benefits. I also wonder how many well-meaning believers have lost the joy of the Christian life because of retirement.

We can concentrate on storing treasure in heaven by examining our hearts using the four tests, and following the stewardship principles we have studied in this book, arriving at old age with just the right amount of money. Isn't it logical that if God is the only one who knows how long we will live, and what our needs in old age will be, that He is the One to decide whether we should have any accumulated savings in old age, and how much?

CHAPTER 18

BIBLICAL ESTATE PLANNING

Should a Christian have a will, and if so, how should he write it? That is, how should he distribute the remaining assets he leaves on this earth when he dies? Is there such a thing as "Biblical Estate Planning?" Is it important to God, i.e., does the Bible speak to this issue, or does it even matter? These are the questions we will seek to answer in this chapter.

YOUR LAST ACT OF STEWARDSHIP

It has been said that a person will spend fifty or sixty years accumulating earthly treasure, then spend another 20 years or more trying to keep from losing it, but will not spend two hours planning the distribution of it when he dies.

The stewardship of what you leave on earth when you die is something I suspect that very few people have ever given serious thought to. I will argue that it's just as important to God how you distribute *what's left* of His property, as it is how you manage it *while you are alive.* You are just as much a steward of what you *leave* as what you managed *while you were here.* And you can lose reward by failing to distribute what's left to God's glory, just as you can lose reward by mismanaging God's property while you are here. **Remember. Distributing what's left will be your last act of stewardship in this life**.

A SENSITIVE AND EMOTIONAL ISSUE

We are embarking upon a subject that is usually sensitive and emotional. That is often the case when we are challenged to surrender our desire to decide what is in our best interest, and submit to what God says is in our best interest. Add to that the fact that the Bible criticizes what the world thinks about this issue, and you have the makings of bitter disagreement and hurt feelings. I believe it would be wise for us to hear the following words from God before we proceed.

"For My thoughts are not your thoughts, neither are your ways My ways," declares the LORD. "As the heavens are higher than the earth, so are My ways higher than your ways, and My thoughts than your thoughts…" [Isaiah 55:8-9].

How much higher are the heavens than the earth? What a great illustration of how far apart God's thoughts, ways, and ideas are from man's, on every major issue in life. Therefore, there will be tension when God's thoughts begin to criticize our thoughts, especially in sensitive, emotional areas. Some may be offended by certain material in this chapter. It is certainly not my intention to offend anyone. My purpose is not to try to convince you of my opinion. My only purpose is to try to faithfully present God's principles of estate planning, then let you decide how to write your will.

GOD'S MANAGEMENT AGREEMENT WITH MAN REVISITED

In Chapter 4 we stated that the central truth in the Bible regarding the handling of money is, "God entrusts His wealth to man to manage for Him." Thus, if we have a biblical philosophy of money, we will never think of ourselves as owners of anything on this earth. That being the case, our primary objective is to increase God's estate, not ours. Our objective is to give Him a good return on His investment in us during the years we manage it, **then give God back what's left when we are finished with it**.

Consider this simple illustration. Suppose someone gave you $1,000 to manage for a year, and said to you, "Invest this for me in any way you choose for one year. At the end of the year, we will settle accounts." What would you do at the end of that year? You would give him back two things. You would give him the profit earned on the money. Hopefully there would be some. But you would also give him back the original $1,000, because it is his property, and you were merely managing it for him.

That is an excellent analogy of how the kingdom of God operates, as we discovered when we studied Jesus' parable of the talents (Matthew 25:14-30).

Again, it (reference to the kingdom) will be like a man going on a journey who called his servants and entrusted his property to them. To one he gave five talents of money, to another two talents, and to another one talent, each according to his ability. Then he went on his journey [Matthew 25:14-15].

As we learned from studying the parable, when the estate owner returned from his journey, the period of stewardship was over, and he brought the three managers to accountability, and settled accounts with them. Each manager gave back the original amount entrusted to him along with the profit he had earned on it. Even the unfaithful steward, who earned nothing on the money, returned the one talent to the owner ... because it belonged to him. Jesus said, "This is analogous to the way the kingdom of God works."

God will entrust certain material wealth to every believer with the expectation of getting a return on it while under the believer's stewardship, and getting back what is left when his management period is over, because it is God's property. I believe if we can grasp and accept this concept, it will do more to teach us the principles of biblical estate planning than any other single thing ... *and it is so simple.* A good steward will give God a good return on His investment each year while he has it, and then when he's finished, he'll give what's left back to God. That is his last act of stewardship.

That is a clear and simple concept, isn't it? But being simple does not mean it is easy to accomplish ... nor free of emotional stress and tension. Most of us will struggle with the decisions we must make. Our only hope of getting it anywhere near right is to surrender our lust to decide what is in our best interest, and learn and submit to what God tells us is in our best interest. Let's see if we can begin to get a handle on the tension and stress that we will face. Eternal responsibility and reward are at stake.

SOLOMON ON ESTATE PLANNING

In the book of Ecclesiastes, Solomon confesses the mistakes he made, and the conclusions he reached as he attempted to find happiness and meaning in this earthly life. Although Isaiah 55:8-9 had not been written when Solomon wrote Ecclesiastes, he came to exactly the same conclusion stated by Isaiah, that man's thoughts and ways are exactly opposite to God's thoughts and ways. Further, he concluded that man's thoughts and ways do not work ... they do not bring fulfillment in life. Quite the opposite, they lead to heartache and defeat.

I think if Solomon were here today, he would admit to being one of the world's leading experts on man's attempts to find happiness and satisfaction. If anyone ever gave it a full run for the money, it was Solomon. He ran the gamut from sex, to alcohol, to wealth, to pleasure, to knowledge, to folly, to work ... you name it, he tried it, and finally concluded that none of it produced contentment, or real meaning in life.

In one portion of the book, where he discussed his experiment with work, Solomon wrote about his struggle with the distribution of his estate. I believe it will be an excellent text for us.

> So I hated life because the work that is done under the sun was grievous to me. All of it is meaningless, a chasing after the wind [Ecclesiastes 2:17].

"All is meaningless," he said. All what? It is very important to understand what Solomon meant by this phrase, because all, in a universal sense, is not meaningless in this life. There are some meaningful things in the earthly life. This is where the little phrase "under the sun" becomes so important, a key phrase appearing throughout the book. Solomon means by this phrase all that men are doing on the earth (under the sun) apart from God ...... all that men are doing independently of God. Or, using the terminology we have used throughout this book, all that men are doing while refusing to surrender their lust for autonomy. All of that is "meaningless and a chasing after the wind."

Today we are still falling into the trap Solomon fell into. It's the original lie of Satan, in which he suggested to our first parents, that you can be like God without being in submission to God. You can be godly without God. In essence, "If you eat of this tree, you will have the knowledge to decide for yourself what is in your best interest. You will not need God to tell you what is in your best interest. You can be independent of Him."

Solomon embarked upon a series of experiments (described in Ecclesiastes) to find meaning and happiness in life *independently* of God. One of them was work. Labor. That's the one he's discussing in this text, and his thesis is that working, or laboring, when engaged in as an attempt to find meaning or happiness in life leads only to despair. He does not condemn the work ethic in this passage. He wrote many verses in the Proverbs which support the work ethic. That's how important this phrase "under the sun" is. He is saying that work as a means of attaining happiness apart from God, is futile, like grasping for a fistful of wind. Work *for God* ...... good stewardship of God's property, is a blessing. Work *as a god* is a curse. Workaholics, please take heed.

> I hated all the things I had toiled for under the sun, because I must leave them to the one who comes after me [Ecclesiastes 2:18].

Here Solomon refers to his son, Rehoboam, who succeeded him as king in Israel.

> And who knows whether he will be a wise man or a fool? Yet he will have control over all the work into which I have poured my effort and skill under the sun. This too is meaningless [Ecclesiastes 2:19].

Can you sympathize with Solomon's dilemma? He was probably thinking, "I've accumulated this enormous amount of wealth, only to die and leave it to someone else. That's bad enough. But add to that the probability that the one I leave it to will be a fool ... who will mismanage it, and waste it, and probably even damage my reputation in the process, and you are driven to despair." And that's exactly what he says next.

> So my heart began to despair over all my toilsome labor under the sun [Ecclesiastes 2:20].

If you want to find out how foolish Solomon's son Rehoboam was, read 1 Kings Chapter 12. Any doubt that he was a fool is removed by that passage. And I suspect Solomon knew his son was a fool, or at least feared that he lacked the wisdom to handle his wealth prudently after he was gone. That seems implied in this passage. No wonder Solomon despaired. And the despair Solomon experienced has been repeated over and over all down through human history ... the futility of leaving wealth to a person who will mismanage it ... including, sad to say, many Christian families today.

I pause here to interject a word of hope. We can avoid the despair which Solomon describes by doing two things. First, give God a generous first portion of every dollar of income as we receive it, and second, give back to God what is left when we die. That is the thesis of this chapter and the essence of biblical estate planning.

I am drawn to the conclusion that, if I die and leave wealth to a person who mismanages it ... who does not use it to build the kingdom of God, then I can be held accountable to God for mismanagement. This, of course, brings to mind our children. I'm sure you knew that's where I'm headed here. Obviously, that's what was in Solomon's mind, as verse 20 clearly indicates.

Let's discuss our minor children first. We are responsible for providing financially for our children until they reach adulthood. That could include a college education if we believe that to be the will of God. It could include helping them get started in business, or helping them get a home, if that is our conviction. But once we have fulfilled the obligation to get them to adulthood, we are under no further obligation to them financially beyond that which is clearly the will of God, and **the will of God is that the wealth continue to build the kingdom.** Again, you get to decide where to draw the line, and then be responsible for the portion you decided not to place in the kingdom during your lifetime.

What about our adult children? This, of course, is the sensitive area, because we are emotional creatures. As we begin thinking about this, questions and emotions begin flooding our minds. Let me make clear what I am *not* saying up to this point. I'm not saying whether or not you should leave any money to your adult children, nor how much. All I've said up to this point is two things. First, it is a mistake not to direct how your remaining assets be distributed when you die, that is, it is a mistake to not have a will. Second, I am saying, however you direct the distribution of your wealth, it must be equivalent to returning it to God. It must be kept working in the kingdom of God.

Now we come to the really difficult issue, how to determine distribution of our estates in relation to our adult children. I struggled for two or three years with how to present this critically important issue. I remind us that under the New Testament, we are given the latitude to decide how we will steward God's property. No specific commands are given us regarding distribution of our estates at death. The controlling commands Jesus gave us are, "Do not store treasure for yourselves on earth. Do store treasure for yourselves in heaven." We will be held fully accountable for how well we obeyed those two commands. With that in mind, I came to the conclusion that the best way of helping us write our wills is to suggest five penetrating questions to ask ourselves. If we consider them carefully, search our hearts, spend protracted time in prayer, and search the Scriptures in relation to these questions, we can find the will of God. Here are the questions.

1. Do you want to be an obstacle to your son or daughter learning to walk by faith? By that I mean learning to depend on God for his or her needs. Many children have been hurt, rather than helped, by having money left to them, even in Christian families. There are situations in which it could be the worst thing you could do.

2. Would you want to be an obstacle to your son or daughter learning the biblical concept of work? By this I mean learning to work to eat, and learning the work ethic as it is presented in the Bible. Many verses in the Proverbs teach the work ethic, how important it is, how bad laziness is. In our text, Solomon recognized the danger of leaving money to someone who didn't work for it.

> For a man may do his work with wisdom, knowledge and skill, and then he must leave all he owns to someone who has not worked for it. This too is meaningless and a great misfortune [Ecclesiastes 2:21].

As we are seeing, this misfortune can be avoided by learning and practicing the biblical principles of stewardship. But question 2 is an important question to consider. There is a risk in leaving money to someone who didn't work for it.

3. Do you think leaving money to an unbeliever is good stewardship of God's property? Let this question sink in. Think long and hard before coming to a decision. Suppose you have an adult son or daughter who is not a Christian. What would be accomplished by leaving wealth to that unbelieving son or daughter? Perhaps your first thought is, I hope one day he or she will trust Christ as Savior. Of course you do. But do you think leaving money will help that to happen? Or do you think making financial decisions based on what you hope will happen is good stewardship? If he or she does become a Christian, you can change your will.

Here is an even more difficult question than question 3.

4. Suppose you have an adult son or daughter who is a Christian, but has an established pattern of carnality, one who in your judgment is a wayward Christian. Do you think leaving money to a wayward Christian would be good stewardship? You may say, "I don't have any right to judge the spirituality of my grown son or daughter." I submit that you do as far as the stewardship of your money is concerned. Ask yourself this, "What is a wayward Christian going to do with money? What is a materialistic Christian going to do with money?" I do not know what they will do with it, but I can tell you one thing they will not do with it. They will not invest it in the kingdom of God. You can be fairly assured of that. What is a Christian with a drinking problem going to do with money? Perhaps you're thinking, I hope and pray they will repent and get back in God's will, and begin growing spiritually. That would be wonderful. If it happens, then change your will.

This is serious business. I hope these questions will help convince you of that. We are under a management contract with God (see Chapter 4). We are bound by the terms of that contract. God is not playing games with the stewardship of His property.

I think we can reduce all these questions to one key question, question five.

5. Would leaving money to a particular son or daughter be the same as investing it in the kingdom? Would it be the same as giving it back to God? In the final analysis, this is the question you must answer. Let me explain what I mean by giving it back to God. Would that particular son or daughter give God a good return on the income as he or she received it, and then would he or she pass what's left on to another faithful steward when finished with it? If you cannot get a yes answer to this question, then you would probably be guilty of mismanagement by leaving money to that son or daughter.

Please understand that I realize this is an emotional issue. I know what goes on in the heart of a parent of grown children, because I am one. I know how the heart can be torn. I understand the stress and tension which can be created as we face these issues. But let's remember that Jesus said, "This is the way the kingdom operates ..." (Matthew 25:14). In that illustration which He gave, the steward who mismanaged the estate owner's property was severely reprimanded, "You wicked, lazy servant! ..." (Matthew 25:26). The servant was denied any further privilege of management, and his reward was taken away. Stewardship is very serious business. It is not fun and games.

Facing these questions is an excellent application of the following instructions Jesus gave His disciples.

> If anyone comes to Me and does not hate his father and mother,
> his wife and children, his brothers and sisters – yes, even his own
> life – he cannot be My disciple [Luke 14:26].

Elsewhere, Jesus taught us to love others. But here he makes it clear that obedience to His commands is a higher priority than our relationship with any family member. One good application of this passage is in the area of biblical estate planning. The issues we are dealing with in this chapter should give us a greater understanding and appreciation of this command of Jesus. And they are issues involving eternal consequences. Which is more important, what our children think, or what Jesus says? In a sense our personal dealings with our heavenly Father are private and exclusive. Even our families cannot enter some discussions.

We continue Solomon's discourse on work.

What does a man get for all the toil and anxious striving with which he labors under the sun? [Ecclesiastes 2:22].

Let me re-phrase that question in light of our study. This is what I think he is asking, "What does a man pursuing a humanistic philosophy get for all his anxious striving?" He answers his own question in verse 23.

All his days his work is pain and grief; even at night his mind does not rest. This too is meaningless [Ecclesiastes 2:23].

The question is, what does a man get for acting independently of God? The answer is pain, grief, despair, unhappiness, sleepless nights. Are there any exceptions? I doubt it. I know I'm not one.

A man can do nothing better than to eat and drink and find satisfaction in his work. This too, I see, is from the hand of God, for without Him [i.e. without God, apart from God, or independently of God], who can eat or find enjoyment? [Ecclesiastes 2:24-25].

Implied answer: No one. The next verse refers to "the man that pleases Him (God)." Who is the man that pleases God? He's the man that acts in dependence on God. He's the man that doesn't try to order his life independently of God. He surrenders his thirst for self rule. Let's read what Solomon says about him.

To the man who pleases Him, God gives wisdom, knowledge and happiness, but to the sinner He gives the task of gathering and storing up wealth to hand it over to the one who pleases God. This too is meaningless, a chasing after the wind [Ecclesiastes 2:26].

Men who are disobedient to God may accumulate wealth on this earth, sometimes even large amounts of it. But God decides who enjoys wealth in this life. Enjoyment and fulfillment come to those who are obedient stewards of God's wealth, those who act in dependence on God.

Let me summarize what I think this passage is saying in relation to biblical estate planning. If we die and leave wealth to the wrong person or persons, it is a form of mismanagement of God's property. I believe I can find in this passage at least four results which can occur from such mismanagement. (1) We can lose at least some of the enjoyment of the wealth as we manage it. (2) We can lose reward in eternity. (3) The money we leave will likely not be a blessing to the one who receives it. (4) God will likely move the wealth. God constantly moves wealth from hand to hand on this earth like pawns on a chessboard in order to compensate for the mismanagement of men.

Therefore, leaving money to children should be done only after careful thought, prayer and meditation in Scripture. Ask yourself the five questions as part of your decision making process, and ask God for conviction and confirmation of your decision.

Here is a suggestion you might consider. It is not Scripture, just a suggestion. If you are considering leaving money to one of your children who is a Christian, who from all appearances is seeking to walk with God, and growing spiritually, consider giving some of your property to that son/daughter while you are alive, and see what he/she does with it. Help him/her learn the principles of stewardship, how to become a faithful manager of God's wealth. If you like what you see, tell that son/daughter you plan to include him/her in the will, with the understanding he/she will give God the first portion of every dollar of income as it comes in, then pass anything left to another faithful steward at death.

ONE WAY TO ELIMINATE THE PROBLEM COMPLETELY

In Chapter 15, I mentioned John Wesley's approach to finances. His three simple rules for managing money were: (1) Earn all you can. (2) Save all you can. (3) Give all you can. By "save," John Wesley meant keep your expenses as low as possible. Spend only what you have to in order to survive.

So his three rules were: (1) Earn all you can. (2) Keep your expenditures as low as you can. (3) Give all you can. Keep studying his life, and you soon realize his real goal was to give God everything by the time he died. On one occasion he said, "When I die, if there is more than 100 pounds (perhaps equivalent to a few thousand dollars today) in my estate, you can call me a failure." On another occasion he said, "These hands will be the executors of my estate," which simply meant that he had every intention of distributing his estate before he died, and in fact, there were 28 pounds left in his estate when he died. He made a lot of money during his life, and distributed it all but a few hundred dollars.

Think about that. No doubt he made that commitment to God years before he died, and had complete faith that God would honor it. What a neat solution to estate planning. If you can do this, your will wouldn't need to be more than a page or two. I mention this because it profoundly affected my heart as a young man. God may use it to touch the heart of someone who reads this.

WRITING THE WILL

Usually the husband and wife do not die at the same time. Therefore, it is important to plan the estate following each death. The ideal situation would be a husband and wife who are both born again, who love the Lord and love each other. Both are dedicated to living in obedience to God, and they share common biblical convictions on stewardship. That's an ideal marriage relationship. Such a model couple will jointly plan the distribution of their assets following each death, no matter who dies first, in such a way that the property they managed for God will continue working in the kingdom. That's the ideal.

In a fallen world, the ideal is not always achieved. One spouse may be an unbeliever, or a believer who is not interested in biblical stewardship. The wife may not be submissive to her husband, or the husband may not love his wife sacrificially, as Christ loved the church. The husband may not look upon the marriage as a partnership. It is an equal partnership according to Scripture. They are "heirs together of the grace of life" (1 Peter 3:7). "The two will become one flesh" (Genesis 2:24).

These are situations which are less than ideal. They can be dealt with only by confession and repentance of sin, prayer, intake of the Word, counseling, etc. What I want you to understand is the ideal situation, which can be a goal or model for your estate planning. The ideal is two born-again marriage partners, who love each other and love the Lord, and who are in agreement concerning the stewardship of God's property entrusted to them. They will write a will directing how the estate will be handled if the wife dies first, and how it will be handled if the husband dies first. They will do this with the assistance of a lawyer. Don't attempt to do this without a lawyer.

The details of writing the will are beyond the scope of this study. We are looking only at the biblical principles of estate planning. For assistance in the details of writing the will, and handling the many details which must be handled when death occurs, there are good books available. I recommend an excellent book entitled *Leave Your House in Order*, by John Watts. This book is available on Amazon.com. It is written from a non-technical view and is thoroughly biblical in its approach to the subject, and will tell you what you need to be thinking about as you write your will.

If our ideal couple has minor children, they will include provisions for them in the will. These provisions will remain in the will until the children reach adulthood. One of those provisions will be the appointment of a guardian to take custody of their children in the event both parents die before the children reach adulthood. This provision alone is reason enough to have a will. Without it, some judge could decide who the guardian of your children will be.

After all children reach adulthood, this ideal couple should review the will and change it. The guardian appointment provision can be removed. They will plan distribution of their estate in a way that will ensure good stewardship of God's property after they leave this life, as we have discussed in the paragraphs above. And they will review their will at regular intervals with the help of their lawyer.

ESTATE TAX CONSIDERATIONS

If the ideal couple has an estate small enough not to create any estate tax (i.e. less than the combined gift-estate tax exclusion under the law), the will can direct distribution of the entire estate to the surviving spouse after the first death. The surviving spouse can continue managing the estate for the glory of God without any estate tax expense. But if the estate is larger than the gift-estate tax exclusion, then the couple may wish to leave a portion of the estate directly to the Lord at the first death, if the surviving spouse does not need it after the first death. That is often the case with larger estates. The portion left to God is free of estate tax. This is very efficient stewardship of God's property.

WHAT IF YOU HAVE A VERY SMALL ESTATE?

Some readers may be thinking, "I don't have enough money to even worry about having a will." I can understand that, and sympathize with that feeling. But I don't want you to miss a truth, which if planted as a seed in the heart, could have eternal consequences. That truth is based on the central truth of stewardship with which we began this study (Chapter 4): God owns and controls all wealth on this earth. "The earth is the Lord's, and everything in it" (Psalm 24:1). God owns the cattle on a thousand hills. He also owns the hills (Psalm 50:10). Furthermore, God is in control of who gets stewardship of His property.

> Rich and poor have this in common. The Lord is Maker of them all [Proverbs 22:2].

God decides who gets five talents and who gets one talent. Has it ever occurred to you that if you thoroughly mastered the principles of biblical stewardship (and you don't have to have any money to do that), and then committed yourself to follow those principles, what God might do? He is in control. He might decide to entrust much larger amounts of His property to you because He is looking for faithful stewards.

> For the eyes of the Lord run to and fro throughout the whole earth, to show Himself strong in behalf of them whose heart is perfect toward Him [2 Chronicles 16:9 (KJV)].

I am afraid there aren't many in the 21st century church who measure up to this standard. The church today is full of materialistic Christians. Many have large amounts of wealth, but it is not committed to God, at least the evidence suggests it is not.

God is looking for faithful stewards whose hearts are set on storing treasure in heaven. When He finds one, He may entrust more wealth to him to manage, which brings me to my final point of this chapter. **The time to become a faithful manager of God's property is now, no matter how little of it you have, so that God can safely trust you with wealth should He decide to do so**.

Now it is required that those who have been given a trust must prove faithful [1 Corinthians 4:2].

God's managers must be proven faithful. Faithfulness cannot be demonstrated in a short time. Meditate on that. Faithfulness is a pattern of life. To be proven faithful, time must pass … a lot of time. A believer must start where he is and persevere, and over time establish a pattern of faithfulness.

I suggest to you that the only way you can be sure you will do the right thing with the assets you are managing when you die, is to establish a pattern of faithfulness before you die. It's not likely you will be any better steward of what you leave than you were of what you managed while you were alive. If you haven't been a faithful steward of God's money as you earned it over the years, you are not likely to distribute what's left to God's glory.

If you haven't been a faithful steward of God's money, you have done one of two things with His money. You either spent it, or you hoarded it. If you spent it, it's gone, and there's nothing you can do about it. You will lose eternal reward you could have earned with God's money. You will also lose enjoyment of the things you bought with God's money. Ask Solomon about that.

If you hoarded it, the result is the same. You have lost both reward and enjoyment. And it is not likely that you will distribute your hoard to the glory of God. It just isn't likely to happen. Therefore, **the time to become a faithful steward is now, before it's too late**.

For further meditation you might like to read questions 10, 12, 13, 18, 33 and 40 in the Appendix.

CHAPTER 19

WHO OWES WHO?

I end this study with a truth that transformed my life. In fact, the day this truth clicked in my brain, the change was every bit as dramatic as was my conversion to Christ, and my coming to realize the truth of Square One - that God is in control and He has my best interest at heart. In some sense I have saved the best for last. And as I write this, there is a prayer in my heart that everyone who reads it will experience a similar change.

The demographics of our nation tell us that in the next 50 years the elderly will become a huge ministry test, not only for society as a whole, but especially for the church. Nearly every one of you who reads this will at some point in your life have one or more elderly loved ones or close friends brought into your life by God for the purpose of desperately needed ministry. It will probably come at a time that seems the most inconvenient or burdensome to you. You had better understand *who owes who*.

Ministry to the elderly can become very tedious, tiring, discouraging and inconvenient, and nearly always involves personal sacrifice. If you understand who owes who, you'll be able to invest your life in other lives out of a heart of unconditional love. And you'll become indebted to those who permit you to serve them because they will become a source of your eternal reward, your treasure in heaven. If you can get hold of this truth, **it will transform your life**.

Let's begin with a text. The apostle Paul writes:

> And I do not want you to be unaware, brethren, that often I have planned to come to you (and have been prevented thus far) in order that I might obtain some fruit among you also, even as among the rest of the Gentiles. I am under obligation both to the Greeks and the barbarians, both to the wise and to the foolish. Thus, for my part, I am eager to preach the gospel to you also who are in Rome [Romans 1:13-15 (NASB)].

I was in a Bible class a few years ago with five other businessmen. We were studying Romans, Chapter 1. When our teacher came to verse 14, he paused and said to the class, "Gentlemen, why was Paul indebted to the Greeks and barbarians?" Nobody answered the question. In my mind I could think of only one possible answer, "God called Paul to preach the gospel, so I assume he was indebted to all men. He owed them the opportunity to hear the gospel." But in this passage Paul gives us a different reason why he was indebted to them. He said, "I plan to come to Rome in order that I might obtain some fruit among you also." By fruit, Paul meant eternal reward. He was saying that by coming to Rome and preaching the gospel, he would earn some more eternal reward, just as he had by preaching to other Gentile groups. And you can tell he was excited about this reward, for he said, "I am eager to come and preach to you."

So why was Paul indebted to the Greeks and Barbarians? Because *they were a source of his eternal reward or profit.* (The word translated "fruit" in verse 13 is translated "profit" in Philippians 4:17.)

The truth we are seeing here is both counter-intuitive and counter-cultural. Let me explain. If I minister to you, the world says you owe me. Scripture teaches the opposite, that if you permit me to minister to you, I owe you, because you will be a source of eternal reward for me. Paul said, "If you Romans permit me to preach the gospel to you, I will owe you. I'll be indebted to you just as I am to the Greeks and barbarians, because you will be one of the sources of my eternal reward." This changes the whole dynamic of interpersonal relationships.

Aunt Nila had married a cowboy with some oil wells. She is now sick and the prognosis is poor. Maybe if I help her, and play my cards right, she will feel obligated to me and include me in her will. Can you imagine yourself having thoughts like that? I can and I have. That is typical of the world's response to the health crisis of an ailing aunt.

God's plan is that her situation is an opportunity for those who understand it to minister to her with the attitude that **they owe her.** Then her pain and irrational responses are not irritants that drive people away, but a source of even greater eternal profit for the one wise enough to see it. When God brings an aunt Nila into your life, don't fail to remember *who owes who* in the ministry transaction.

If you meditate on this and begin to apply it to your relationships, it can become one of the most relaxing and freeing truths in the Christian life. It solves the problem of unrealized expectations. Every one of us is human. Every one of us is selfish by nature. It is all too human for us to expect someone we minister to, or do a favor for, to respond with some measure of gratitude. I look back over my own life. I remember times, before I learned this truth, I would do what I thought was a good deed for somebody, or minister to them in some way, and they wouldn't respond like I expected. And I would think, "Well the least they could do is thank me, or show their gratitude in some way." *That is straight from the devil.* The truth is, if a person permits me to minister to them, **I become indebted to them**, not the other way around, because they become a source of my eternal reward. Getting this straight has changed my life. I try never to forget who owes who in the ministry transaction.

A word of balance and caution. Not every contact with another person will develop into a relationship that will lend itself to ministry. You cannot have a relationship with another person who doesn't want you to have it. So we must not try to knock down doors that God has not opened. We must remember Square One. God is the One who is in control. We must relax, be ourselves, and let God bring us into the relationships He wants us to be in for ministry purposes.

THE IMPORTANCE OF THE PROFIT MOTIVE

Let us learn from Paul and the New Testament that the profit motive is a legitimate motive for ministry. God created it in us, then asked us to surrender our natural instinct for seeking profit in this life, and instead seek profit in the next life ... eternal reward. It's the same thing He did with our desire for autonomy. He created us with the desire, then asked us to surrender it and submit to His authority. He created in us the profit motive, then asked us to forego seeking profit in this life in exchange for even greater and lasting reward in eternity. Paul's way of saying it was, "Set your minds on things above, not on earthly things." (Colossians 3:2), which I suspect is his commentary on Jesus' command to store for ourselves treasure in heaven, not on earth.

God does not expect us to work for Him for nothing, and Paul understood this. Until this clicked in my mind, I had never noticed the word "profit" in the love chapter, 1 Corinthians 13.

> And if I give all my possessions to feed the poor, and I deliver my body to be burned, but do not have love, it *profits* me nothing [1 Corinthians 13:3].

I had never focused on that last phrase. It clearly implies that if I do not minister in love, it profits me nothing. But it also equally clearly implies that if I do minister in love, I will have profit. And it further seems to me that Paul is interested in earning a profit, just as he was when he wrote to the Romans.

The Greek word for love in 1 Corinthians 13 is *agape*. The essence of agape is that you do what is in the best interest of the person loved, no matter how it feels, and no matter how the person responds. You may or may not enjoy the relationship. The person you minister to may be grateful, or he may hate you. There may be great sacrifice required on your part, or little at all. The defining characteristic of agape is acting in what you perceive to be the best interest of the person loved. It's the love God has for us. It is unconditional love. It is the kind of love that earns eternal reward.

But what I am going to suggest to you is that that kind of love is not possible without an understanding of the profit motive. God made us that way.

Unless you understand the profit motive combined with love, you will find it extremely difficult, or impossible, to love that unlovable person in your life.

Unless you understand the profit motive combined with love, you will find it extremely difficult to remain in an unhappy marriage. You'll find it extremely difficult to obey Jesus' commandments on marriage and divorce.

Unless you understand the profit motive combined with love, you will find it difficult, if not impossible, to give sacrificially of your financial resources.

Unless you understand the profit motive combined with love, you will find it difficult to minister to the elderly.

As I conclude this, there is a prayer in my heart for all who will read it, **but especially for younger people**. I say to you younger people, don't wait until you are 60 or 70 years old to learn this, like I did. Don't do that. You'll waste too many years of your life. **Get hold of this truth. Now. It will transform your life.**

Never forget who owes who in the ministry transaction.

EPILOGUE

THE COUNSEL I NEEDED BUT NEVER GOT
By Dan A. Bentley

If God determines our standard of living on earth, and promises to meet the needs of His "faithful servants", how do I determine my needs? When Israel gathered manna day by day in the wilderness, they didn't line up at the local soup kitchen. They gathered for themselves varying amounts. Everyone's need was not the same. I think God still chooses differing needs for different individuals. It occurs to me that God in His wisdom chooses at various times to withhold needs from His children so that others in His family may participate in providing those needs. Paul spoke of this when he was describing the condition of the Jerusalem church to the Corinthians. God gives us the opportunity to participate in His work of providing the needs of some of His children. Do you think He depends on us to come through? No, He allows us to earn reward. Their need is for our benefit.

Maybe the following illustration will help you determine your own needs, and the needs of anyone you might counsel financially. Anyone can get off the track as God complicates his circumstances and chooses to entrust him with more responsibilities. It is certainly permissible and honorable to eliminate debt, but it is usually the case that the excess income used to get to that point will not cease to flow when the debt is over. Now comes another test that strains camels and stretches eyes of needles. I use the following illustration without recommending it for anyone's own experiment. I must admit, however, that this is a loose testimony of what my wife and I actually did before we first realized our desire to eliminate our debt.

You attend graduate school where you master a trade which you also have student loans for. You borrow for operating expenses in the business. Then, you and your wife learn you will be blessed with a second child and you are convinced you need a bigger house. The old clunker finally gives out, and since the bankers seem eager to help you spend money you have yet to earn, you let them grant you another loan … again!

What I just described is close to what really happened. Our debt did not seem to be unmanageable at the time. By the hard work of my wife and God's provision, we weren't having trouble making the payments, but through some biblical financial ministries, we both became convinced that continuing this path was not God's best for us.

Then we discovered the gap between need and want. I found that as I began to eliminate debt, in order to apply extra payments to the principal, expenses must decrease. It is good if income increases (there is a catch here: the taxes continue to rise when I am ridding myself of debt, and God expects me to honor that commitment). **He** provides the wisdom to see where to cut expenses and raise revenue. Willingness in the heart to apply God's best is met by God's provision, and He will get the credit for reducing and eliminating debt. He will also determine how quickly this happens. Disobedience will surely slow the process down.

If I continue this course of using all extra income beyond the essentials (food and covering) as a dedicated debt reducer for very long, I will identify God's exact provision that He calls my "need". That figure is my living expenses while I am straining to apply all excess to my creditors' accounts. I am dedicated to spending no more than absolutely necessary on "self". **Need is apparent right here**. I only want to spend what I must on myself and my family. I am not attempting to raise my standard of living; I am cutting it to the bone. Of course it will vary from one to another. I now understand that need is independent from income. I now know God's definition of my *needs*. It wasn't that painful. I admit God is generous in meeting my needs.

As the end of the debt comes into sight, as the last few checks are posted, what happened to me may happen to you. Getting out of debt was exciting. My wife and I were both committed to it. I assumed we were content because the reduction in standard of living would soon be over, and our ensuing standard of living would be even more wonderful. In reality, contentment resided in the fact that we were exactly where God wanted us financially. We were gathering more than we needed, then applying all the excess beyond our needs to the debt. Make sure you get that. **When you are only using what God wants you to use from His resources, financial peace will follow**.

The big question then hit me and I felt like a crash test dummy: "**Now what**? The financial gurus all failed me!" But it wasn't their fault. My sight stopped at the wall where the debt ended, and I didn't know how to see beyond that wall.

You could assume the role of financial counselor and see the vision beyond the wall for me. I want you to help me see the joy of shared manna. God provided me with more than enough to eliminate the debt, and still allowed my income to grow. Why did He do that? Did He want me to hoard it? Did He think I was not consuming enough? All my needs were already met and I was content.

You already know the counsel to give me. "Continue the lifestyle and ideal standard of living you already said you are happy with. Don't slow down your momentum! Use balance in determining your stores for foreseeable needs, then press yourself as firmly as you did during debt reduction and **apply the same strategy used to eliminate debt toward storing treasure in heaven.**

"God guided you and provided for you during debt elimination. He let you in on the secret of your real need. You understand your lifestyle and standard of living have little to do with your income, don't you?

"Go ahead and give like you paid the lenders. You won't blow it if it is in God's hand. Apply the balance to His kingdom and it will invisibly grow in your account, and it will be there long after the 'elements have melted with fervent heat.' Go back to the old days and thrill yourself to find a misplaced coin you want to deposit to the Kingdom. Let it thrill you like it did when you applied it to your debt."

Those last statements, in your own words, could be your message to me. You are truly helping me only if I will follow through all the way to storing treasure in heaven and seeking a "Well done" from my LORD. Otherwise I will fail to be another camel through the eye of the needle. I will either never understand that I am to manage God's assets for God, and thereby squander my opportunities to give the Master a good return, or I will get to the wall having mastered the debt, and proceed to become a rich young ruler. This era has too many of those already.

When you present this radical message to me, you might affect our relationship. I hope you do it anyway. If you love me with agape love as discussed earlier in this book, regardless of how I respond, you then will act in my best interest. You ought to think about how we will spend eternity, not how we will interact over the next twenty years, as I either work on manipulating God's standard of living for myself, or attempt to shield myself financially from every potential pitfall. Why would you only care if I respond positively to the Gospel when the great commission clearly instructs you to teach me everything Jesus commanded? I need to know I can follow the Master only when the funds in my possession are readily returning to Him. How could it not be so? Make me grapple with this life-altering question. Whose assets are we holding anyway?

Neither the church (for the most part) nor the world will commend you for encouraging me to take such a radical course of action. You will not be picked up by the syndicated radio networks and there won't be publishers clamoring for your next offering. Would you please consider talking to me anyway? I really am interested in laying up treasure in heaven, but no one ever told me this was a possibility. I thought my options consisted of tax-deferred retirement funds, a diversified portfolio of stocks and bonds, and perhaps a nominal increase in monthly giving commitments. After all, I am working very hard! Can I really depend on God to take care of me if I give too much? I guess that if He can't be depended on to do such a small thing, how can I depend on Him to save me from my sins, take me to heaven, and give me eternal life? I really am going to need some counsel to break this attachment to mammon. By the way, how are we going to tell my wife about this?

APPENDIX

FORTY QUESTIONS TO ASK GOD
ABOUT YOUR GIVING

The forty questions listed below are taken from *Money, Possessions and Eternity*, by Randy Alcorn (Tyndale House Publishers, Inc. Wheaton, Illinois, 2003), pages 218-222. Mr. Alcorn's web site may be accessed at www.epm.org. I recommend this book to all who want to study the subject of biblical stewardship in depth.

1. Father, with the financial assets and opportunities you've entrusted to me, have you raised me up for just a time such as this? (Esther 4:14). Have you called me to join a great team of your children in freeing up money and possessions to reach out to the needy and fulfill the great commission?

2. Is the fact that you have entrusted me with so many resources an indication that you have given me the gift of giving and want me to exercise it more frequently and skillfully?

3. What am I holding on to that is robbing me of present joy and future reward? What am I keeping that is preventing me from having to depend on you? What am I clinging to that makes me feel like I don't have to depend on you to provide, like I used to before I had this much? What do you want me to release that would restore me to a walk of faith?

4. In light of 2 Corinthians 8:14 and 9:11, do you want me to assume that each financial blessing you entrust to me is not intended to raise my standard of living but to raise my standard of giving?

5. Am I being held in orbit around the mass of treasures I have stored up? Have I overaccumulated? Have you multiplied "my" assets not so I would stockpile them, but so I would distribute them to the needy?

6. Where in the world (and in my community) do you want me to go, to see, and participate in Christ-centered ministries meeting physical and spiritual needs?

7. Am I treating you as owner and CEO/CFO of "my" assets, or am I treating you merely as my financial consultant, to whom I pay a fee (of 10% or greater)?

8. When I make a list of all the assets you've entrusted to me and ask you what you want me to give away, is there anything I'm leaving off the list? Is there anything I'm treating as if it were untouchable, as if it were mine and not yours? Do my retirement funds belong to you too? What doesn't?

9. Do you want me to set a basic level of income and assets to live on, then give away whatever you provide beyond that (regardless of whether that's 50%, 90%, or 99%, or more)?

10. How can I be sure that the assets you've entrusted to me will serve you after my death? How do I know that those to whom I leave them, or those to whom *they* leave them, will use them for your glory? If I want money to go to your kingdom later and it's more than I presently need, why wouldn't I give it to your kingdom now?

11. If the world and everything in it will burn at your second coming (2 Peter 3:10-13), will my assets, accounts, and the holdings I've stored up on earth be wasted if you return in my lifetime? Once my present opportunity to give is lost, will I get a second chance? Do you want me to adopt a "use it or lose it" approach to my current opportunities for eternal investment?

12. Once they've finished college or are working on their own, would inheriting wealth (beyond items of special sentimental and heritage value) help my children's eternal perspective and walk with God? Or would it have a corrupting influence on their character, lifestyle, work ethic, or marriage?

13. If my children would resent my giving money to your kingdom instead of leaving it for them, does that indicate they're

not qualified to receive it? If so, why would I give them your money? If my investment manager died, what would I think if he left my money to his children? Does the fact that you entrusted your money to me, not others, indicate that you want me, during my lifetime, to invest it in eternity? Will you, in turn, provide my children with the money you expect them to manage?

14. What's the eternal downside to giving now? What's the eternal downside of delaying giving until later? Am I really in danger of giving too much too soon? Or is the only real danger giving too little too late? If I give away most of my assets now, what will I have available to give later?

15. If I don't give something now, is it possible I may no longer have it to give later?

16. If I don't give something now, is it possible I may die before I get a chance to give it later? If my desire is to give it away before I die and I can't know when I'll die, should I give it now?

17. If I don't give it now, am I in danger of my heart getting further wrapped up in earthly treasure? (Matthew 6:21). Will the same heart that's prompting me to give today later persuade me to keep something because I ignored your prompting to give?

18. Because I have no choice but to leave money behind when I die, is it really "giving" to designate money to ministries in my will? (Although these may be the wisest places to leave my assets – and all of us will have some assets remaining at our death – it involves no sacrifice or need for faith.) Will I rob myself of joy and rob you of my trust by holding on to significant assets until death that I could have given while I was still alive?

19. In James 4:13-17, you tell me I can't know how much money I can make (or lose) tomorrow, or even whether I'll be here. Is it presumptuous of me to accumulate a large amount of "confederate money" that may not be used for you in the future, when it could definitely be used for you in the present?

20. When I stand before your judgment seat, would you ever say to me, "You blew it – you sold those shares and gave them to feed the hungry and evangelize the lost, and then two years later the market peaked"? Or would you say, "Well done, my good and faithful servant"?

21. Can you produce higher eternal returns from money I give you today than Wall Street can? Can anything match your promise of a hundredfold return (10,000 percent)?

22. Is it ever wrong to give to you now rather than wait until later? If Christ commended the poor widow in Mark 12 for giving to you everything she had – considering her faithful, not irresponsible – how much would I have to give away before you would consider me irresponsible?

23. Do you want me to set up a foundation or give money away as you bring it in? If I have a foundation, do you want me to give assets away now, or implement a phase-out plan so the principal doesn't end up wasted at your return?

24. Because you called the rich young ruler in Matthew 19:16-30 to give away all that he had and follow you in faith, is it possible you might call me to do the same? Do you want me to ask you?

25. Why do I want to hold on to my wealth? Am I trying to prove something? What am I trying to prove – and to whom? Is it pride? power? prestige? selfishness? insecurity? fear? Am I a control freak? Or is it just because possessiveness is normal in our society, and I'm merely going with the flow? Do you want me to go with the flow or do something different – maybe radically different?

26. Am I living to hear others say of me, "He [or she] is a great success" or to have you say to me, "Well done, my good and faithful servant"?

27. Instead of asking "Why should I give this away?' do you want me to ask "Why shouldn't I give this away?" Should I put the burden of proof on *keeping* rather than *giving*? When money

comes in, which should be the rule and not the exception: *giving* or *keeping*? Unless there's a compelling reason to keep, should I normally give?

28. Am I hanging on to money as a backup plan in case you fail me? Is my fear of dire health catastrophes and old age scenarios creating an inertia in my giving, because I imagine I must provide everything for myself if something goes wrong? Considering that the vast majority of people in history and most in the world today have nothing stored up for retirement, am I preoccupied with putting too many treasures in retirement funds? Are you calling me to work without a net – trusting you'll catch me in case of a fall?

29. Has Money become my idol? Are material assets competing with you for lordship over my life? Is generous giving your lifeline to rescue me from bondage, your leverage to allow me to tear down the idols? If materialism is the disease, is giving the only cure?

30. I want to submit everything to your review and ask you to guide me as to what I should do with your money and possessions. What specifically am I hanging on to that you want me to give away?

31. Am I giving your money to people of weak character and materialistic values? Although they may be good causes, are the Humane Society or opera as close to your heart as evangelism, church planting and helping the poor? Do the ministries I am supporting financially help the poor in Christ's name, not just in the name of humanitarianism? Is the gospel offered to dying people once they've been fed?

32. How can I better communicate with and pray with my spouse so we can walk together down this exhilarating road of giving, leading each other and not leaving the other behind?

33. What am I doing to train my children to be generous givers – not just donors, but disciples?

34. What handful of people in my unique sphere of influence do you want me to pray for and talk with about generous giving? Have you called me to mentor others in giving, that they may end up giving more than I do? In helping someone become a great giver, will I be like the man who led D. L. Moody to Christ?

35. What giving-oriented, mission-oriented, and eternity-oriented books and magazines can I pass on to those in my sphere of influence? What tapes or videos can we listen to and watch together?

36. What simple reminder of God's call to stewardship and giving can I make for myself, then pass on to others? Maybe I can give them something to put in their Day-Timer or on their PalmPilot, in their wallet or Bible, on their dashboard or refrigerator or exercise machine, such as a business card or a bookmark with central verses such as Deuteronomy 8:17-18 or Matthew 6:19-21.

37. What can I set up to provide a discussion forum concerning stewardship and giving? A dinner? A weekly breakfast? A weekend retreat? A weekly study using *Money, Possessions and Eternity, The Treasure Principle,* or materials from Crown Ministries?

38. What conferences can I invite others to attend? What ministries can I introduce others to? What vision and ministry trips can we go on together?

39. How can I help my pastor(s) encourage biblical training in stewardship and giving and assist them in creating an open church dialogue regarding lifestyle choices and kingdom investments?

40. Five minutes after I die, what will I wish I would have given away while I still had the chance? Would you help me spend the rest of my life closing the gap between what I'll wish I had given then and what I'm actually giving now?